How to T
Like a
Social Scientist

How to Think Like a Social Scientist

Thomas F. Pettigrew
University of California, Santa Cruz

HarperCollins*CollegePublishers*

Acquisitions Editor: Catherine Woods
Project Coordination, Text and Cover Design: York Production Services
Electronic Production Manager: Mike Kemper
Manufacturing Manager: Helene G. Landers
Electronic Page Makeup: York Production Services
Printer and Binder: R.R. Donnelley & Sons Company
Cover Printer: New England Book Components,Inc.

How to Think Like a Social Scientist

Library of Congress Cataloging-in-Publication Data

Pettigrew, Thomas F.
   How to think like a social scientist / Thomas F. Pettigrew
      p. cm.
   Includes bibliographical references (p.168) and index.
   ISBN 0-673-99709-X
   1. Social sciences—Methodology.   I. Title.
H61.P5284   1995
300'.72—dc20   95-8952
                                                                          CIP

95 96 97 98   9 8 7 6 5 4 3 2 1

Contents

Chapter 3 In Comparison With What?   37

· Chapter 4 Searching for Causes and Changes   70

Chapter 5 Sampling, Selecting, and Socializing   95

Chapter 6 Keeping Our Levels Straight   109

Chapter 7 Thinking in Systems Terms   124

Chapter 8 Try Out Your Healthy Skepticism!   143

Preface

The special nature of social science thinking has long fascinated me. Since my first social science courses at the University of Virginia, this way of understanding the social world has impressed me as being unique and interesting. It differs markedly from "common sense" and mass media approaches to the same phenomena.

Yet introductory textbooks rarely discuss this direct way of thinking. Their primary task is to cover the many facts of the field. So I wanted to write a brief volume that treats the underlying ideas of social science thinking as its only focus. The hope is that the book will serve for general reading as well as a useful supplement for basic texts in social science courses, especially introductory and methods classes.

The volume pursues its topic throughout—the distinctive ways social scientists think about social life. It argues for a *healthy skepticism* and contrasts this approach with popular social analyses as reflected in the mass media. It is a book that would have been useful to me when I was an undergraduate, but I can only write it now after years of teaching and research.

Several features involve the reader. First, I have used a concise, personal, and narrative writing style, stocked with examples drawn from throughout the social sciences. Second, by emphasizing the complexities of understanding social life, the volume encourages critical thought—including critically judging the book's own arguments.

Finally, the book engages the reader with an opening quiz, and each chapter closes with an extensive summary, provocative issues for discussion, and recommended reading. The last chapter completes this theme. It asks readers to apply their newly acquired healthy skepticism by evaluating actual newspaper articles reporting social science findings. The emphasis throughout, then, is not on facts and theories, but ideas and thinking.

A favorite chess book, *How to Think Like a Grandmaster,* inspired the title; Germany's University of Muenster offered me the opportunity to write the book. During an enjoyable summer, Professor Amelie Mummendey and Dr. Bernd Simon kindly provided me with the time, facilities, and quiet necessary to begin the task.

I want to thank Catherine Woods of HarperCollins for her extensive help and the dozen anonymous reviewers who supplied invaluable suggestions. I wish also to thank my family—all published writers themselves and rigorous editors and critics: my wife, Ann Hallman Pettigrew, M.D.; my daughter-in-law, Noha M. Radwan; and my son, Mark F. Pettigrew. Unlike most authors, I am happy to share the blame for any errors in this volume with my entire family!

Thomas F. Pettigrew

Chapter

1

—

Everybody Is a
Social Scientist!

People do not think of themselves as astrophysicists. No one, that is, save those specially trained in astrophysics. And only those few among us with the necessary training regard ourselves as biochemists, mathematicians, or neurosurgeons.

Most people, however, can fancy themselves social scientists. After all, we are all human beings. Each day we observe and interact with other human beings. So we can regard ourselves as lay-psychologists. Moreover, we all participate daily in social institutions and live out our lives in human societies. So we also can claim to be lay-sociologists. We also exist embedded in our own cultures. We can sample other cultures through travel and at ethnic restaurants. So we are lay-anthropologists as well.

Consider, too, our participation in politics. Political news from the mass media bombards us daily; we try to vote in elections regularly. So are we not also lay-political scientists? Finally, we deal daily with money. Unlike neutrons, synapses, and laser beams, money is something we have to think about often—to make, spend, and save. So do we not also qualify as lay-economists?

In short, social science deals with the social lives we all lead. So we naturally come to think we know a lot about it. In varying degrees, maybe we do. If so, what makes social scientists different from the rest of us?

The most obvious difference is that social scientists have had specialized training. They have learned particular bodies of collected knowledge; they have learned special methods to test new ideas and gain new knowledge. Social scientists have also developed special ways of thinking about social life, of how to approach new problems, and what patterns to look for in new events. In fact, experts in many areas are distinguished by their skill at detecting common patterns in their specialties (Dawson, Zeitz & Wright, 1989).

The knowledge bases of the social sciences, organized and expanded by computers, are now so vast that no would-be Leonardo da Vinci could master them all. So, as in other areas, social scientists increasingly become narrow specialists. Hence, most social psychologists know little of economics, or economists of anthropology. Even within a discipline, few can encompass the entire range of their field.

The methods that the various social sciences use to explore new ideas have also expanded. And methods have also become more specialized. Quantitative approaches have advanced rapidly—with economics setting the pace. Qualitative approaches have also advanced in those social sciences that employ them.

Weighty textbooks in each discipline introduce students to these exciting stores of theories, facts, and methods. This thin volume, however, focuses on the third difference between social scientists and others—the type of critical thought used to understand social life. To be sure, the disciplines differ markedly in their approaches. Yet there are basic principles that underlie social scientific thinking that contrast sharply from popular thought. These basic principles are the focus of this volume.

1.1 FIRST, A LITTLE TRUE/FALSE QUIZ

How easily do you think in social science terms? Take a few minutes and try using "common sense" to determine whether each of the findings in italics is largely *true* or largely *false*. Try also to think about the underlying factors that support your choice. Each of these descriptions derive from American research conducted in the various social sciences over the past half-century. They vary widely to provide a flavor of the vast range of interesting topics studied across the social sciences.

[1] *Black Soldiers' Satisfaction*   A major sociological study during World War II studied the morale of black American soldiers. *These black soldiers were more satisfied with Army life when stationed at a military base in the northern United States than at a base in the then-tightly segregated southern United States.* TRUE OR FALSE?

[2] *Promotions and Satisfaction*   The same World War II investigation also looked at differences in morale among various branches of the Army. It noted that members of the Army Air Corps received promotions far more rapidly than those in the Military Police. *So the airmen were much more satisfied with their promotions than were the Military Police.* TRUE OR FALSE?

[3] *Religious Voting and Kennedy's Election*   A political science study of the 1960 presidential election found that voting along religious lines was intense that year. Many Protestants cast anti-Catholic ballots. They opposed John Kennedy because of his religion, as he was only the second Roman Catholic

ever to run for President. *So, while President Kennedy barely won, religiously-oriented voting nearly cost him the election.* TRUE OR FALSE?

[4] Dr. King's Murder and Attitude Change   After a white gunman in 1968 assassinated Dr. Martin Luther King, Jr., the major black leader of the Civil Rights Movement, a curious phenomenon occurred among white Texans. *Surveys found that many of those whites who had most strongly opposed Dr. King and racial justice now felt especially guilty. And it was these whites who, following the assassination, changed their attitudes the most toward favoring racial change.* TRUE OR FALSE?

[5] Lonely, Isolated Inventors   An anthropologist looked at when and where major inventions, such as the telescope and the telephone, occurred. He found that *developing new inventions is largely an act of individual geniuses working alone. Typically one person creates inventions largely apart from other influences.* TRUE OR FALSE?

[6] Post-War Homicide Rates   A sociological study of homicide throughout the world noted an interesting trend in murders following wars. *Homicide rates within countries throughout the world fall sharply following their participation in war. War brings unity to the population. Perhaps, too, killing the enemy exhausts the total potential for homicide.* TRUE OR FALSE?

[7] Birth Rates and Prosperity   Demography is the social science that studies populations. Americans know it best for its work on the mammoth U.S. Census, but it also studies population issues around the globe. In these investigations, demographers repeatedly find that one of the strongest correlates of birth rates is economic prosperity. *When families can better afford to have more children, they do.* TRUE OR FALSE?

[8] Economic Development and Poverty   Economists who study the economic progress of developing nations uncovered an encouraging phenomenon. In the past, these countries have typically had small, rich elites with the rest of their populations in dire poverty. *When modern development brings some prosperity, it opens new job opportunities for those who had lived at the subsistence level. Thus, the poorest segments soon benefit from development, and a more equitable social class system begins to take shape.* TRUE OR FALSE?

[9] Payment and Lying   In a famous social psychological experiment at Stanford University, researchers asked college students to do a boring task. Then the researchers paid them either $20 or $1 to tell the next student subject that the task was actually interesting and stimulating. *Rewarded handsomely, those subjects paid $20 later came to think the task they had performed really had been interesting. Those paid the miserly $1 did not.* TRUE OR FALSE?

[10] Finding Good Jobs   How do people find out about suitable employment—especially highly-skilled jobs that pay well? The research of labor economists and sociologists shows that *people typically locate good jobs through formal channels, such as newspaper advertisements and employment agencies. Others find out about these employment openings through close friends and relatives.* TRUE OR FALSE?

1.2   ANSWERS TO THE QUIZ

Here are the correct answers to these items with brief descriptions of how the social scientists who uncovered these findings explained them.

[1] Black Soldiers' Satisfaction   FALSE. Black American soldiers in northern camps were in fact *objectively* much better off than those in southern camps in World War II. Yet objective status does not necessarily translate into *subjective* feelings. Human beings are too complicated for such simple assumptions. This famous sociological investigation of Army morale found the black troops in *southern* camps to be more satisfied (Stouffer, Suchman, DeVinney, Star & Williams, 1949).

The tricky element here concerns with whom the soldiers were *comparing* themselves. Or, as sociologists prefer to ask, what group is their **reference group?** (*All terms in bold letters throughout the book are defined in the Glossary.*) "Common sense" leads us to think that the black troops in northern camps would compare themselves with their black counterparts in southern camps. Think about that a minute. Few of these soldiers knew of conditions in both types of camps. How could they have made that comparison to determine how satisfied they should be in relative terms?

Stouffer and his colleagues who conducted this study reasoned differently. They suggest the comparisons the soldiers knew and used were the black civilians who lived near the camps. As soon as you frame the problem this way, the surprising finding makes sense. Black civilians in the South in the 1940s endured intensive segregation and discrimination. Black soldiers in southern camps had their difficulties. Yet, in comparison with the black civilians they saw regularly, their Army life seemed much better.

By contrast, black civilians in the North were experiencing wider opportunities with new, higher-paying jobs opening in the war industry. Using this reference group, black troops in the North felt **relative deprivation** and hence were less satisfied with Army life.

This example introduces us to the importance of *relative* comparisons in social life. They are more typical than absolute comparisons, and social scientists must always compare their results relative to some benchmark. The benchmark chosen can determine the conclusions drawn. We will consider this point in detail in Chapter 3.

[2] Promotions And Satisfaction   FALSE. The same study of Army morale found that the Military Police were far more satisfied with their slow promo-

tions than the airmen were with their rapid promotions. Again, the key point is with whom each group was comparing its promotions. It was not with each other. The two groups had minimal contact and knew little of the other group's promotion rates. Hence, they could not serve as reference groups for each other.

This time Stouffer reasoned that the soldiers of these two U.S. Army branches were comparing *within* their groups. A military policeman worked hard and long to move up in the ranks. When he succeeded, he took satisfaction in knowing that his hard earned promotion was comparable to that of his colleagues in the Military Police. However, the high-flying airmen typically had many comparisons of colleagues who had received promotions even more rapidly than they. Surrounded by comparisons of extremely fast promotions, many airmen were dissatisfied with their own fast gains.

[3] Religious Voting and Kennedy's Election   FALSE. If you thought this item true, you are in good company. Most of the American mass media thought heavy anti-Catholic voting had almost cost John Kennedy the presidency in 1960. A careful **simulation** of the election using massive amounts of survey data, however, showed that actually the opposite was true (Pool, Abelson and Popkin, 1964). Religiously-motivated voting helped Kennedy *win* the election of 1960!

The best-fit simulation showed Kennedy did indeed lose popular votes from this divisive religious voting. The study indicated he lost about 4.3 million Protestant votes that otherwise would have been cast for a Protestant running as the Democratic Party candidate. This suggests a staggering amount of religious bigotry at the polls in 1960. At least it appears staggering today, for the religious backgrounds of candidates in American elections is now of little interest.

Overlooked by many observers at the time was that Kennedy also *gained* votes by being a Roman Catholic. The simulation estimated that he garnered about 2.8 million Catholic votes that otherwise would have gone for the Republican Party candidate. Overall, then, Pool and his colleagues estimated Kennedy had lost about 1.5 million votes on the religious issue (4.3–2.8 million).

What these researchers remembered, and the media forgot, was that direct popular votes do not win American presidential elections. The Electoral College decides the victor by a winner-take-all principle of casting electoral votes by state. Here lies the reason for the surprising result of the religious issue actually aiding Kennedy's election.

Kennedy lost most of the 4.3 million Protestant Democrats in the South and West. He would have lost some of these states anyway. Other states he lost because these voters had few electoral votes. Montana, Idaho, and Utah, for instance, had only four electoral votes each. Hence, the anti-Catholic voting against Kennedy cost him only about 110 votes in the Electoral College.

The 2.8 million pro-Catholic votes, however, were another story. These voters lived largely in big eastern and midwestern states such as New York,

Pennsylvania, and Illinois. These states were critical for Kennedy; without them he would not have become President. He won each by only a whisker. Hence, the pro-Catholic votes made the difference in these swing states. Together these states contributed about 132 electoral votes. All told, then, Kennedy *gained* about 22 electoral college votes from the religiously-motivated voting of 1960 (132–110).

The larger issue here involves multiple levels of analyses. Popular analyses often err by focusing on just the level of individual people—such as individual citizens voting on their religious prejudices. The problem is cast in an entirely new light when the issue is placed in a larger structural context—such as state-by-state voting in the Electoral College. We shall return to this issue in Chapter 6 on "Keeping Our Levels Straight."

[4] Dr. King's Murder and Attitude Change   FALSE. Those types of white Texans who were already the *most* favorable to racial change became even more favorable after the murder of Dr. King. Those types initially most unfavorable to racial change revealed no feelings of guilt after the tragedy. On the contrary, they became still more resistant to racial change.

These are the findings from a study by Robert Riley and the author (Riley & Pettigrew, 1976). We had sampled white Texans' opinions toward race relations for another project during November 1967 and February 1968. Then bullets struck down Dr. King in April of 1968. So we rushed back to Texas to conduct two more surveys during May and August of 1968.

We could not secure interviews with the same respondents on each occasion. Hence, we analyzed our data by types of people—such as young working-class whites from rural East Texas. When we did this, we discovered two opposite trends. Those types of respondents open to racial change before the assassination became still more open after it. Those closed to change earlier became more closed.

We interpreted these results as showing that white Texans viewed the slaying of the black leader within the perspectives of their prior racial views. Those types responsive to King's message for racial justice during his lifetime saw in his death further need for such justice. Similarly, those types who had rejected his message earlier saw in his death the disproof of his views.

This investigation used a **longitudinal research** design. Such a design collects data at different points in time and compares them across time to search for changes. More common are **cross-sectional research** designs which collect the data at one time. Though expensive and time-consuming, longitudinal research is important for all social sciences. Many questions, especially those that demand causal explanations (and most do), require some form of a longitudinal design. Longitudinal studies are important, because they provide another type of comparison—one made across time. We will return to this topic in Chapter 4 on "Searching for Causes and Changes."

[5] Lonely, Isolated Inventors   FALSE. The popular conception of lonely inventors locked up in their laboratories and conducting their work apart from outside influences is incorrect. According to Alfred Kroeber (1948), the distinguished anthropologist, the timing and location of major inventions is anything but random.

In fact, different people independently discover most major inventions within a few years of each other. The famous Alexander Graham Bell and the forgotten Elisha Gray filed patent petitions for the telephone within hours of one another in 1876. The following year, Thomas Edison in America and Charles Cros in France introduced the phonograph. Similarly, four people working in four countries invented the steamboat between 1783 and 1788. Louis Daguerre, the Frenchman, and William Talbot, the Englishman, introduced photography six months apart in 1839. Five inventors from Great Britain and the United States developed the telegraph around 1837. Today we remember only one of these men, Samuel Morse, for the telegraph code named for him.

Kroeber discerned a similar pattern for scientific discoveries—which, like inventions, are innovative cultural creations. Thus, four different scientists, including Galileo, reported sunspots in 1611. John Napier and Joost Burgi each introduced logarithms between 1614 and 1620. Isaac Newton and Gottfried Leibnitz each introduced the calculus in the 1670s. Major achievements in chemistry—nitrogen (1772–73), oxygen (1774), that water equals H_2O (1781–83) and the Periodic Law of Elements (1869)—were also multiply discovered. So too were such achievements in biology as the theory of natural selection (1858) and the rediscovery of Mendel's laws of genetics (1900).

From many such examples, Kroeber concluded that inventions were not just the creations of individual inventors. They were also part of the **zeitgeist**—the spirit of the times. The basic antecedent ideas, as well as the need, for the invention had entered the inventors' cultures. This is not to deny their genius. It does suggest, however, that had they not stepped forward when they did, others would have done so soon after.

[6] Post-War Homicide Rates   FALSE. Again the answer is false, although "common sense" dictates that homicide rates would decline after wartime. Dane Archer and Rosemary Gartner (1984), in their prize-winning volume *Violence and Crime in Cross-National Perspective,* found that murder rates typically *rise* after wars compared to a similar pre-war period. In a **control group** of nations that did not go to war during these years, no rise in murders occurred. We can be confident of this surprising result. The two sociologists diligently pursued the finding across 110 countries, 14 wars, and two different measures of change in violence rates. The result replicated repeatedly. We shall see in Chapter 4 that such **replication** is a major means social science has of gaining confidence in the **validity** (soundness) of its results.

Like the notion of an invention zeitgeist, Archer and Gartner explain their finding as reflecting a cultural rise in the acceptance and legitimization of violence during wartime. That is, violence against the enemy legitimatizes violence in general—even against your own group. The further finding that postwar homicide rates rose especially in those countries that won their wars yet suffered high percentages of battle deaths supports this interpretation of a *violent culture*.

Their idea of a culture that legitimatizes homicide fits with other analyses. For example, both a historian (Franklin, 1956) and social psychologists (Pettigrew & Spier, 1962) have demonstrated such a culture in the southern United States. The **concept** becomes important in such heated debates as those concerned with capital punishment. Can, as its advocates claim, the legal killing of convicted murderers actually deter homicide? Or does capital punishment itself, as its opponents claim, lend further support for a violent culture?

Archer and Gartner also provide worldwide data on these questions. They uncover no data to support the deterrence effect of capital punishment. Actually, they found the opposite. Consistent with their emphasis on the legitimization of violence, homicide rates decline on average following the abolition of capital punishment. This finding reveals how scholarly work in social science is often relevant to controversial public issues.

[7] Birth Rates and Prosperity   FALSE. Speaking of controversial issues, birth control is a topic of focal interest for demography. Writers often cite studies of birth rates as evidence that greater birth control is necessary if the world is to avert a disastrous population explosion in the making.

One consistent result of this demographic work is that economic prosperity is a strong predictor of birth rates. Yet prosperity acts in precisely the opposite manner from the reasonable sequence offered in the item. It is the poor of the world living in the poorest nations who have the most children. As prosperity comes to an area, birth rates begin to *decline*.

Why should families have fewer children just when they can provide them with a better life? There are many reasons behind this interesting phenomenon. We shall cite two major ones. First, families have many births in poor regions because wretched health conditions create tragically high rates of infant mortality. One must have many births to assure enough surviving children to aid family subsistence. Prosperity improves health conditions and care, and reduces the subsistence value to families of extra children.

Second, expectations for the future are important. As times improve, parents begin to dream of a better life for their children—and a better life requires investments in education and other previously unattainable opportunities. So such dreams for the future are only practical when there are fewer children in whom to invest.

Thus, one way to motivate families to have fewer children is to bring economic prosperity to these nations. Yet it is not the only way. Even the poorest of the world's countries can still mount effective family-planning programs. In Bangladesh, for example, such programs achieved a 21% decline in fertility rates between 1970 and 1991—from seven to five-and-a-half children per woman of child-bearing age (Robey, Rutstein & Morris, 1993).

[8] *Economic Development and Poverty* FALSE. If only it were true that development aids the poorest citizens the most! Albert Hirschman (1981), the distinguished economist, notes that precisely the opposite happens in the initial stages of economic development. The rich elite gets richer, maximally benefiting from the new development. The poor see little "trickle-down" from the new prosperity. Hence, the social class patterns of these nations become even more inequitable. The disparity between the haves and the have-nots grows even larger.

Why does this situation, Hirschman (1981:39–58) wonders, not rapidly trigger revolutions throughout the developing world? He likens the situation of the poor in these nations to that of an automobile driver stuck in unmoving traffic in a two-lane, one-way tunnel. (The idea actually occurred to Hirschman while he was stuck in Boston's Sumner Tunnel. Note how social scientists usefully spend their spare moments!) After both lanes have stopped for some time, one rejoices to see the next lane begin to move. You expect that means the traffic is finally opening, and your lane will soon proceed. Suppose, however, your lane fails to budge, while cars in the adjoining lane continue to rush past. After a while, your mood shifts from relief to anger over the unfairness. You may suspect foul play, and even consider illegally crossing over into the other lane.

Applied to the poor of developing countries, Hirschman's analogy predicts calm in the initial stages of development. Then it predicts growing unrest in later stages as the unequal economic situation worsens. In fact, this is precisely the pattern that we have often witnessed in developing countries during the past half-century of "rising expectations."

[9] *Payment and Lying* FALSE. If you thought this item correct, you should know that so did some psychologists at the time of the study. In simple reward-and-punishment terms, one would predict the $20 subjects would change their minds more than the $1 subjects. However, on average, it was the $1 subjects who more often changed their minds. This famous experiment by Festinger and Carlsmith (1959) offers support for Festinger's theory of *cognitive dissonance*. This theory holds that certain conditions reverse reward-and-punishment predictions.

The researchers reasoned that the subjects who had received $20 for lying could later easily explain to themselves why they had done it. They did it to earn the $20 (over $100 today when corrected for inflation). The $1 subjects had no such easy explanation. Their memory for the event was in "dissonance." That is, their knowledge that the task was quite dull conflicted with what they had said to the next subject. The theory of cognitive dissonance predicts that such a situation sets up a tension that people need to resolve. To ease the discomfort of this cognitive dissonance, many of the $1 subjects later remembered the task as fairly interesting after all.

[10] *Finding Good Jobs* FALSE. While some people secure high-paid employment through formal channels, even fewer secure it through close friends and relatives.

So how do qualified people find out about good jobs? Mark Granovetter (1973, 1982, 1983) discovered it was through word of mouth from distant acquaintances. He called the phenomenon "the strength of weak ties." With this finding, Granovetter helped to open an exciting new area of sociology called *network theory.*

The basic idea is that information flows through loose networks of people who do not know each other well. Maybe they were classmates in high school or college, but not close friends. Relatives and friends are of limited help, Granovetter found, because they know about the same information as you do. "Weak ties," however, indicate the two people are in different **social locations.** Therefore, they have access to different flows of information. So, in chance meetings, your old acquaintances can tell you about new openings at their firms that require the skills you possess.

This network analysis is an intriguing example of **social structure** in action—a topic we will discuss throughout the book. It has direct implications for understanding how society filters opportunities by social class, race, and sex. These networks with critical employment information were in the past largely upper-middle class, white, and male in America.

This network perspective offers one reason African Americans who attend interracial schools as children get better jobs than comparable African Americans who attend all-black schools (Braddock, 1989; Braddock, Crain & McPartland, 1984). Integrated education enables them to break through the white monopoly and gain access to critical information about jobs and other opportunities. This explanation does not require that the blacks actually learned more in the interracial schools, or even had particularly close white friends.

In sum, false is the correct response for all ten items of the quiz. If you correctly thought most of the items were false, then three possible conclusions arise. Perhaps you have already taken social science courses. Maybe you have a genuine talent for social science thinking. You will make a prudent consumer of social science findings, and you might even consider specializing in one of these fields. Possibly you shrewdly detected that the context of this opening chapter was to show that social science findings are not as obvious as many think, so you responded accordingly. Such sensitivity to social context suggests you have a talent for thinking like a social scientist.

If, however, you thought many of these items were true, then you share this with most people. You can take heart that I purposely selected tricky items. Not all social science results are so surprising. Yet "conventional wisdom," a less polite term for "common sense," often leads one astray in understanding the complexities of social life. For the fact remains: social life *is* complex.

1.3 THE COMPLEXITIES OF STUDYING SOCIAL LIFE

There are many reasons social life is so complex and difficult to study. Here we shall describe five of the most important reasons.

1.3.1 Multiple Causation

Few events in the social world are caused by only one factor. Multiple factors shape most phenomena, especially the important ones. Popular analyses often search for the *one* key factor to explain an entire social phenomenon. For example, research in criminology (the study of crime) shows that many factors contribute to America's high rates of crime today. Yet many in political life act as if it were caused by only one simple factor—the so-called "breakdown in family values," or not enough fear of punishment by criminals, or whatever. Social scientists have learned not to expect the social world to be so simply constructed. An important part of thinking like a social scientist is to expect and search for multiple causal agents.

Making it more complicated, the many causal, **independent variables** used to predict a phenomenon (the **dependent variable**) are often tightly interrelated themselves. The difficult problem for the social analyst in interpreting such data is how to extract the causal relationships from a mass of possibilities. While this exercise is usually painstaking and time-consuming, it also can be great fun. It is not unlike Sherlock Holmes solving a baffling mystery, so it is my favorite task as a social scientist.

The difference between this situation and that of much research in chemistry and physics is striking. Social science, even in laboratory experiments, must work in **open systems**—situations in which the key **variables** under test are not the only ones operating. Physical science can often approximate **closed systems** for its research. Such closed systems isolate the few variables of interest from contaminating external variables.

1.3.2 Multilevel

As noted in the presidential vote example, significant aspects of social life occur on different levels of analysis. Popular analyses often stay at only the best known and most immediate level of the individual. Yet this is not enough to capture the complexity of social life. All the social sciences have found it necessary to work at higher levels as well.

Hence, macroeconomics considers the economy from the broadest structural perspective. Political science views the entire political **system,** not just individual voters. Cultural anthropology treats whole cultures and societies, not just the individuals within them. Demography studies whole populations. Sociology looks at whole societies, as well as institutions within societies. Social psychology is the most individually oriented of all. Yet it also specializes in groups of people, particularly in face-to-face situations where people interact.

Those new to social science usually find the broader structural levels of analyses the most difficult to understand at first. We are not as accustomed to thinking of social structures as we are of individual people. The basic idea, however, is straightforward. Social science uses the term social structure to represent two basic aspects of organized social life. First, social arrangements are *patterned*, not random. Second, these patterns are *relatively persistent* over time. Social structure, therefore, translates to *relatively persistent social patterns*.

Institutions, such as colleges, are one type of social structure. To see how social structure works, consider student life at your college. The social world is always changing, so college life this year is not exactly the same as it was last year. Yet events this year on campus are more similar to last year's events than life on other college campuses. In other words, campus life at your college is *patterned* from year to year, and it is relatively *persistent* even though social change is always occurring. In Chapters 6 and 7, we shall return to this basic concept of social structure that underlies much of what is distinctive about social scientific thinking.

1.3.3 Relational

Social life does not merely consist of separate entities at different levels of analysis. These entities relate to each other in complex but patterned ways. So the many aspects of student life on your campus—from dormitory routines to academic expectations—are related to each other. It is these relational links between various aspects of the social world that make up social structure.

There is a direct analogy here with the human body. The human organism does not consist just of its separate parts—the ears, eyes, nose, bones, etc. The essence of the organism is how these various parts interact with each other to form a patterned, organized system. So it is with social systems. This systemic pattern of relational links between parts is why "the whole is more than the sum of its parts." This truism holds throughout social science. We will see the concept of system used at all levels of analysis—from personality system to political system.

Chapter 7 will focus on this feature of social life. There we will learn how social systems, like the human body, are open systems. They are not self-contained; rather they depend on an exchange with the environment. Just as the body ingests food and excretes, so does a factory take on raw materials and produce products. This open quality of social systems means that we also must study the relations *between* systems. Thus, open systems are more complex to study than closed systems because the links *between* open systems become important.

1.3.4 Reactivity

Human beings present a constantly moving target. This fact is a fourth reason underlying the complexity of social life. This complication, too, differs from physical science. Many of the major variables of physics and chemistry are inert and change over time only because of the causal variables under test.

Reactivity refers to human beings reacting to each other, to being interviewed, to hearing an economic forecast or a political prediction. Human beings are constantly changing because they are reacting to their environment. In reacting, they affect what caused them to react in the first place. So the subject matter of social science is always in perpetual flux, often changing as a direct function of social science research itself. For example, people interviewed by political surveys become, as a result of the interview, more likely to vote on election day.

Consider the effects of economic forecasts. These widely-broadcast predictions lead many people to change their economic plans. A forecast of bad times ahead, for instance, might cause many investors to sell their stocks. If enough people do this, their actions can affect the accuracy of the forecast itself. If the stock sales drive down share prices, they may help confirm the forecast. Thus, a **self-fulfilling prophecy** occurs. The economic prediction itself helped to cause the prediction to come true.

In a similar vein, some worry the mass media practice of announcing survey predictions during election campaigns may affect voting results. Television coverage of American presidential elections makes this problem more acute. The networks announce early survey results and voting returns from the East long before voting has ended in the West. People may become less likely to vote when they see their favorite candidates far behind. Or, perhaps, people may be less likely to vote when the media predict their favorites to win and their single vote seems less necessary.

Human reactivity often operates through expectancies (Rosenthal & Jacobson, 1968). If elementary school teachers think Linda is bright, they will *expect* her to do well in her classes. This expectation can cause the teachers to behave differently toward Linda. They wait longer than usual for Linda to respond to questions because they are certain she will know the correct answers. These behaviors are so subtle that teachers themselves are usually not aware of them, yet they can create a self-fulfilling prophecy. The teachers' expectations that Linda will perform well shape a situation in which Linda does indeed perform well! Unfortunately, teachers' expectancies also can work in the opposite direction to the disadvantage of those students thought to be less intelligent.

Laboratory experiments in social psychology show how powerful such expectancies can be in interpersonal situations. One study had two students interact who had not met before (Snyder & Swann, 1978). Before the interaction, the experimenter led one of the subjects to expect that the other student would behave in a hostile manner. This expectation caused the subject to act in a way that provoked hostile behavior from the other subject. Thus, the misinformed subject's expectations actually shaped the other subject's behavior into a self-fulfilling prophecy. Many similar studies show this intense reactivity of human beings to subtle, non-verbal cues.

Reactivity is so powerful that social research must take care not to allow it to distort results. Toward this end, social scientists use an array of "nonreactive" measures ranging from covert observations to **archival data** (Webb, Campbell, Schwartz, Sechrest & Grove, 1981).

1.3.5 Measurement Error

Measurement refers to the assignment of numbers to objects or events so that we can study them systematically. Such number assignment must be done according to established rules if it is to make sense (Stevens, 1968:850). An I.Q. test score of 110 makes no sense unless we know how this score was obtained, that 100 is the average score, etc. Any distortion in this score in how it reflects what it is supposed to be measuring is **measurement error.**

By the nature of its phenomena, social science must contend with large amounts of measurement error in its research compared to that of the physical sciences. The accuracy and calibration of measures in chemistry and physics are often quite fine compared to the size of the effects studied. For the reasons we have just reviewed, it is difficult to measure with such precision the complexities of social life.

There are two types of measurement error—**variable error** and **constant error.** Variable error is random **error.** Research can reduce it by having more observations or subjects. More serious is constant error—non-random error that deviates in one direction from the "true" data. Simply increasing the number of observations or subjects will not correct constant errors. Such expansion will only magnify them.

A measure's **reliability** refers to the problem of variable error. A highly reliable measure has less variable error. There are two types. **Test-retest reliability** involves the stability of measures recorded at different times. If you take an achievement test today, will you get a similar score when you take the same or equivalent test a few weeks later? **Internal consistency reliability** gauges the cohesion of a measure. Do the various items of the achievement test correlate with each other?

A measure's validity refers to constant error. Here the focus is on how well the measure captures the essence of the abstract **construct.** Are the various tests of intellectual skills *valid* measures of the abstract construct of intelligence? If so, constant error is relatively low.

There are several ways to estimate validity. **Face validity** is just a matter of judgment: Does the measure look (on the *face* of it) as if it measures the construct? Do the questions asked in the I.Q. test look to you like questions that measure intelligence? **Convergent validity** goes a step further. It asks if the measure relates positively with other measures of the same construct. Does I.Q. test A correlate closely with I.Q. test B? **Divergent validity** is exactly the opposite. It checks to see if the measure *fails* to relate with measures of *other* constructs. Does the I.Q. test *not* relate with measures of personality that are thought to be unrelated to intelligence? Finally, **criterion validity** asks: Does the measure relate with other variables as theory holds the construct should? Do the I.Q. test scores predict grades in school?

Business sections of daily newspapers routinely recognize measurement error. When the U.S. government announces its economic indices each month, they often carry with them a correction for data advanced in earlier months. Sometimes these monthly corrections are large enough to change conclusions about the trends of the current economy. These changes may alter "housing starts"—the number of new houses on which construction began each month—by several hundred thousand units. They may alter unemployment data by hundreds of thousands of workers.

These changes are important. Major decisions of economic policy as well as many individual investment decisions rely on them. Government agencies carefully collect and analyze these data precisely because they are so important. However, by the nature of the measurement of social variables, some error is inherent in them.

It is informative to note the difficulties of a non-social science that also experiences large degrees of error in its predictions. The study and prediction of earthquakes has made marked advances in recent years, but it shares error problems with social science. So earthquake specialists grapple with difficulties that resemble those of social science. Since people are deeply concerned with and react to these results and predictions, this field's work also gets entangled with controversy.

1.4 SO WHO DIDN'T KNOW THAT?

The study of social life, then, is complex for many reasons. The task of social science is anything but simple. Yet this fact is neither commonly understood nor accepted. Why? We have already discussed one reason—we all can fancy ourselves as a social scientist though we cannot similarly imagine ourselves to be an astrophysicist. We think we understand the social world because we negotiate our way through it each day.

Another reason is that social science findings often appear obvious—*after the fact*. The findings seem that way because every culture develops sayings (aphorisms) to prepare us for common social eventualities. These aphorisms in time gain the ring of true wisdom. The problem is that one can use them after the fact to "explain" whatever happens. So, "absence makes the heart grow fonder," but "out of sight, out of mind." "There is no place like home," but "the grass is always greener on the other side of the fence." "Think before you jump," but "he who hesitates is lost." Thus, no matter what direction social scientific findings take, a cultural aphorism can *later* "explain" them.

Social science teachers learn the hard way how obvious many research findings appear to many students. Most of us have had the experience of giving a spirited lecture on our favorite research findings only to hear the dreaded refrain: "So who didn't know that? Do you mean to tell me that it took a research grant of thousands of dollars to find that out? You could have just asked my mother!"

Samuel Stouffer, a distinguished sociologist who taught at Harvard University, would fume at this response. He decided to do something about it. He devised a true-false test that was the inspiration for the one you have just taken. In fact, the first two items from his Army morale study were part of his version of the test. Stouffer handed out his test on the first day of class in his undergraduate courses. All 20 items were false, yet most of his Harvard students marked the majority of the items as true.

Stouffer would collect the tests before announcing the answers. Then, with considerable satisfaction, he would make his preemptory strike. Breaking into a broad smile, Stouffer would shout out, "Who didn't know that? *You* didn't know that!" Having answered the dreaded question before anyone had even asked it, Stouffer then proceeded to give his inspired lectures on survey research.

There is another more emotional factor involved in the resistance to social science. Social scientific theories and findings can threaten our established beliefs and understanding of the world. Aphorisms are often wrong; cultural truisms turn out to be mistaken; new ideas and data challenge comfortable positions of privilege. I shall later argue that social science is most useful precisely when it is advancing discomforting insights against the tide of dominant opinion.

Little wonder, then, that social science receives more than its share of harsh criticism. Economics has long been called "the dismal science." The poet W. H. Auden coined the phrase, "to commit a social science" to mean to make a silly or outrageous statement. Witty, but one can easily detect a note of threat.

Likewise, former Senator William Proxmire from Wisconsin enjoyed entertaining the U.S. Senate with contemptuous citations of social science studies. Each month the senator would attract publicity by announcing his "Golden Fleece Award." These dubious awards would cite an instance of what Proxmire considered an outrageous example of government waste. Often he would rip out of context an obscure-sounding project from the records of government sponsored research. Without having read the investigation, Proxmire would rage against its having been funded.

In one celebrated incident, he attacked a psychological study of aggression in monkeys (Kiesler & Lowman, 1980). The researcher soon lost his federal funding for the research. He then surprised the senator by suing for defamation. He argued that Proxmire's attack had seriously damaged his standing as a psychologist and researcher. After lengthy court battles, the Supreme Court of the United States ruled in the psychologist's favor.

Whatever the merits of this case, the general point is well taken. By definition, social science treads on subjects of great and immediate interest to people—money, power, culture, even personal matters. Of necessity then, controversy will always surround social science. It will often be "hot in the kitchen," whether social scientists like it or not. The Audens and Proxmires of the world will always be around.

Moreover, every field needs critics. Many critics chafe particularly about social science writing. Why must it be so awkward, so abstruse and filled with new words (neologisms)? I partly agree. I think social scientists should write more clearly, though there is far greater variety than critics allow.

I will, however, defend the use of neologisms. No one criticizes physical science when it finds it necessary to employ new terms. Yet there is an unstated assumption by critics that social science should conduct its work while limited to popular terms of the language. When social science does adopt popular terms, such as "intelligence," it often causes confusion. Typically, the popular term has additional meanings (such as "intelligence" being a single, one-factor entity) that turn out to be imprecise. New terms have the distinct advantage of being precisely defined without such erroneous connotations.

The deeper problem caused by the immediate relevance of social science for everyday life involves values—judgments of right and wrong and what "ought to be." Social scientists are human beings with their own values who study human beings. So value assumptions in their theory and research are unavoidable. In addition, the work of social science may influence public policy in ways that directly affect people's lives. For these reasons, the work of social science necessarily involves values.

To be sure, the natural sciences cannot escape the involvement of values either. One need only think of the painfully difficult value questions raised by atomic energy or DNA research. Yet social science is especially open to charges of value **bias** by those unhappy with its results and conclusions.

Social scientists are not of one mind on the role of values. Unfortunately, some simply deny the issue. They come to regard themselves as completely "objective." They might agree it is a problem for others, but not for themselves. Nonetheless, most social scientists, I believe, would agree with the Swedish economist, Gunnar Myrdal (1944:1043), when he argued that values are inherent in social science. Be aware of your values, Myrdal maintained, struggle against their biasing effects in your work, and alert your readers to them. Objectivity becomes, then, a sought-for goal of social science, one that you must strive for even if you can never fully attain it.

1.5 SUMMING UP

The social sciences study social life. As such, everyone can think of themselves as a social scientist. This closeness to life has significant consequences for social science, consequences we have considered in this chapter.

It is all too easy to ignore the deep complexities of social life. In doing so, some come to regard the work of social science as obvious—*after the fact*. The short quiz revealed the not so obvious character of many social science findings.

We noted five reasons for the complexity of social life. It is multiply determined, highly interrelated, and simultaneously operates at several levels. Social life is also reactive. Human beings present a moving target; they generally react back to each other and their environment. Finally, social scientists must work with a high level of error in their measurements of this complex scene. Effective measures must possess both reliability (stability over time and internal consistency) and validity (accurate representations of the abstract constructs they are intended to tap).

In the midst of this complexity, social science deals with matters that matter—issues that affect people's lives. Not surprisingly, then, social science has more than its share of critics—many of them thoughtful, some just abusive. Moreover, its most policy-relevant work will necessarily be controversial. This relevancy also means that the values held by social scientists themselves will be involved in their work. They can and should strive for objectivity, yet complete objectivity is unobtainable.

With all these problems—from complexity to controversy, one might wonder how social science can operate at all. The principal weapons any science has to combat these problems are the rigor of its theory and methods, peer review and criticism, and a special form of critical thinking that is the subject of this volume. Basic to this manner of thinking is a *healthy skepticism*.

By "*healthy,*" I mean an open stance to new ideas and research results. A nihilistic negativism that virtually rejects the possibility of advancing our understanding of social life is not constructive. Such a rejection is self-fulfilling. If we do not expect to advance knowledge, we will not do so.

By "*skepticism,*" I mean a full appreciation of the rich complexities of social life as discussed in this chapter. Such a view includes being skeptical of your work, too, and being prepared—even expecting—for later work to prove you wrong. Such a humbling prospect is usually in the cards. Advances in science are social products, the work of many scientists and many efforts—not the result of lonely scholars working in pristine isolation. Science advances by adopting a critical stance and subjecting its work to critical review.

Throughout the book, we will define the many forms this healthy skepticism assumes. The final chapter will ask you to play the **role** of a healthy skeptic yourself. You will review articles drawn from leading newspapers and try out what you have learned about thinking like a social scientist.

ISSUES FOR DISCUSSION AND REVIEW

A> Does the subject matter of social science pose more—or fewer—difficulties than those of physics and chemistry? Why?

B> Some social scientists believe that it is best not to discuss values. They strive for "objectivity." They do not think they need to inform others about their personal values. Other social scientists disagree. They believe they should publicly express their values so others can better judge how "objective" their research is. What do you think?

RECOMMENDATIONS FOR FURTHER READING ON ISSUES RAISED IN THIS CHAPTER

On the Complexity of the Social World:

For readers who wish to read a basic source:

H. M. Blalock, Jr. 1984. *Basic Dilemmas in the Social Sciences*. Beverly Hills, CA: Sage.

On Expectancy Effects:

For readers who wish to read a basic source:

R. Rosenthal and L. Jacobson. 1968. *Pygmalian in the Classroom*. New York: Holt, Rinehart & Winston.

On Values in Social Science:

For readers who wish to read a basic source:

G. Myrdal. 1944. *An American Dilemma*. New York, Harper & Row. Appendix 2.

Chapter
2

Thinking Theoretically

Theory has a bad name in popular American thought. It often connotes high-flown, unrealistic ideas too impractical to be useful. Moreover, many view scientific theories to be so abstract as to be impossible to understand. Perhaps Einstein's famous theory of relativity led to this view.

This prevalent attitude goes with the stereotype of scientists in general—genial people, perhaps, but so hopelessly wrapped up in their impractical theories they can barely navigate through their daily lives. Yet thinking theoretically is an essential part of science. Indeed, theory is essential for everyone. Our actions are based on predictions that derive from our unstated "mini-theories" about the social world.

To see why theory is essential to thinking like a social scientist, this chapter sketches the broad outlines of social theory. Just what is a theory? How do you define a theory's key concepts? What makes a theory useful? From where do theories come? We shall see that theories are part of larger scientific perspectives (**paradigms**). Finally, we shall consider how theories take different forms across the social science disciplines.

2.1 WHAT IS A THEORY?

Social science theories are answers to puzzles. They arise from conflicts between our observations and our present understanding of the social world. They are attempts to explain unexpected research results, contradictions, inconsistencies—anything that does not logically follow from our present grasp of how social life operates. When successful, theories advance our knowledge of social life.

Social theories take many forms, yet they all express *ideas* about the social world. They do so with abstract statements that attempt to add to scientific knowledge in five important ways. (1) Theories help to *classify* "things"—entities, processes, and causal relationships. (2) They also help to *predict* future events as well as (3) *explain* past events. (4) Theories are especially important for *understanding* what *causes* events. (5) Finally, they *guide research* in useful directions by specifying on what to focus and what to ignore. Not all theories perform all five tasks. Yet a theory wins acceptance within social science by how well it accomplishes these tasks.

Theories, then, are formal statements of ideas to advance science in these five ways. They do so by proposing particular concepts (or constructs) that classify and describe the phenomenon; then they offer a set of interrelated statements using these concepts. These statements must use a common language others will understand—often this language is mathematics. Theories put in verbal form usually must be translated into statistical terms before they can be rigorously tested (Blalock, 1969, 1984).

Hence, we must formalize theories to communicate clearly with other scientists and to allow research tests of the idea. The statements are systematically related to each other and include causal **generalizations** that are directly testable. Science values simply stated theories, because such theories are more easily understood and tested. Yet, given the complexity of the social world, we cannot always achieve this desirable feature.

We will be discussing social theories throughout the book. Recall examples from Chapter 1. In the question on military morale, we saw how two concepts—reference groups and relative deprivation—helped to explain the surprising results. These concepts expressed the theory's basic idea—that comparisons with significant others shape human satisfaction (Walker & Pettigrew, 1984). In the question on homicide after wars, the concept of a violent culture captured the theory's basic idea. Homicide increases after wars, the theory holds, because war culturally legitimizes violence. In the question on payment and lying, the concept of cognitive dissonance explained why subjects paid only $1 changed their views of the boring experiment more than those paid $20.

Observe in each example that the facts do *not* speak for themselves—as the adage claims. Observations must be part of a broader context, a *theoretical* context, before they gain importance and are generalizable to other situations. This needed context, then, must be *abstract*. So, social scientists state their broad theories in a general way that is universal and not unique to a particular location or time. Any test of the theory, however, is *concrete* and limited to the specific conditions of the test.

2.2 DEFINING A THEORY'S KEY CONCEPTS

Concepts (or constructs) are terms needed to shape and communicate ideas. We have seen how they form the building blocks with which we *construct* theories. New theories often introduce concepts, such as relative deprivation, that present a novel approach to an old problem.

Many social science concepts are *fuzzy*—that is, precise definitions are not possible and their boundaries are unclear. This imprecision can cause difficulties for social theory. This is especially true when, as Chapter 1 mentioned, the concept has popular meanings different from those of social science usage. For example, the popular idea of public opinion turns out to be extremely difficult to define. V. O. Key, Jr., the political scientist, quipped it was harder to define than the religious conception of the Holy Ghost!

Yet fuzzy concepts cause fewer problems in social science than you might think. This is true in part because agreement among social scientists about a concept's meaning is more important than its formal, verbal definition. Fuzzy definitions are also often adequate, because the concrete variables that represent the concept in research define it more precisely. Hence, the specific procedures that measure the variables are called **operational definitions.**

For example, *intelligence* is an abstract construct (or concept). Psychologists measure it by a set of variables thought to be *valid* representations of the abstract concept. The actual procedures for measuring these variables with an intelligence test comprise the operational definition of intelligence. Some would argue what the test measures defines what we mean by intelligence, that the operational definition is itself sufficient. Most social scientists reject this view. They regard this measure of intelligence to be only one among many acceptable operational definitions; the abstract concept is much broader than what any particular test measures.

Social scientists may disagree over a concept's exact verbal definition. If they agree on the variables that measure it, however, research can proceed. For example, there is debate over the verbal definition of social class—a central concept in sociology. Yet there is general agreement that three variables measure social class—years of educational attainment, annual income, and the prestige of one's occupation. As with these three measures of social class, it is highly desirable to have multiple measures of a single concept. Each measure contains its own unique error. So the core meaning of the concept is captured by what the measures have in common.

The problem of fuzzy definitions varies according to the type of concept. **Primitive concepts** are the most basic terms, but the hardest to define precisely. Shared agreement about primitive concepts is vital, because other concepts cannot describe them. **Derived** (or **nominal**) **concepts** are, as their name implies, derived from primitive concepts. Obviously, the whole theoretical stack of cards depends on our having a common understanding of the basic, if fuzzy, primitive concepts.

2.3 WHAT MAKES A THEORY USEFUL?

If concepts are the building blocks of theory, the relational statements that comprise the theory form the structure. The bare bones theoretical statement can simply state A *causes* B. In Chapter 4 we will see that the idea of cause is complicated. So even this simple statement requires careful testing. It may turn out that A causes B only under condition X. When the situation is different from X, A does not lead to B. In such common situations, the X condition is a **moderator variable,** since it *moderates* the relationship between A and B.

In social psychological experiments, for example, female subjects often conformed more than male subjects. Alice Eagly (1978; Eagly & Carli, 1981) reviewed these studies. She found this relationship held primarily in studies conducted before 1970 by male experimenters who used tasks in which males have an advantage. In recent studies conducted by females with tasks familiar to both sexes, gender differences in conformity disappear. Thus, the date of the study, the sex of the experimenter, and the type of task *moderate* the relationship between sex and conformity. This simple five-variable theory now allows us to predict *when* females will conform more than males and *when* they will not. It also suggests how traditional gender roles operate in our culture. These roles were stronger before 1970 and are triggered by male experimenters and male-oriented tasks.

A may relate to B only because they both relate to C. In this causal statement, C, the **mediator variable,** explains directly *why* A relates to B. Taller people usually weigh more than others. So height (A) and weight (B) positively relate with each other, yet no direct causal connection exists between them. Such mediators as genes and diet explain the relationship. Thus, genetic and nutritional factors *mediate* the positive **correlation coefficient** between height and weight.

More commonly, mediators account for some, but not all, of the link between A and B. That is, A partly causes B, but the relationship is also influenced by mediators that relate to both A and B. For instance, many studies show that older white Americans are on average more prejudiced against minorities than others. Education mediates *some* (but not all) of this relationship. Older people have had on average less education than younger people, and better educated people are usually less prejudiced. The link between age and prejudice involves other mediators as well. Continued work might uncover many more mediators, each explaining a portion of the original relationship. In time, a large array of mediating factors might account for the full correlation between age and prejudice. At that point, we would fully understand why older people are often more prejudiced.

By such means, theories become useful by helping with the five tasks specified above—to classify, predict, explain, understand, and guide research. The **surplus meaning** of both concepts and theories helps in accomplishing these tasks. Surplus meaning refers to the extra meanings and ideas conveyed by concepts and theories that go beyond their formal definitions and statements. The importance of surplus meaning suggests a rough rule of thumb for how useful a new concept or theory is: *Does it lead to new ideas that you would not have had without the new concept or theory?* If it does, then clearly the new idea is useful.

This rule of thumb is not as simple as it may first appear. It contradicts a popular notion about ideas in general—namely, that they are useful only when they are "true." In Chapter 4 we will learn that the assessment of "truth" is neither easy nor direct. Hence, we must place such terms in quotation marks to remind us of this problem.

Scientific theories that later prove to be wholly or largely "wrong" often lead to scientific advances. They do so by setting off the sparks of sound ideas in others. Often such theories shape later advances by forcing critics to counter them with rival theories and research. By our rule of thumb, then, these theories are useful although they later prove to be "wrong."

Popular misconceptions about science fuel this difference between scientific and non-scientific thinking. As emphasized in Chapter 1, science is a social enterprise, not the creation of lonely individuals uninfluenced by others. Scientific advances, then, are social products made possible by the work of many people. Even those who advance theories that later prove to be inadequate contribute to the advances.

Theories are also necessary guides to research. We noted the complexity of social life and the almost limitless number of possible variables and causal links that we could study. Remember high school algebra. When there are too many unknowns in a set of equations, solutions are impossible. The social researcher routinely faces this situation. Theory must supply the needed unknowns for work to proceed.

There is, then, a need to narrow our search and avoid *fishing expeditions.* Aimless investigations, unguided by theory, are wasteful of resources and usually fruitless. Well-specified theories provide research direction. They suggest which variables to measure (to represent the key concepts) and what causal relationships to test. Hence, theories reduce the many possibilities to a manageable context for research. Therefore, we need theories to guide research just as we need research to test theories. Science requires a constant interchange between theory and research, with each shaping and guiding the other.

2.4 FROM WHERE DO THEORIES COME?

Puzzles motivate scientists to formulate theories. The ideas advanced in theories come from experience and imagination. This is a major reason social science benefits by having people among its ranks from a wide variety of backgrounds. The more diverse the origins of social scientists, the wider the net of special experiences and knowledge upon which to draw. This provides an additional reason for affirmative action efforts to recruit more women and minorities into social science. To be sure, these efforts are steps toward greater opportunities and fairness for underrepresented groups. In addition, such efforts aid social science by widening its range of ideas and theories.

Science at the theory-building stage is open to influence from all sources. It is a mistake to think that science consists only of quantitative research and statistics. Qualitative research is particularly important at this stage. It can get close to social life to gain new ideas and insights before we learn how to conceptualize and quantify the phenomena under study.

There are, however, two major differences between scientific and non-scientific theories. First, scientists design their theories to be testable and open to disproof (*falsifiable*). Second, rigorous research then tests the scientific theory.

We can learn from where theories come by reviewing three examples of social theory development at different levels of analysis. In each case there is a puzzle to solve, a contradiction to explain. And in each, social scientists draw on their special experiences to propose a solution for the puzzle.

The puzzles that social theorists must solve take many forms. flicting research results present the puzzle. So does the failure of generalize to a new time, situation, or group of people. Our first e: this type. It describes how sociologists expanded their theory of self-esteem when it did not apply to children.

Sometimes the contradiction arises from the failure of theory to explain what you think you know from your personal experience. My work illustrates this situation. Sometimes a glaring contradiction between abstract theory and societal events present the puzzle. This situation describes our final example. Keynesian theory, a major advance in economics, developed as a direct result of a clash between theory and events.

2.4.1 Rosenberg's Theory of Self-Esteem

Often puzzles come from within social science itself. Discrepancies in empirical findings arise from studies conducted by different investigators on different samples in different locations. Social scientists then alter their theories to explain such discrepancies.

Similarly, **error cases** can suggest a puzzle. Error cases are instances where the theory's predictions are clearly incorrect. Such cases are important and worth careful attention. They inform us about the weakness of the theory under test. Suppose close inspection of a study's data reveals there are many error cases of a particular type. This circumstance suggests not only the theory's inadequacy, but how to improve it.

Such an instance occurred in the sociological study of self-esteem. Rosenberg and Pearlin (1978) set out to reconcile a series of conflicting findings. Among adults, higher social class standing relates to higher self-esteem. However, among adolescents this relationship is weak, and among younger children it disappears. How can we explain these differences? The two sociologists formulated and tested four different explanations for this puzzle.

(1) *Social comparison.* Adults meet a far wider class range of persons than children and perceive class differences more than children. (2) *Reflected appraisal.* Since we see ourselves in part as others see us, the wider class contacts of adults also shape self-esteem through how others react to us. (3) *Self-perception.* We also form our self-image by observing our own behavior as others observe it. Children are born into their social class standing (**ascribed status**), while adults often achieve theirs. Hence, adults are more likely to make inferences concerning their self-worth from their social class standing. (4) *Psychological centrality.* The more centrally important social class dimensions are to a person, the more they influence self-esteem. Hence, income and self-esteem relate strongest for those adults who most value money. Children are often confused about their social class position—thus, it cannot be as central for them.

Once they had specified these four processes, Rosenberg and Pearlin had accomplished more than merely explaining the original empirical puzzle. They had developed a broader, more inclusive theory of the social development of self-esteem.

2.4.2 Explaining Anti-Black Prejudice Among White Southerners

Less sweeping theories often arise out of a social scientist's personal experience. Like most social scientists, I can illustrate the point with an example from my experience. I grew up in the American South in the midst of intensive racial segregation. Anti-black prejudice and discrimination were deeply ingrained in the traditions of Virginia during the 1930s and 1940s. As an undergraduate at the University of Virginia, I became interested in social science because I wanted to study and combat these phenomena. I read extensively on the subject. There I confronted theoretical arguments that did not fit with my southern experience. The conflict between what I read about racial prejudice and what I thought I knew about it posed the puzzle for me.

The classic work on *The Authoritarian Personality* (Adorno, Frenkel-Brunswik, Levinson & Sanford, 1950) appeared when I was a college sophomore. Its exciting research and analysis became the dominant theory of prejudice in social science in the 1950s, inspiring thousands of follow-up studies. It emphasized the personality basis of prejudice. It did not study the South, however, and it virtually ignored power, culture, and social structure in race relations.

Using insights from Sigmund Freud's psychoanalytic theory, the book focuses on the well-established fact that prejudiced people typically reject not just one but many outgroups. The study showed that people with multiple prejudices often have a particular personality syndrome—called *the authoritarian personality*. Though originally inspired by German Nazis, research throughout the world supports many of the personality tenets of the book.

The authoritarian personality gets its name from its central feature. Authoritarians have an up-and-down (hierarchical) view of society; they see people as ranked in status from top to bottom. Toward authorities at the top, such people are compliant, even obsequious (authoritarian submission). Toward those perceived as beneath them in status, they aggressively demand compliance (authoritarian aggression). In addition, the multiply-prejudiced do not like to think deeply about themselves. They try not to look inside at their own personalities (anti-intraception).

As an undergraduate, I found this analysis fascinating. It *was* a major advance in the understanding of prejudice at the individual level of analysis. Yet it did not help me to understand the pervasive southern patterns of racial hatred and discrimination that surrounded me.

Most of the people I knew well—friends and family members—expressed varying degrees of anti-black prejudice and acceptance of racial discrimination, although few of them exhibited features of the authoritarian personality. From my "up close" experience, then, I doubted if greater authoritarianism among white Southerners could explain the region's racist patterns.

The theory is not so wrong as it is incomplete. In ignoring cultural and structural factors, it omitted the South's peculiar history that fashioned its racial problems—slavery, frontier values, a lost civil war, and deep poverty. I drew up a survey research design that could test my ideas. Later I followed the design for my doctoral thesis research.

Surveys of the white populations of four southern and four northern towns provided the data for my thesis (Pettigrew, 1958, 1959, 1961, 1991a, 1993). I found the attitude measure of authoritarianism (the F-Scale) correlated with anti-black prejudice about the same in the two regions. Moreover, the average score on the measure was the same in the North and South. Authoritarianism, then, proved to be an important factor in racial prejudice in both regions at the individual level. Yet it did not explain the greater intensity of such prejudice in the South.

My research showed that the racial **norms** of the South, shaped by its special history, accounted for the regional difference. Norms are widely-shared expectations regarding how people should think and act (Pettigrew, 1991b). Conformity to the South's norms in other domains predicted the racial attitudes of the white Southern respondents. I repeated the study in South Africa with college student respondents with similar results. Later Middleton (1976) followed up this work in the South with larger samples, and both replicated and extended the results.

My questioning of an important social science analysis proved useful. Research supported my theoretical hunches, stemming directly from my experience in the South and extended them to another society. The point for the reader is to have confidence in your ideas about how the social world operates. When what you learn in social science does not fit with your experience, question the social scientific material. Then formulate your idea in testable terms and gather data. You may be right!

2.4.3 Keynesian Theory in Economics

John Maynard Keynes was an English economist with wide experience in public policy. A critic of classical economic theory, he was a successful financier and journalist before he became the most famous economic theorist of the 20th century. He developed his influential theory in direct response to his criticism of British economic policy.

Keynes' interests in public policy were of long standing. The son of an economist, he showed skill in political debate with Cambridge University's student government. He later served as an economic advisor to the Versailles peace conference following World War I. Events at this 1919 conference horrified Keynes. The Allies required Germany to pay enormous amounts as reparations for war damage. Keynes believed these payments were excessive, could never be paid, and would deter European economic development. He correctly foresaw disaster.

Keynes left the peace conference in protest and ill health, and wrote a stinging indictment of the treaty (Keynes, 1920). Out of government throughout the 1920s, Keynes wrote frequently in leading newspapers on economic policy. He worried about the persistent unemployment of workers in major sectors of Britain's economy—such as coal miners and shipyard workers. His widely-read commentaries advocated public work projects to supply useful jobs for these long-term unemployed workers.

Dominant economic opinion, however, flatly rejected Keynes' remedy. It placed its faith firmly in classical economic theory; an unfettered **market** would somehow right the economy's imbalances. Besides, went the argument, the unemployed could secure jobs if they would accept less pay. Similarly, business could sell more goods if it would lower prices. Such concessions would reactivate the nation's economy. To his critics, Keynes' arguments were misguided—kind hearted, perhaps, but lacking a theoretical base. Without an alternative to classical economic theory, his popular articles had scant impact on British policies during the 1920s.

Soon thereafter, the Great Depression struck throughout the world. Keynes' worst fears came to pass. Mainstream economic theory could not account for the near-total collapse of both the British and world economies. The opportune time had arrived to challenge much of classical theory and to supply a different economic perspective.

Keynes, a political activist, seized the moment. Only now did he become a forceful theorist. First, he wrote *A Treatise on Money* (Keynes, 1930). Developing his ideas further, he produced his masterwork, *The General Theory of Employment, Interest and Money* (Keynes, 1936). Though technical and complex, this volume had direct relevance to the Depression. It held a government-sponsored policy of full employment could best achieve economic recovery.

Keynes questioned much of traditional economic thinking. In a depression, there was no wage so low it could eliminate unemployment. So it was both wrong and unjust to blame the unemployed for their plight. There was a need for an alternative explanation and remedy, and his volume supplied both. The new focus revolved around the concept of *aggregate demand*. This term refers to the total spending in an economy by consumers, business investors, and government. When aggregate demand is high, economic times are good. When it is low, sales of goods suffer and jobs are lost.

Keynes' analysis showed that consumer spending made only a limited contribution to aggregate demand. Hence, variations in business investment and government spending are of primary importance. So, in times of economic slowdowns, there is a need for an increase in spending by business and government. There are many ways government can affect spending. It can make borrowing easier by increasing the money supply and lowering interest rates. Often in mild recessions, such monetary alterations are enough to stimulate business investment and start the recovery.

Deep depressions, such as the devastating one of the 1930s, require stronger economic medicine. Government should change its exchange rates with other currencies, overhaul its taxation policies, and sharply increase its spending. Keynes' most radical break from the past was his remedy of deliberate government deficits for public works and subsidies to afflicted groups.

The world was ready for Keynes' views. They soon won wide acceptance throughout the industrial world, and have shaped American economic policies since 1935. For our purposes, the important point is that Keynes did not set out to be a theorist. The Great Depression that ravaged the industrial world in his time presented the puzzle. His interests in practical economic policy for Great Britain led him to fashion his innovative new theory.

There is a prejudice among many social scientists that holds practical work and policy interests in low esteem. It views such work as mere applications that do not advance social science understanding. This example challenges this narrow view. Keynes' work illustrates how practical work can lead back to exciting theoretical advances. There are many other examples. Theory suggests new ideas for application to social problems, and these applications in turn present new puzzles and ideas for theory. When working at its best, this full-cycle link between social theory and application is helpful to both.

2.5 PARADIGMS PROVIDE THE CONTEXTS FOR THEORIES

Keynes introduced more than a basic theory; he provided an innovative paradigm—a new perspective on economic systems. Our first two examples concerning theories of self-esteem and prejudice were simply additions to established theory within an existing paradigm. Keynesian economics accomplished far more. Classical economics held national governments to be weak, individual liberty paramount, and economic systems the sum of their parts (Hutton, 1986:218). In contrast, Keynes held governments to be powerful, individual liberty one among many values, and economic systems more than the sum of their parts. Such a shift in view encompasses far more than social research can test.

By making aggregate demand the centerpiece, the Keynesian paradigm offered a new form of macro-economics. Keynes' ideas suggested new theories and ways to conduct research on economic systems. These ideas posed new puzzles for solution while offering explanations for old puzzles other paradigms could not explain.

These are the five functions of new scientific paradigms. They (1) present a broad, new perspective, (2) suggest new theories and (3) types of research, and (4) pose new problems while (5) solving old ones.

There is, however, more agreement over what paradigms do than precisely what they are (Cohen, 1992). They are *not* theories. Theories are testable propositions about causal relationships. Paradigms are much broader. They provide the wider perspective within which a large set of interrelated theories and research studies develop. So paradigms are *meta-theoretical*—that is, they guide a whole scientific tradition. Thus, a paradigm offers a model that inspires a group of scientists to develop a coherent tradition of theory and research (Cohen, 1992:1412).

As extensive scientific traditions, paradigms become deeply established. When they shift, it is a major event. The most famous examples of dramatic paradigm shifts have occurred in the natural sciences. These *scientific revolutions,* in Thomas Kuhn's (1970) terms, change both scientific and popular thinking. Newtonian physics replaced earlier "natural laws," only to be overturned itself in the 20th century by the theory of relativity. In biology, Charles Darwin's theory of natural selection replaced earlier biblical and "natural law" explanations for the harmony between living forms and their environments.

Social science has no examples of such sweeping "revolutions." The nearest instance is the rejection of simple biological explanations for social phenomena following World War I (Pettigrew, 1980). The complexity of the social world has led to less agreement within the social sciences on any one supreme paradigm reigning unchallenged.

However, paradigm shifts do occur in social science. They are less decisive than the Newtonian and Darwinistic examples, but they serve similar functions. What typically happens is that the new perspectives add to, rather than replace, existing paradigms. Often the new ideas meld with older conceptions to form even broader perspectives.

Thus, Keynesian theory did not replace classical economic theory. Modern economics blends the two. Neo-classical analyses of *supply* remain while economists widely accept Keynes' emphasis on aggregate *demand*. Similar examples exist throughout social science. In sociology, conflict and consensus paradigms coexist and represent two sides of social reality (Turner, 1990). Conflict theories seek to explain social change, while consensus models seek to explain social order. Both are necessary concerns, though the two paradigms disagree in many ways. To witness paradigm shifts in social science, consider how perspectives on social deviance have shifted over the years.

2.5.1 Paradigm Shifts in Thinking About Social Deviance

Initially, social science regarded deviance from societal dictates as simply a problem of deviant individuals. That is, the cause of deviance rested entirely *within* those who committed the deviant acts. From this perspective, criminality, drug addiction, even mental illness show individual "weakness" for the condition. Early explanations held these individual conditions to be unchangeable (immutable), often genetic. Thus, society had no obligation to help deviants. What good would it do when cures were impossible? This *immutable dispositional paradigm* caused England to send debtors to prison although that made it impossible for them to repay their debts.

The next paradigm of deviance was less heartless. The *mutable dispositional paradigm* still thought the problem existed wholly within deviants themselves. However, it granted that the deviants could be cured. So people expected prisons, asylums, and other institutions to "treat" their inmates and end their deviance so they might return to society. Yet the basic responsibility of these institutions remained that of isolating these deviants from the general population. One needs only to look at most prisons today to see that their remedial mission remains secondary at best.

By the 19th century, social scientists began to propose a more complex *interactive paradigm*. This view held that deviance was a combined result of individual dispositions and social factors. Criminals and others seen as deviants were still held responsible in part, but social causes of their behavior were also important. This model of deviance did not gain full acceptance in social science until the 1950s.

The most striking paradigm shift on deviance came in the 1950s and 1960s. The *labeling and stigma paradigm* turned the view of deviance completely around. It saw the problem not with those labeled and stigmatized as deviants, but with those who had the power to label and stigmatize.

This new perspective questioned the whole concept of deviance. Was it not merely a *social construction?* That is, was it not a concept developed by society rather than a genuine phenomenon inherently existing in acts labeled "deviant?" After all, society's laws socially define criminality. That which is criminal in one society can be acceptable behavior in others. Hence, many nations do not tolerate the widespread ownership of guns allowed in the U.S. Some societies accept drug addiction; others label it deviant. Even the same society can accept some addictions while stigmatizing others. Western society has long tolerated addiction to alcohol and tobacco, while labeling other drug addictions as deviant.

There are limitations to labeling and stigma theory. Its analysis usually ignores the act regarded as deviant. Moreover, it often neglects society's involvement in these acts. Yet this theory provides a strikingly different vantage point from which to view deviance. Like other paradigm shifts, it broadens the range of inquiry and makes us think of issues ignored by older paradigms. Though it has not replaced the interactive paradigm of deviance, the labeling and stigma paradigm is now an important component of how social science regards deviance.

2.5.2 Kuhn's Model and the Struggle for Paradigm Acceptance

Paradigms in social science, then, are more modest in scope than those in the natural sciences. Nevertheless, Kuhn's (1970) analysis of scientific revolutions is useful in thinking like a social scientist.

Kuhn (1970) states that *normal science* works within a widely-accepted paradigm. This perspective becomes the cognitive cocoon within which *scientific communities* carry through in theory and research the many implications of the paradigm. It goes unchallenged until puzzling research results (anomalies) repeatedly arise. The existing paradigm cannot account for these anomalies. This situation brings on a scientific crisis that sets the scene for a scientific revolution.

At first, there is great reluctance to abandon the old perspective. In time, however, established scientists either convert to the new, more promising paradigm or die off (**cohort replacement;** see Chapter 5). This **conversion** process from one perspective to another is complex and not entirely rational. Neutral rules of theory construction and research remain important—they are what distinguish science from other ways of establishing knowledge. Yet, Kuhn maintains, political and other biasing factors also are involved. This is true for natural science, and it may be more true for social science.

Kuhn's model of scientific change is widely debated. It exaggerates the sharpness of paradigm shifts. These shifts consist less of a conversion than a slow, gradual process of melding and **replacement.** As we noted, the combining rather than substitution of paradigms is typical of the social sciences.

A second problem comes from a misreading of Kuhn's model by some commentators. Seizing on Kuhn's point concerning irrational factors involved with shifting perspectives, some claim the model shows that neutral rules of theory and research do not operate in science. With no valid ways of choosing between paradigms, goes the argument, scientists are no different from others who have no way to test their claims. Kuhn's model of scientific change has no such implication. Non-rational factors influence science as with any human enterprise. Nonetheless, the neutral procedures of science—the focus of this book—remain important and unique.

These issues aside, Kuhn's model has special strengths. Its basic concepts of paradigm, normal science, scientific community, and scientific revolution provide a useful perspective. Its denial of the romantic view of science as a completely rational enterprise marching relentlessly to final truth is a helpful corrective. Its emphasis upon scientific resistance to change is of special interest to social science.

That science resists new paradigms should not surprise us. Since science is a social product, it is subject to many of the barriers to change other social institutions exhibit. Dominant paradigms become the conventional wisdom. They get deeply rooted; careers of celebrated scientists are based on them; entire research traditions revolve around them. The paradigm's primitive concepts gain common meanings and acceptance. Thus, those on the periphery often introduce new paradigms. They are less enmeshed in the dominant paradigm, have less status, and less access to the leading journals. For these reasons, the acceptance of new scientific paradigms can be problematic (Kuhn, 1970).

Observers who romanticize science as a noble pursuit of truth decry this conservatism. They cite many instances where science was slow to adopt innovative breakthroughs. True enough, but the selection of these instances is biased. We need to know, as control comparisons, the frequency of other types of cases. The critics cite dramatic advances that science was slow to adopt. Yet we also need to know how often science adopted or rejected *negative* cases. The conservative stance of science has its drawbacks, to be sure, but it also screens out many false leads.

2.6 THE WIDE RANGE OF THEORIES IN SOCIAL SCIENCE

In addition to the range of competing paradigms in the social sciences, a variety of theories exist within paradigms. Theories range widely across the various social sciences both as to their level of analysis and how specific they are.

Experimental social psychology's theories are the narrowest in scope. Reflecting its root discipline of psychology, this field typically regards specific hypotheses and predictions as theories. Chapter 1's relative deprivation explanation is an example. From our perspective on theories, these specific predictions are more accurately regarded as parts of a more inclusive theory. Indeed, one prominent social psychologist complains that his field should advance broader theories (Kelley, 1983). He compares social psychologists to mining engineers instead of geologists. They dig down deeply, but they do not connect their insights with more general theories.

Broader theories in social science, however, often suffer from being too vague to allow direct empirical testing. Such broad theories represent general approaches, since their vagueness makes them impossible to disprove (falsify). General approaches can be useful in social science as paradigms, but we should not confuse them with theories. Those who prefer specific theories grumble that social science needs fewer "approaches" and more "arrivals."

The most effective theories for guiding social research are middle range in scope. These theories are more general than specific hypotheses, but not so broad and vague as to be untestable. Such theories are also broad enough to be generalized across cultures and nations. We will review such middle-range theories in Chapter 6.

Keynes' "general theory" shows how a more sweeping approach can be effective. We noted how this major contribution is basically a paradigm, for it introduced a perspective that countered classical economics. Yet Keynes also provided an array of middle-range theories within the paradigm that are testable. Little wonder, this work won wide attention.

Sociological theory is often even broader. Although called "grand theory," these contributions border on being paradigms. They cast a wide net for detailed work, but direct tests are not possible. Nineteenth-century sociology began the tradition of grand theory. A 20th-century example is Talcott Parsons' theory of action (Parsons, 1937, 1951, 1970; Parsons, Bales & Shils, 1953; Parsons & Shils, 1951).

The complexity of Parsons' ideas defy summary. Yet a brief description of his paradigm's aims provides a glimpse of its enormous sweep. Taking the systems approach we will discuss in Chapter 7, Parsons viewed the structural, cultural, and personality components of social life as interlocking systems. As such, these systems have common problems and processes. From 1937 until his death in 1979, the Harvard professor elaborated on these common problems and processes. Though criticized for its breadth, Parson's contentions have had a lasting influence on sociology. Like most grand theory, it provided a valuable paradigm even if further specification was necessary to allow empirical testing.

2.7 SUMMING UP

Theories are attempts to solve puzzles. Inconsistencies that arise from our present understanding of social life pose these puzzles. Theories advanced to explain these inconsistencies offer new ideas about the social world. They are essential to social science thinking, for they contribute to knowledge in five ways. Theories help to (1) classify, (2) predict future events, (3) explain past events, (4) understand causes, and (5) guide research.

Theories propose concepts (or constructs) to classify and describe the phenomena under study. They then advance a set of interrelated statements that propose how these concepts relate to each other. We formalize theories to communicate clearly and to allow research tests of the idea. Science values simply-stated theories, but the social world's complexity does not always permit them. Social theories must be abstract so we can generalize their ideas across locations and time. However, any test of the theory must be concrete and limited to the specific conditions of the test.

Concepts are the building blocks of theories. Social science concepts are often fuzzy, with imprecise definitions and unclear boundaries. This difficulty creates fewer problems than one might imagine. Agreement among scientists on a concept's measures is more important than agreement on its verbal definition. In addition, *fuzzy* definitions are often adequate, because the concrete variables that represent the concept in research define it more precisely. The specific procedures that measure the variables are called operational definitions. It also helps to have many variables to measure each concept. Each variable has unique variance of its own, but what the several variables have in common captures the concept.

In addition, we must distinguish between primitive and derived concepts. Primitive concepts are the most basic terms. Yet they are the hardest to define because other concepts cannot describe them. By contrast, we can define derived concepts with primitive concepts. Thus, the theoretical enterprise depends on a common understanding of the basic, but fuzzy, primitive concepts.

Relational statements constitute a theory's formal structure. Such simple statements as A causes B are rarely possible in a complex social world. Typically, social theories must specify the moderators and mediators of the relationships. Moderators predict *when* and *where* the relationship between A and B will hold true. Mediators tell us *why* a relationship exists.

The usefulness of new concepts and theories can be gauged by a rule of thumb: *Does it lead to new ideas that we would not have had without it?* Note that even theories that later prove to be incorrect may, by this rule, be useful. Many advances in science are the result of countering erroneous theories.

Theories are also useful guides to social research. They supply the needed unknowns to limit the possibilities to a manageable context for effective research. *Fishing expeditions*—aimless research unguided by theory—usually prove fruitless.

Theories come from many sources. At this initial stage, science is open to all forms of inspiration. There are two differences, however, between scientific and unscientific theories. Scientists design their theories to be testable and falsifiable, and then they test them with rigorous research. Since we often draw our theories from our own experiences, social science benefits by having people within its ranks from diverse backgrounds.

We discussed three examples of theory development. Some puzzles come from contradictions that arise from within social science itself. Rosenberg's broadening of self-esteem theory came from research that found social class did not relate to self-esteem among children as it did among adults. Other puzzles come from the scientist's own life experiences. Theories of prejudice contradicted what I thought I knew about racial prejudice in my native southern United States. I devised and tested a rival theory that stressed conformity to a society's norms.

The third example shows how applied interests in social policy can lead to major theoretical advances. For John Maynard Keynes, the English economist, opposition to his economic policies preceding the Great Depression inspired a radically different approach to macro-economics. His theory, emphasizing *aggregate demand,* advocated massive governmental spending for public works.

Keynes' views constituted more than a theory; they introduced a paradigm. New paradigms (1) offer broad, new perspectives, (2) suggest new theories and (3) research, and (4) pose new problems while (5) solving old ones. Paradigms, then, are much broader than theories. They provide the contexts within which interrelated theories and research studies develop. Thus, paradigms guide an entire scientific tradition. As such, they become deeply entrenched—virtually the air scientists breathe. So when a paradigm shift occurs, it represents a scientific revolution. Sweepingly new paradigms, such as Darwin's natural selection perspective, are more common in natural than social science. More typically in social science new paradigms meld with, rather than replace, older paradigms. Recall the shifts in viewing social deviance— from the *immutable and mutable dispositional paradigms* to the *interactive and labeling paradigms.*

Kuhn's (1970) model of *scientific revolutions* is instructive. He emphasizes the resistance in science to shifting paradigms. The process is often slow and gradual, rather than dramatic. Like any human enterprise, irrational factors retard these shifts. Such resistance can slow the acceptance of important advances, yet it also screens out many false leads.

Finally, we saw that theories vary widely in scope across the social sciences. At their narrowest, theories in experimental social psychology consist largely of specific hypotheses and predictions. At their broadest, "grand theories" in sociology represent virtual paradigms, and are beyond empirical test. Middle-range theories, neither narrow nor sweeping, are the most effective guides for social research. Major contributions, such as Keynes' theory in economics, manage to include testable, middle-range theory while offering a major new paradigm.

ISSUES FOR DISCUSSION AND REVIEW

A> The author holds theories to be valuable if they lead us to ideas we would not have had without them. Others disagree. They believe theories are valuable only if they are "true." What do you think?

B> We have seen that theories often come from one's own experience. Use *your* experience to question any current social science idea. How would you put your objection in the form of a rival theory? What research would you want to carry out to test your new theory?

C> Can you think of two conflicting paradigms operating today in social science? How do they conflict? Is the discipline combining the two perspectives, or is one paradigm replacing the other?

RECOMMENDATIONS FOR FURTHER READING ON ISSUES RAISED IN THIS CHAPTER

On the Structure of Social Theories:

For readers new to the subject:

P. D. Reynolds. 1971. *A Primer in Theory Construction*. Indianapolis, IN: Bobb-Merrill.

For readers who wish to read a basic source:

H. M. Blalock, Jr. 1969. *Theory Construction: From Verbal to Mathematical Formulations*. Englewood Cliffs, NJ: Prentice-Hall.

On Scientific Paradigms:

For readers new to the subject:

B. P. Cohen. 1992. Paradigms and models. In E. F. Borgatta & M. L. Borgatta (Eds.), *Encyclopedia of Sociology*. Volume 3. New York: Macmillan.

For readers who wish to read a basic source:

T. S. Kuhn. (1970). *The Structure of Scientific Revolutions*. 2nd Ed. Chicago: University of Chicago Press.

On the Range of Social Theories:

J. H. Turner, 1990. *The Structure of Sociological Theory*. 5th Ed. Belmont, CA: Wadsworth.

Chapter
3

In Comparison
With What?

A 1991 survey asked a sample of American adults about happiness (Davis and Smith, 1991:193). "Taken all together, how would you say things are these days—would you say that you are very happy, pretty happy, or not too happy?" Almost a third (31%) reported being "very happy." The majority (58%) chose the middle response, "pretty happy." One in nine (11%) said they were "not too happy."

How shall we interpret these isolated data? How do we know what a third of Americans saying "very happy" means? Does this represent an increase or decrease in reported happiness among adult Americans? How does it compare to samples of adults in other countries asked the same question? Obviously, we need additional data for comparison. *Data do not make sense until compared with meaningful benchmarks.*

Actually, we do have 18 previous surveys that asked Americans the same question since 1972. The total results from these previous studies shows little change: about a third (33%) over these years reported being "very happy," a majority (55%) "pretty happy," and one in eight (12%) "not too happy." With this additional comparison, we can now conclude that the 1991 results are not unusual for adult American samples.

How do these data compare with those of other nations? Suppose half of adult Canadians reported they were "very happy." This comparison might tempt us to conclude that Americans were not especially happy. Or suppose that only a tenth of the adult French reported being "very happy." This comparison might tempt us to conclude that Americans were quite happy. Hence, *completely opposite conclusions can flow from different comparisons.* The skeptical social scientist, then, always asks of any data—*in comparison with what?*

Examples throughout social science illustrate this point. For instance, current German economic policy reacts more extremely than other western nations to the threat of mild inflation. In the 1920s and early 1930s, Germany endured a devastating period of massive inflation (as foreseen by Keynes). The value of money changed drastically almost daily. What you could buy this month for 10 deutschmarks might cost you twice as much next month. Some observers regard this as a major reason for the rise to power of Adolph Hitler and his Nazi Party.

At the close of World War II, Germany again experienced an economic crisis. An entirely new financial system left previous money worthless. With this history, Germans understandably developed a deep fear of inflation and what it can do to a society. Today, a half century later, the German government still follows extremely conservative economic policies, designed to combat inflation with high interest rates. The salient German comparison is not with the economic policies of its European neighbors, but with its own financial crises of the past.

3.1 DIFFERENT COMPARISONS CAN LEAD TO DIFFERENT CONCLUSIONS

Modern Germany also provides a pointed example of how comparisons shape conclusions at the individual level of analysis. Before reunification in 1990, East Germany was a Communist-ruled nation in the eastern European Communist Block. Compared to its poor eastern neighbors, East Germany was the undisputed flagship. It was more prosperous and industrialized than Poland, Hungary, Czechoslovakia, Romania, or Bulgaria. Though economically limited by western standards, East Germans thought well of themselves in comparison with their Communist neighbors.

Then came reunification with West Germany. This historic event caused the East Germans' reference group to shift suddenly from East to West. West Germans, one of the world's most prosperous peoples, replaced the less-developed Eastern Europeans as the standard of comparison. Now, compared with West Germans, East Germans no longer sailed on the flagship. Self-esteem and morale declined alarmingly in East Germany. Depression and suicide rates rose. Reunification also resulted in massive disruptions—widespread unemployment, new laws and regulations, and other threats to the old lifestyle. These disruptions added to the malaise. Yet at the heart of the East Germans' distress was their sudden shift in comparisons.

Changes in black America illustrate how different comparisons can lead to contrasting conclusions at the societal level of analysis. Three types of comparisons are available: black American conditions in the past, white American conditions in the present, and varied conditions within black America. Each is useful—though for different purposes. Making use of all three comparisons provides us with a rounded perspective. They give different answers, but the answers are to different questions.

Figures 3.1, 3.2, and 3.3 provide an outline of the economic and social trends of African Americans over recent decades. The first set of bar graphs (or histograms) suggests that black American progress has been impressive. In 3.1A, we see the rapid rise in the number of black elected officials throughout the nation. In 3.1B, we observe the sharp decline in black infant mortality over recent decades. In 3.1C, we note how black life expectancy at birth has climbed over the past half century. In 3.1D, we see large increases in both black physicians and lawyers since 1950. In 3.1E, we view the gains in black home ownership, though they virtually ended after 1970. Figures 3.1F and 3.1G show black progress in education. For those 25 years and older, the median number of school years has more than doubled since 1940. This advance represents steady increases in both high school and college graduates among African Americans.

The progress shown in these graphs is genuine. Yet the positive impression they create results from the particular comparison Figure 3.1 employs—past black conditions. Black American conditions have improved in absolute terms across a range of indices—political, health, the professions, housing, and education. Relative to their own past, then, African Americans have made considerable strides. However, Figure 3.1 does not consider how other Americans were faring during this period.

Figure 3.1   Black Progress
A: Number of Black Elected Officials

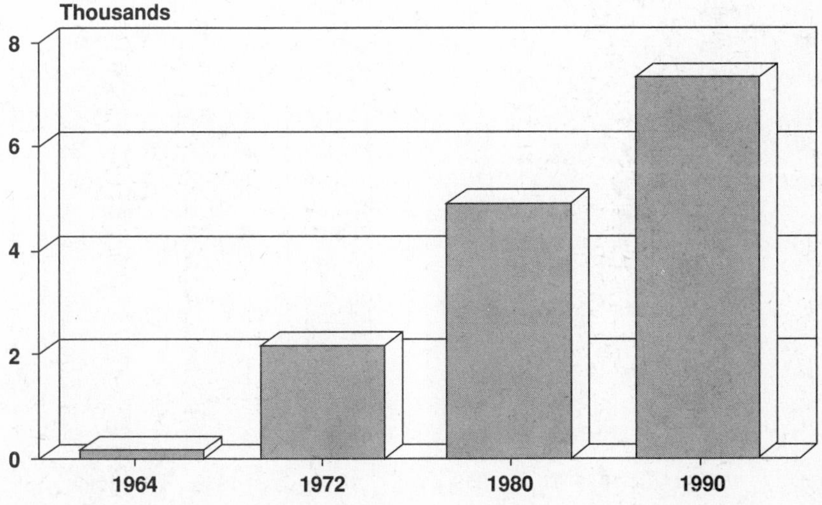

Source: U.S. Bureau of the Census, 1992a.

B: Black Infant Mortality (1st year)

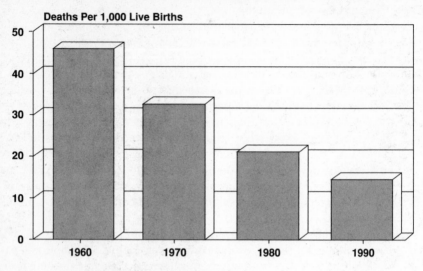

Deaths Per 1,000 Live Births

Source: U.S. Bureau of the Census, 1979, 1992a.

C: Black Life Expectancy at Birth

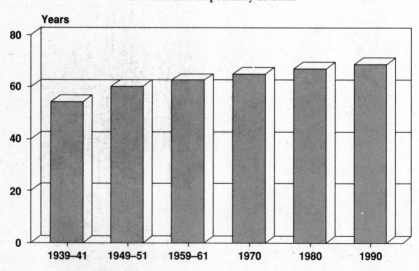

Years

Source: U.S. Bureau of the Census, 1979, 1992a.

D: Number of Black Physicians & Lawyers

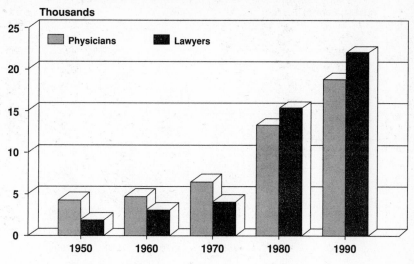

Source: U.S. Bureau of the Census, 1992a.

E: Black Owner-Occupied Housing

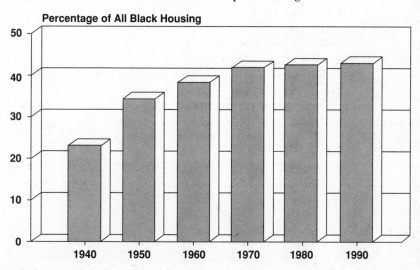

Source: U.S. Bureau of the Census, 1979, 1992a.

F: Black School Years Completed (25+)

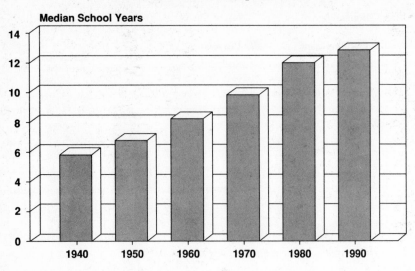

Median School Years

	1940	1950	1960	1970	1980	1990

Source: U.S. Bureau of the Census, 1979, 1992a.

G. Black School Graduates (25+)

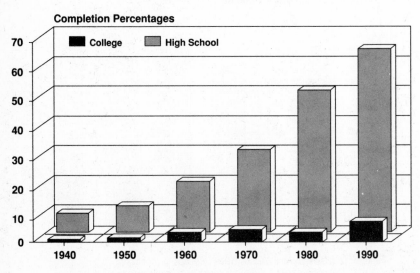

Completion Percentages

■ College   ▨ High School

Source: U.S. Bureau of the Census, 1979, 1992a.

Figure 3.2 shows another story. Here a different comparison is used—the position of white Americans on these indices over these years. A rather mixed picture now emerges. While black infant mortality rates have rapidly decreased, so have those of white Americans. In 3.2A, we note that the roughly two-to-one ratio of black to white infant deaths remains constant. In 3.2B, we see that white life expectancy at birth has also climbed over these years. Nevertheless, black gains have closed about half of the racial gap. In 3.2C, the racial gap in home ownership remains about the same despite black improvement since 1940.

It is in education where we find narrowing racial gaps. In median school years and high school completion (3.2D, 3.2E), black gains have been faster than those of whites and closed much of the racial gap. Rapid increases in black college graduation, however, have been more than offset by even greater white increases (3.2F). Figure 3.2G shows how recorded unemployment rates swing widely across different economic periods. One thing does not vary: African American rates of unemployment stay more than twice those of white Americans regardless of the economic climate.

In 3.2H, we see the lack of progress in black family income relative to that of white families. While there was improvement in 1970, the ratio by 1980 had returned to that of 1950 and 1960—just over half the median family income of whites. These data actually understate the economic problems of black people, since they do not consider accumulated wealth—where whites have an even greater advantage.

Figure 3.2   Racial Comparisons
A: Infant Mortality (1st Year)

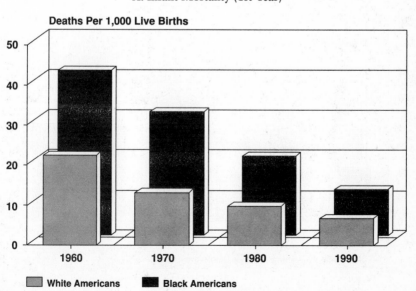

Source: U.S. Bureau of the Census, 1979, 1992a.

B: Life Expectancy at Birth

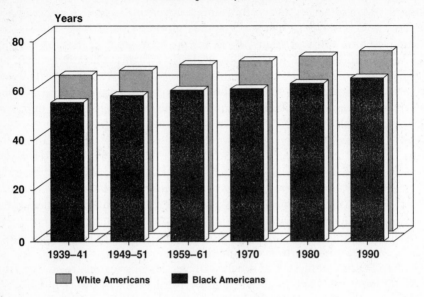

Source: U.S. Bureau of the Census, 1979, 1992a.

C: Owner-Occupied Housing

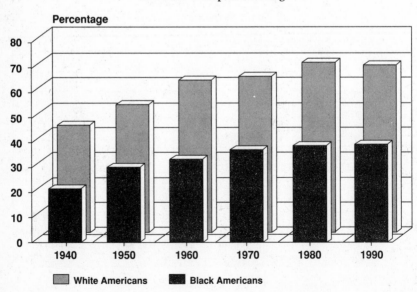

Source: U.S. Bureau of the Census, 1979, 1992a.

D: School Years Completed (25+ years)

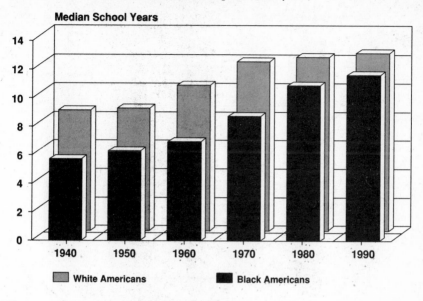

Median School Years

Source: U.S. Bureau of the Census, 1979, 1992a.

E: High School Graduates (25+ years)

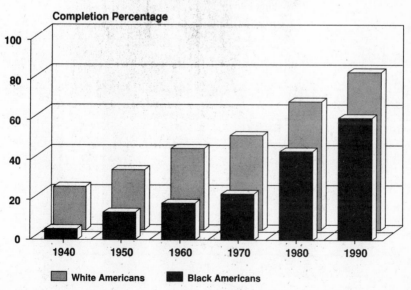

Completion Percentage

Source: U.S. Bureau of the Census, 1979, 1992a.

F: College Graduates (25+ years)

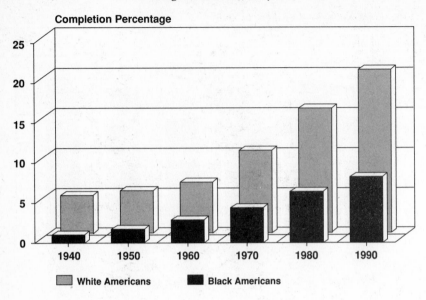

Completion Percentage

Source: U.S. Bureau of the Census, 1979, 1992a.

G: Unemployment Rates (16+ years)

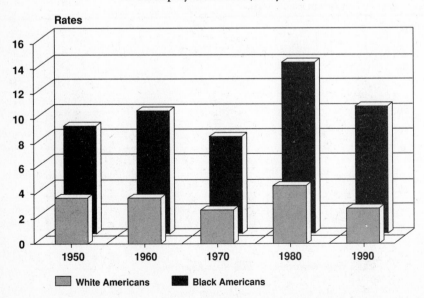

Rates

Source: U.S. Bureau of the Census, 1979, 1992b.

H: Median Family Income: Black/White

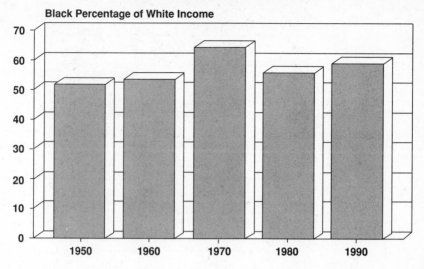

Source: U.S. Bureau of the Census, 1991.

Figures 3.1 and 3.2 provide only averages for the whole African American population. Changes have also been occurring within black America, as shown in Figure 3.3. In 3.3A, we see two diverging trends occurring over the past generation. Using 1990 dollars, the percentage of black families with annual incomes of less than $10,000 has been increasing. Also, the percentage of black families with incomes over $35,000 has been rising. Using 1990 dollars in 3.3B, median family income has actually declined in the North and West for black Americans since 1967. It is in the South that black family income has risen. The two trends together cause the regional gap to close considerably over these years.

Figure 3.3 reveals what 3.1 and 3.2, using only averages for the entire group, could not. Black gains over recent decades have been uneven within the group. Some black Americans have made major strides, while others remain mired in poverty.

Which of these comparisons—the black past, the white present, or the intragroup differences—is the correct one? None of them is right or wrong. Each answers a different question. Figure 3.1: Have black Americans improved their lot in America in absolute terms? Figure 3.2: Have black Americans closed the gap in opportunity with white Americans? Figure 3.3: Have all sectors of black America benefitted from the changes? All three are important questions that deserve answers.

Taken together, these three comparisons tell us much more about black advances in the last half of the 20th century than any of them alone. These

Figure 3.3 Black Comparisons
A: Black Family Income Changes

Percentage of All Black Families

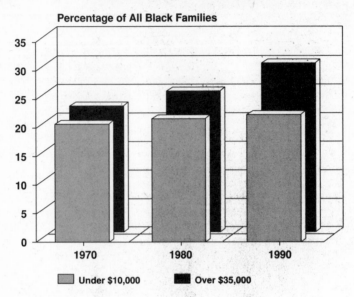

Under $10,000   Over $35,000

Source: U.S. Bureau of the Census, 1991.
Note: In constant 1990 dollars.

Median Family Income (Thousands)

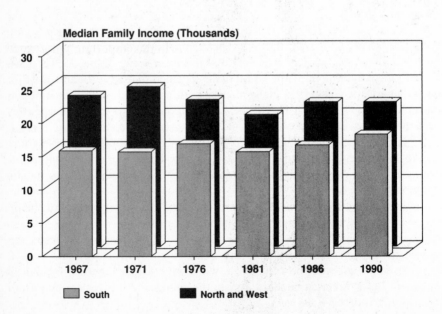

South   North and West

Source: U.S. Bureau of the Census, 1992b.
Note: In constant 1990 dollars.

data show that blacks as a group have made genuine advances in absolute terms over these years. Yet their progress compared with white Americans has been slow and uneven. Moreover, their gains are unevenly shared within the group.

To draw conclusions about American race relations based on one of these comparisons while ignoring the others is highly deceptive. Commentators of various political persuasions routinely present precisely this type of limited analysis. Armed with a healthy skepticism, the social scientist (and you!) can detect such misuses of selected comparisons and recognize their limitations.

3.2 WHY CONTROL COMPARISONS?

The importance of comparisons underlies a basic tool of scientific method and thinking—*controls*. The simplest example occurs in a laboratory experiment with two groups. Treatment of the control and **experimental groups** is identical except for the test variable. If a difference emerges between the groups, it suggests that the variable under test *caused* the difference. After all, we set up the experiment so the test variable would be the only difference between the groups. Cause, however, is a complex idea, as we shall learn in Chapter 4. The point is that without the control group we would not know how to interpret the data from the experimental group alone.

The control group eliminates a **plausible rival hypothesis** for explaining the results of the experimental condition (Cook & Campbell, 1979). Its data tell us if we would get the same results without the test variable. *This is the basic idea of controls in social science: to exclude plausible explanations for the results other than those we wish to advance.* In this important sense, then, controls are conceptual and empirical tools.

Perhaps the best known example of control groups involves drug research. People who take a pill typically think they should feel differently. Even if we are not sure what effect the drug has, we are still likely to expect some effect after taking it. So drug research has long used an experimental group that takes the drug and a control group that takes a pill with no effects (**placebo**). In a **single blind study,** subjects do not know the group in which they are participating (the real drug versus the placebo). The measured effects of this control—the placebo group—are then compared with those from the experimental group that took the test drug. Note how the difference between the experimental and control groups' results answers a plausible rival hypothesis for the real drug's effects. Namely, are these effects simply the arousal induced by *any* pill?

Soon, however, drug researchers learned that the single blind procedure was inadequate. Though subjects did not know which pill they were taking, the experimenters did. Often the experimenters' expectations unwittingly influenced the results—another instance of human reactivity discussed in Chapter 1. So the **double blind study** technique became the standard controlled experimental design in drug research. In this design, neither the subject nor the experimenter knows in which group the subject is. Similar precautions are necessary in experiments in social science.

These examples of control groups involve **between subjects comparisons.** The subjects serve in either the experimental or control group, but not both. Another experimental design uses **within subjects comparisons.** In this design, all subjects participate in both the control and experimental groups. The experimenter randomizes the order in which each subject participates in the two groups—so subjects serve as their own control.

3.3 CONTROL GROUPS IN SOCIAL SCIENCE EXPERIMENTS

The key distinguishing feature of experiments is the random assignment of subjects to the experimental and control groups. In the between subjects study, there must be no biased selection of which subjects go into each group. This feature insures that prior differences between the subjects cannot later provide plausible rival explanations for the results. Chapter 5 will discuss **selection biases.** In the within subjects study, random assignment refers to the order in which each subject takes part in the control and experimental conditions. Such assignment insures that order effects will not bias the results.

Another advantage of true experiments is that the researcher controls the independent variable (hence its name). Such control means the experimenter can alter both the timing and form of the treatment or intervention whose effect is under test. Such control allows the researcher to reach more precise conclusions about the results.

The random assignment of subjects as the basic criterion of experiments does not limit their use to laboratory studies. If researchers can achieve random assignment, experiments are possible outside the laboratory—*in the field,* as social scientists call it. For example, opinion surveys can experiment on the effects of the ordering of its questions by randomly asking them in different sequences to their respondents (Schuman & Kalton, 1985).

Most concerns of social science do not lend themselves easily to experiments either in or out of the laboratory. Researchers cannot manipulate many independent variables of interest and importance. Sometimes the variable is beyond our ability to arrange (such as natural disasters). Often it would be unethical to manipulate the variable (such as extreme fear in subjects). And ethics require that social scientists not hurt their subjects in any way.

There are experiments conducted in all the social sciences. They are rare, however, except in social psychology. This is the discipline within social science that has a branch for such work—experimental social psychology. This branch specializes in studying social processes in laboratory experiments.

Earlier we mentioned several of these laboratory experiments. Recall the self-fulfilling prophecy experiment in which one subject expected hostile behavior from another subject (Snyder & Swann, 1978). The control group consisted of the same arrangement, except there was no such expectation of hostility. The independent variable, then, was the expectation of hostility. The self-fulfilling effect of this manipulation, you remember, was that the students with this expectation unwittingly induced hostile behavior in the "target" subject. This induced hostile behavior, then served as the dependent variable—since it *depends* on (is caused by) the independent variable.

The experimenters carried their research one step further. They wanted to see if this induced hostility of the target subjects would generalize (extend) to a second session with a different subject who had no prior expectations. For this second stage of the study, Snyder and Swann (1978) split the experimental target subjects into two groups. They led one group of subjects to believe that their hostile behavior was dispositional—that is, it reflected their personal characteristics. They led the second group of subjects to believe their hostile behavior was situational—that is, only a reaction to their partner's behavior. Each group now served as a control for the other. The study showed the target subjects continued their hostile behavior only when they thought it derived from their own personalities—a dispositional cause.

Because of the complexity of social science discussed in Chapter 1, there are usually many plausible rival explanations in social research. Therefore, one control group is often not enough.

3.4 CONTROLS IN FIELD RESEARCH

We noted that experiments are not possible for most social science problems. You cannot squeeze entire social, economic, or political systems into experimental designs. Forced to work in "the real world," random assignment of subjects to experimental and control groups is rarely practical. Society does not come neatly packaged into research groups. Social scientists typically have to make do with what they find naturally occurring in society.

Even when it is possible to set up true experiments in the field, political and other pressures often defeat the effort. I once consulted for a massive federal study of new educational programs. The researchers randomly set up experimental schools (that received new federal money to provide the new programs) and control schools (that received no new money and had no new programs).

It was a noble effort. Soon, however, parents of children in the control schools throughout the country heard that the study had left out their schools. They angrily demanded that their childrens' schools also get extra funds for new programs. Under intense pressure, many local school boards began sending some federal funds intended only for the experimental schools to the control schools.

The study later revealed few differences between the two sets of schools. This negative finding is now hard to interpret. Were the new programs actually ineffective? Or did the leakage of monies from the experimental to the control schools enhance student learning in the control schools so few differences emerged? Hence, learning may have improved in both types of schools as a result of the extra funds. The inability to maintain true experimental and control groups prevented clear conclusions and left open a highly plausible rival hypothesis to explain the negative results.

Control comparisons in non-experimental research are essential. There are many sources of bias that offer plausible rival hypothesis. These biases, called **threats to validity,** are especially troublesome in social research where randomized experiments are not possible (Cook & Campbell, 1979). As the term implies, these biases *threaten* the accuracy and interpretation of a study's results. These distorting biases occur frequently, and they *invalidate* social research.

3.4.1. Multiple Comparisons with Quasi-Experiments

Why is randomization so important? The answer is that it helps to limit rival hypotheses by making less likely common types of threats to validity. If randomization is so important but experiments so difficult to conduct, what can social science do? How can we get control comparisons in non-experimental settings? The three types of comparisons discussed for assessing black American gains illustrate one approach. We gather data on as many relevant control comparisons as the situation allows. This procedure permits, as we saw, a rounded perspective through multiple comparisons.

We increase comparisons with **quasi-experiments.** These research designs are not true experiments, because they do not assign subjects randomly to experimental and control groups. Yet quasi-experiments are the strongest possible designs available in most field settings. When true experiments are impossible, researchers do the next best thing and enlarge the number of control comparisons. Though they lack the main feature of true experiments, quasi-experiments retain another advantage of experiments. Experimenters still control the timing and form of the independent variable.

First, let's review inadequate research designs. Figure 3.4 diagrams three such designs (Campbell & Stanley, 1966; Cook & Campbell, 1979; Kercher, 1992). The Figure's I's represent the exposure to the treatment (the independent variable) whose effects are under test. The D's represent the measurement of the effects (the dependent variable). Diagrams 1a, 1b, and 1c are *not* examples of quasi-experiments, because they do not provide the relevant comparisons for rigorous research.

Diagram 1a is the lean case study. It involves only one measurement of the effect (D) following one treatment (I). Such case studies can be of value to generate ideas and hypotheses for further testing. They cannot test hypotheses, however, because there are no comparisons.

However, this design does appear in social science journals. One such study interviewed 21 parents of children who attended a day-care center (Wilson & Golub, 1993). The interview informed the parents about methods to teach children how to prevent sexual abuse (the independent variable). Then, the researchers asked each parent if such methods "should be taught as

Figure 3.4   Inadequate Research Designs

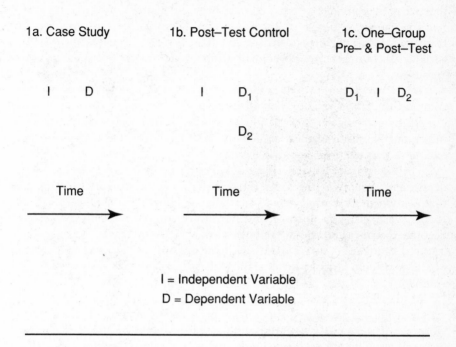

INADEQUATE RESEARCH DESIGNS

1a. Case Study   1b. Post–Test Control   1c. One–Group
                                                        Pre– & Post–Test

   I   D   I D_1 D_1 I D_2

                                  D_2

   Time   Time   Time

                    I = Independent Variable
                    D = Dependent Variable

early as preschool" (the dependent variable). All 21 agreed it should. The investigators concluded that parents informed about child sexual abuse will support prevention programs. Do you see the problems with this conclusion? As in Diagram 1a, there is neither a control group nor pre-intervention measures of the dependent variable. Without any benchmark whatsoever, we cannot assess the fact that all 21 parents agreed. Maybe they would have all agreed without the interview. Maybe a control group would have also unanimously agreed.

Nor can the two-group post-test only design (Diagram 1b) provide adequate tests. Another published study underscores the problems here (Spitz & MacKinnon, 1993). It gave a personality questionnaire to 60 volunteers *after* a program of the Big Brothers–Big Sisters Agency. Twenty-five had successfully completed the program, and the remaining 35 had not. The research found that the successful volunteers had higher scores on trust, imagination, and self-assurance and lower scores on social inhibition. The investigators concluded that future use of these variables could screen for successful volunteers.

See the difficulties in this case? As in 1a, there are no pre-program measures, and only the one comparison between the two groups is available. Perhaps the program caused these personality differences; one might feel less self-assured after not completing the Agency's program. Moreover, the two groups may differ in other ways that account for the personality differences. In fact, the successful volunteers were older and better educated.

The one-group pre- and post-test design (Diagram 1c) is also inadequate. Here we measure the dependent variable (D) before and after the independent variable (I), but there are no control groups. Again, only one comparison is possible.

To see why Diagram 1c is inadequate provides a useful review of the most common threats to validity. For illustration, think of a field investigation of the effects of being on unemployment assistance. Do such payments reduce the recipients' motivation to find work? Or do they just tide the recipients over until they can find employment?

The first threat is **history.** Here a specific event exerts an influence on the dependent variable at the same time as the independent variable. Suppose that just when our sample gets its first unemployment checks, the nation suffers a severe recession. Jobs become hard to get, so our unemployed subjects become discouraged about seeking work. We could easily confuse their lowered motivation to get a job with the receipt of their check. Diagram 1c's lack of comparisons do not allow us to rule out this history threat to validity.

Maturation presents a second threat. This refers to changes in the subjects simply from the passage of time. They grow older, hungrier, more tired, or whatever. It is also easy to confuse these changes with the effects of the payments. If growing old decreases work motivation, this maturation effect could mistakenly make the unemployment checks look as if they lessen efforts to find employment. Again, the design of Diagram 1c does not permit the needed comparisons to reject this plausible rival hypothesis.

Testing effects are a third threat to validity that would go undetected in Diagram 1c's design. They occur when we measure the dependent variable twice, and the first test influences the second. In our study, suppose the recipients became sensitized by the initial measure of their motivation to seek a job. Realizing what the study is about, they report on the second measure greater eagerness to find work than is the case. Without a control group, there is no way in Diagram 1a's design to uncover this testing threat to validity.

Instrumentation is still another threat to validity. If we changed the measures used to gauge the dependent variable in Diagram 1c, this shift could cause a difference. Suppose we measured the subjects' motivation to work before the payment by how often they came to the employment office. Then, following the payment, we measured their work motivation with a questionnaire. The contrasting measures make any changes between them hard to interpret. It is best to use both forms of measurement on both occasions, since multiple indicators of key concepts are essential.

Selection and **mortality** are additional and related threats. We shall treat them in detail in Chapter 5. They refer to different types of people being assigned to (selection) or dropping out of (mortality) the experimental and control groups. Non-random assignment of subjects is a serious threat to all non-experimental research. Diagram 1a has no control group, so these threats are not a problem except for generalizing the results.

In Diagram 1b with a control group, a selection bias could easily occur. If, for instance, older persons suffering from long-term unemployment made up more of the experimental than the control group, selection could bias the results. It would cause the experimental group's work motivation to be unduly low. Hence, it could lead to the mistaken conclusion that the payments diminish the seeking of employment.

The mortality problem involves a biased selection among those who *leave* the study. If subjects who are likely to seek jobs leave the control more than the experimental group, this bias also could distort the findings. As we shall see in Chapter 5, this is a common problem in longitudinal research. Using Diagram 1b, suppose those unmotivated members of the control group are mostly unavailable for the second testing. This mortality bias also would lead to the erroneous conclusion that the payments deter work motivation.

Note how each of these six threats provide a plausible rival hypothesis to explain the results. To meet these and other threats to validity, we turn to quasi-experimental designs that provide additional control comparisons. Figure 3.5 diagrams five of the most common of these designs. Observe that the diagrams boast many more measurements and comparisons than the three inadequate designs. These multiple comparisons make it possible to test the plausible rival hypotheses offered by various types of threat.

The non-equivalent control group design (Diagram 2a) is a widely-used approach. It uses both experimental and control groups as well as pre- and post-measures of the dependent variable. The design does not randomly select the groups. Rather, it uses readily-available collections of people in such places as employment offices and classrooms.

With its five possible comparisons, Diagram 2a's design checks on four of the threats to validity just discussed. Did events occurring at the time of the payments to the experimental group affect work motivation (the history threat)? Were there any changes from the passage of time (maturation)? Were there effects of the first measurement upon the second (testing), or from any differences in the measures of work motivation between the pre- and post-tests (instrumentation)? The comparison between the pre- and post-tests of the control group $(D_4–D_3)$ answers these questions in a gross way. One can subtract any control group difference from that of the experimental group for a net effect $([D_2–D_1] – [D_4–D_3])$.

The random groups design of Diagram 2b is popular, though not as efficient. Here researchers randomly assign groups, but not individuals, to the control and experimental conditions. The pre-test for the control group, however, is missing. This omission means we cannot check on either the history or

Figure 3.5   Quasi-Experimental Research Designs

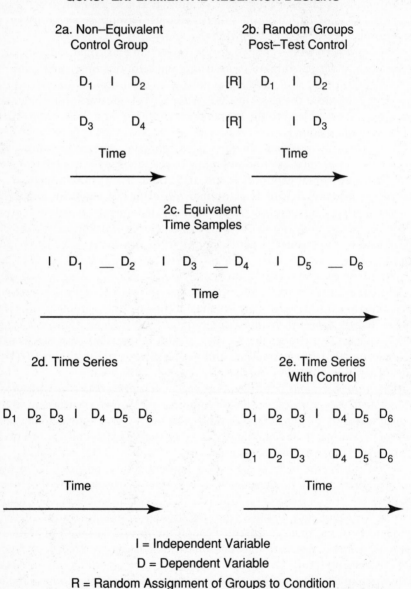

QUASI–EXPERIMENTAL RESEARCH DESIGNS

2a. Non–Equivalent Control Group

D_1 I D_2

D_3 D_4

Time

2b. Random Groups Post–Test Control

[R] D_1 I D_2

[R]   I D_3

Time

2c. Equivalent Time Samples

I D_1 __ D_2 I D_3 __ D_4 I D_5 __ D_6

Time

2d. Time Series

D_1 D_2 D_3 I D_4 D_5 D_6

Time

2e. Time Series With Control

D_1 D_2 D_3 I D_4 D_5 D_6

D_1 D_2 D_3 D_4 D_5 D_6

Time

I = Independent Variable
D = Dependent Variable
R = Random Assignment of Groups to Condition

maturation threats to validity. For our illustrative study, this design would involve randomly selecting different unemployment offices to get our experimental and control subjects. However, we could not secure the pre-test at the control office for some reason.

Many quasi-experimental designs use extended time series to provide the many comparisons needed. We shall look at three of these designs. The equivalent time samples design (Diagram 2c) has a single group receive the treatment (independent variable) or the control condition (no treatment) at random intervals. (A regular pattern is shown in Diagram 2c, but an extended and random pattern is intended.) In effect, the one group serves as its own control.

The random timing of Diagram 2c allows a check on the various rival hypotheses suggested by the history, maturation, testing, and instrumentation threats. The selection and mortality threats are not present with only one group involved. In our example, this design would test one group of unemployed people over a long period. At random intervals, we would administer the measures of work motivation following payments or no payments.

Diagram 2d's time series design is also popular in social research. It is the basic design of most longitudinal research that Chapter 4 will discuss. Here there is only one group and one occurrence of the independent variable. The design gets its power from the multiple testing of the dependent variable both before and after the one treatment. This approach allows a check on all the threats we discussed except that of history. In our investigation, it would mean following one sample of unemployed persons for an extended period. We would test their work motivation repeatedly both before and after their receipt of a payment.

The multiple time series (Diagram 2e) further strengthens the design. The addition of a control group that receives the same multiple tests allows a check on all six threats, including history. In our example, this control group would consist of a comparable unemployed group that receives no assistance.

3.4.2. Multiple Comparisons with Passive Research Designs

Quasi-experiments require that the experimenter manipulates to some degree the treatment or independent variable. Yet often social science cannot meet this condition. Manipulation of many independent variables of interest is impossible. When that is the case, researchers use **passive research designs** that offer as many control comparisons as possible. These designs are "passive," because the independent variable is out of the researcher's control. Such restricted settings present a major challenge to social research.

Figure 3.6 outlines three of the many passive research designs often used in social research. Diagram 3a's passive multiple groups post-test design is the weakest. It is, however, the most common design used in the analysis of sur-

Figure 3.6   Passive Control Research Designs

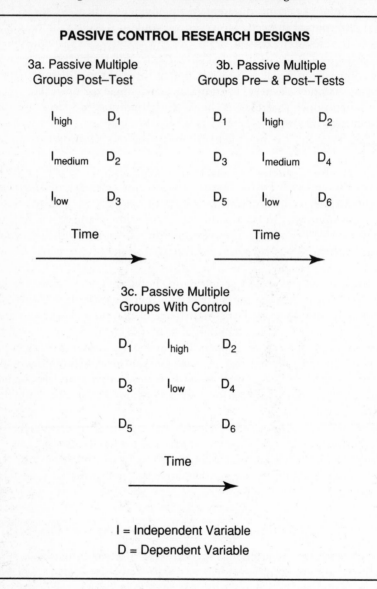

PASSIVE CONTROL RESEARCH DESIGNS

3a. Passive Multiple
Groups Post–Test

I_{high} D_1

I_{medium} D_2

I_{low} D_3

Time

3b. Passive Multiple
Groups Pre– & Post–Tests

D_1 I_{high} D_2

D_3 I_{medium} D_4

D_5 I_{low} D_6

Time

3c. Passive Multiple
Groups With Control

D_1 I_{high} D_2

D_3 I_{low} D_4

D_5 D_6

Time

I = Independent Variable
D = Dependent Variable

veys. It tries to compensate for its lack of pre-tests with multiple groups that experience different levels of the treatment. In our example, this design involves post-measures of work motivation for three or more groups that received different amounts of payment.

Diagram 3b's design represents a marked improvement by adding pre-measures of the dependent variable for three or more groups. Diagram 3c strengthens the design further by adding a control group that does not experience the independent variable. A study we discussed in Chapter 1 illustrates this passive research design.

Recall the Archer and Gartner (1984) study of post-war homicides. These sociologists explained the post-war rise in murders by contending that war legitimatized violence. There are, however, other plausible rival explanations for this surprising phenomenon. The researchers used Diagram 3c's basic research design to consider each of these alternatives. They did so by testing each with an appropriate control comparison.

One rival argument is that homicide increases after wars because of worsened post-war economies. So Archer and Gartner (1984:90–91) tested it with the passive multiple groups and control design (Diagram 3c). They compared the homicide rates for nations whose post-war unemployment rates rose (I_1), those whose post-war unemployment rates declined (I_2), and controls that did not experience war (I_3). There was no difference between I_1 and I_2. Post-war murder rates climbed higher in both sets of nations with wars. Moreover, both had significantly higher increases than those of countries without wars.

Freud's theory of **catharsis** offers another rival explanation. This theory holds that the expression of aggression *lessens* the likelihood of additional aggression. It predicts that those societies whose wartime experiences were the most violent will show the largest post-war declines in violent crimes. To test this hypothesis, the researchers used Diagram 3c in the same way. They compared nations that suffered greater than 500 battle deaths per million post-war population (I_1), those with fewer battle deaths (I_2), and controls without wars (I_3). The Freudian hypothesis was convincingly disconfirmed. Nations with the higher combat death rates had *higher* (not lower) increases in their rates of post-war homicide than other warring nations and the peaceful controls.

A third rival view limits the raised post-war murder rates to veterans returning home and continuing to kill. Archer and Gartner (1984:91–93) test this idea by replicating their study across sex and age. They use Diagram 3c separately for each sex and age group. They cast doubt on the hypothesis by showing that female homicide rates rise like male rates, though women were far less likely to have been in combat. Moreover, all age groups (even those too old to be veterans) reveal elevated homicide rates after wars.

This cross-national study of violence shows how a range of comparisons can use passive research designs to test various explanations for a surprising phenomenon. One by one, Archer and Gartner (1984) disconfirmed plausible rival hypotheses. As they did so, their own explanation of war legitimatizing violence became increasingly more convincing.

The problems raised by non-experimental settings are not as formidable as our discussion may make them appear. A healthy skepticism requires an understanding of these varied threats to validity. It also requires care to create the multiple control comparisons to counter the threats. Diligent researchers, like Archer and Gartner, find clever ways to combat the threats. Their study of the effects of war on homicide illustrates several of these ways.

First, Archer and Gartner custom crafted their research design to their particular problem and setting. Figures 3.5 and 3.6 show only eight general quasi-experimental and passive research designs. Actually, only researchers' imaginations limit possible designs. Combining as many strong design features as appropriate to the problem and possible in the setting leads to countless different research designs. These desirable features include pre- and post-measures of the dependent variable, both experimental and control conditions, multiple groups for each condition, time sampling of the measures, and a time series of the pre- and post-measures.

Archer and Gartner also repeated their tests over many different nations, wars, periods, and measures of homicide. Recall from Chapter 1 that they checked their findings across 110 nations, 14 wars, and two different measures of homicide. Such replication is the most important way social science has to increase the power of its tests. Indeed, it is so important that we shall consider replication further in Chapter 4.

Our discussion has focused upon threats to **internal validity,** that is, those weaknesses of research that threaten the accuracy of a study's results and conclusions. Equally important are threats to **external validity.** These limit the application (**generalization**) of the results to other situations. We saw how the homicide researchers showed through replication how their findings did not apply to just males or one age group.

Consider other external threats to generalization. Had Archer and Gartner used only data from World War II, one could wonder if there were special factors connected with this war that caused inflated homicide rates. If so, one could not safely apply their results to wars in general. The two sociologists handled that problem by testing across 14 wars. Maybe there was something peculiar about their measure of homicide that shaped their results. Archer and Gartner handled this threat by using two different, though intercorrelated, indicators of homicide. Thus, careful repetition of their results across sex, age, nations, wars, times, and indicators of homicide defends against external as well as internal threats to validity.

Well-conducted field research can have an advantage over true experiments in combatting *external* invalidity. By virtue of taking place in "the real world," field research results are potentially more generalizable than data collected in "artificial" laboratory settings. One can easily exaggerate this popular point. Poorly-conducted field research can be artificial, and its results not generalized to other contexts. Well-conducted laboratory research can be highly realistic for subjects and generalized widely.

Aronson, Brewer and Carlsmith (1985:482) make an important distinction between **mundane realism** and **experimental realism.** Field and laboratory research differ most on mundane realism—the likelihood that events in the study would routinely happen in the subjects' lives. The two types of research may not differ, however, in the more important experimental realism—a highly interesting situation that thoroughly involves the subjects.

Take, for example, a famous laboratory experiment about obedience to authority. Milgram (1974) asked his subjects to do something they had never done before—apply electric shock to another human being. So this study lacked mundane realism. However, this research situation proved to be intensely involving for the subjects; it did have experimental realism.

3.4.3 Statistical Controls

One additional means of control in non-experimental research is statistical. After collecting data, social scientists use the power of computers and increasingly sophisticated statistical methods to develop control comparisons. One way to view these methods is to think of them as creating (simulating) control groups after the fact.

Unfortunately, these statistical methods bring with them their own problems. Some methods require assumptions that are questionable in particular situations. Many of these problems involve the dangers of either *over-* or *under-*controlling. Several public debates over studies with educational policy implications have centered on these problems. The basic point is that statistics cannot equal the precision and "hands-on" directness of control groups in experiments.

Nonetheless, these methods allow social science to address its major questions. As we shall see in Chapter 4, statistics are essential to assess the results of experimental research. In addition, statistical methods designed to achieve control comparisons in non-experimental research are necessary both for control and evaluation purposes. Without them, social science, as known today, could not exist.

This fact raises three points that deserve emphasis. First, modern social science is highly dependent on the rapid growth of computers in the last half of this century. When I wrote my doctoral dissertation in 1955, I did not have access to a computer. I analyzed my data on an IBM 101 machine that had no memory. The 101 could only count and sort cards with data punched on them, then print the results.

Today I have a desk-top micro-computer with more computing power than the Harvard University mainframe computer that occupied an entire large room in 1958. On six 3-½" disks, I have all the data gathered in the many General Social Surveys of the U.S. conducted since 1972—over 30,000 interviews with 1,867 variables (Midway Data Associates, 1991). The sweep of the computing revolution since 1950 was a necessary condition for the rapid growth of quantitative methods in the social sciences.

Second, social science has benefited immensely from the work of statisticians who specialize in the unique problems faced by social research. Leo Goodman of the University of Chicago, Frederick Mosteller of Harvard University, John Tukey of Princeton University and others have devoted their careers to devising methods to analyze "the dirty data" of social research. Their many contributions have had a major impact on social science research.

The final point involves students. Often college majors in social science wonder why they must take statistics courses. They may find such courses difficult, and they often do not see how statistics relate to their substantive interests. Statistics are now as critical for understanding modern social science as anatomy is for medicine. Statistics are not just important for analyzing numbers. They also structure social research and how social scientists think. For that matter, statistics have assumed major importance for many fields, such as quality control methods in industry.

To be sure, there are important parts of social science that remain qualitative and do not directly require statistics. Often qualitative research leads to new ideas and theories by being "up close" to the social world. Even this qualitative work is also informed by a general understanding of statistics and the theory of probability that underlies them.

The point for students planning a career in the social sciences is that a firm statistical background is essential. Statistics serve as a foundation of modern social science, and they are central to how most social scientists think. This situation has developed in part because of our immediate concern: the need for social science to exert controls in its analysis of non-experimental data.

The present volume is not a statistics text. It will try, however, to convey the flavor of how statistics help achieve controlled comparisons in social research. We will review several non-experimental studies in which statistics make appropriate comparisons possible.

The first example involves a large multinational study of prejudice in western Europe. Consider the problems of control the author and his Dutch colleague, Roel Meertens, faced in this study (Pettigrew & Meertens, 1995). We analyzed survey data from interviews with 4,000 Europeans about their attitudes toward minorities who have immigrated to their countries. These new groups include Turks in Germany and the Netherlands, Southeast Asians and North Africans in France, and West Indians, Pakistanis, and East Indians in Great Britain. The data are from seven **probability samples** of France, Germany, Great Britain, and the Netherlands. (Chapter 5 will discuss probability samples.)

We wanted to study two types of intergroup prejudice in these four countries. First, we formed two scales of ten questions each to measure these varieties of prejudice. For this initial task, we employed with the help of computers a variety of statistics. One of the scales measured *blatant prejudice*—the openly hostile, close, and direct form. "The North Africans have jobs the French should have" is an item from this scale with which French respondents agreed or disagreed. The second scale measured *subtle prejudice*—the cool, distant, and indirect form. "The Turks living here teach their children values and skills different from those required to be successful in Germany" is an item measuring subtle prejudice.

The control problem arises when we wish to know what predicts these two kinds of prejudice across the seven samples. No experimental and control groups are available; we have only the minimal passive research design—3a in Figure 3.6. Thus, we must develop controls through statistical methods.

In this study of prejudice, eight basic variables predict prejudice. This provides an example of *multiple causation,* as discussed in Chapter 1. Put in experimental terms, these predictors serve as independent variables, and the two types of prejudice serve as dependent variables.

The **predictor variables** are (1) *ethnocentrism* (generalized prejudice against many outgroups), (2) *approval of racist social movements,* (3) *diverse* *friends* (from other groups), (4) *political conservatism*, (5) *group relative deprivation* (the outgroup is seen as doing better economically than your group), (6) *interest in politics*, and the respondent's (7) *education* and (8) *age*.

We want to know how each of these variables predicts blatant and subtle prejudice. But the close interrelations among these eight predictor variables complicates this task. For example, *ethnocentrism* correlates with *education* and *age*. That is, better-educated and younger people are usually less ethnocentric toward outgroups than poorly-educated and older people. This inflates the simple (zero-order) correlation coefficient between ethnocentrism and our prejudice scales, because it includes part of the prediction by education and age. Hence, we need to know how ethnocentrism predicts blatant and subtle prejudice with the other predictor variables controlled. We want the "pure" relationship for each predictor variable for both kinds of prejudice with the effects of the other predictors controlled.

To accomplish this task, statisticians have developed **multiple regression analysis** that social scientists use for both experimental and non-experimental data. With convenient statistical packages for even personal computers, these techniques are easy to apply to such a problem. Figure 3.7 gives the results, averaged across all seven samples. The taller the bar, the stronger the independent prediction of prejudice of each variable with the other seven controlled.

Figure 3.7 shows that the strongest predictor of both blatant and subtle prejudice is ethnocentrism. This finding means that prejudices against minority outgroups (for example, Turkish "guest-workers" and black Africans) are highly interrelated. A person prejudiced against one minority group is likely to

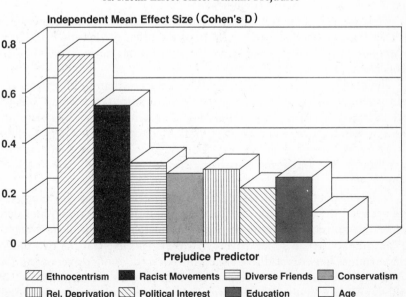

Figure 3.7
A: Mean Effect Sizes: Blatant Prejudice

B: Mean Effect Sizes: Subtle Prejudice

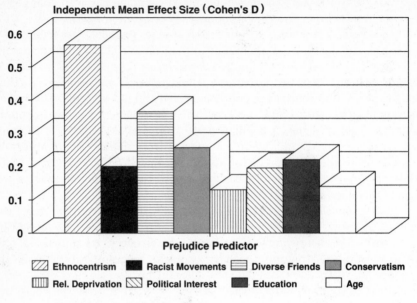

Independent Mean Effect Size (Cohen's D)

Prejudice Predictor

Ethnocentrism   Racist Movements   Diverse Friends   Conservatism
Rel. Deprivation   Political Interest   Education   Age

Source: Pettigrew & Meertens, 1995.

be prejudiced against other minorities. Next, not surprisingly, those who ap-prove of *racist social movements* are more prejudiced. Those with *diverse friends* are less prejudiced. *Political conservatives,* the *relatively deprived,* the *politically disinterested,* and *poorly educated* and *older* respondents also have high levels of both types of prejudice.

We can make these statements about the predictor variables, because for each we have controlled for the effects of the other predictors. Without such techniques as multiple regression, we would be unable to make such state-ments from non-experimental data.

The results of Figure 3.7 are **additive effects**—that is, the effects of the eight predictors add up to explain the two prejudice types. Many social sci-ence data are additive, but many are not. Independent variables also can in-teract in complex ways so that their total effect on the dependent variable is not a simple sum of their separate effects. Such **interaction effects** are al-ways interesting and often surprising. Social scientists learn to look for them.

A simple example contrasts additive and interactive effects. Suppose dri-vers between the ages of 16 and 25 are 25% more likely than older drivers to have an automobile accident. Suppose further that drunken drivers are 50% more likely than sober drivers to have an accident. If the two indepen-dent variables have an additive effect, intoxicated young drivers would have a 75% greater chance of an accident than sober older drivers (25% + 50%). If the predictors have an interactive effect, however, the increased probability of an accident for drunken young drivers would not be 75%. It could be 60%. More likely, the combined risk of youth and alcohol for accidents could be 100% or more. In this case, there is a multiplier effect. Sober young drivers may be almost as careful as sober older drivers. However, intoxicated young drivers are much more at risk than similarly intoxicated older drivers.

In technical terms, an interaction occurs when the effect on a dependent variable (reported accidents) of one independent variable (youth) is not the same at every level of another independent variable (alcoholic intake). Popular thinking, if it even considers more than one predictor, usually assumes simple additive effects. Thinking like a social scientist requires attention to interactive as well as additive effects. Concern for interactive effects provides another reason for controls.

Statistical controls have yet another purpose. They can help to untangle and explain surprising findings. Consider a study from Germany (Lantermann, 1993). This investigation looked at the social and economic integration of the many "Resettlers" who have come to Germany from former Communist countries. Though separated from Germany for centuries, these Resettlers claim ancestral and cultural links with Germany.

Lantermann interviewed samples of these Resettlers. Those from the most "German" enclaves in Poland and Romania had the *most* difficulty integrating into modern Germany. This unexpected result presented a paradox—the more "German" the Polish- and Romanian-Germans had been, the more difficulties they had in adjusting to becoming Germans in Germany!

Lantermann and his colleagues clarified the apparent contradiction by applying statistical controls. In the first place, the German culture that the Resettlers had clung to in Poland and Romania consisted largely of such traditional elements as old songs and speech patterns. What constitutes modern German culture often sharply conflicts with these older traditions and ways of life.

Moreover, as embattled minorities in Poland and Romania, the Resettlers had developed largely *collectivist values*. That is, they looked to their group for support and help rather then relying on personal initiative and achievement. Thus, collectivist values emphasized the group and de-emphasized individualistic values. Yet the *individualistic values* that many Resettlers had not developed lead to success in modern Germany.

Using controls related to collectivist versus individualistic values helps to explain the study's surprising finding. The more traditionally "German" the communities back in Poland and Romania had been, the more deeply were collectivist values held by these refugee Germans. Then, when they migrated to modern Germany and assumed their new status as Resettlers, these collectivist values deterred their integration.

Thus, values—collectivist versus individualistic—help to explain the unexpected result by serving as a mediator variable (as discussed in Chapter 2). That is, these values mediate *between* the independent and the dependent variable. The explanation takes the form: traditional German culture maintained in Poland and Romania led to collectivist values that in turn led to less integration into modern German society.

Observe the comparisons made in this analysis with the help of statistics. First, the researchers compared Resettlers who lived in traditional German enclaves in Poland and Romania with Resettlers who did not live in such environments. This comparison reveals a difference between the two groups in the degree with which they hold collectivist values. Second, the researchers compared those Resettlers who hold largely collectivist values with those who hold largely individualistic values. This second comparison reveals the difference between the two groups in social and economic integration. Together these two comparisons provide an explanation for the surprising result.

3.5 SUMMING UP

Comparisons are important. To make sense of any data, one must compare them to one or more benchmarks. We have seen how different benchmarks can lead to contrasting conclusions. When East Germans suddenly shifted their reference group from poor eastern Europe to rich West Germany, they experienced a general malaise and decline in self-confidence. How one assesses black American conditions depends on the comparison used—past black conditions, present white conditions, or intragroup conditions among blacks. None of these comparisons is the lone correct one. All three are important, for each answers a different question and provides a useful perspective on a complex phenomenon.

The importance of comparisons explains why controls are a basic tool of scientific method and thinking. In the basic experiment, researchers compare a control group's results with those of an experimental group. The only difference between the groups is that the experimenter gives the test variable (such as a new pill) to the experimental group, but not to the control group (that receives a placebo). The basic idea, as with all controls, is to eliminate plausible rival hypotheses for explaining the results. As, one by one, researchers reject other possible explanations, their own explanation becomes increasingly more credible.

Controls are often necessary to remove subtle biasing effects. For example, experimenters who know which group the subject is in (experimental or control) may unintentionally bias the results. So many drug and social science experiments use a double blind design (neither the subjects nor the experimenter know which group is involved) instead of a single blind design (where only the subjects do not know in which group they are).

An experiment features random assignment of subjects to the experimental and control groups. It also features control over the timing and form of the independent variable. While all the social sciences occasionally employ experiments in and out of the laboratory, only social psychology routinely uses them to test its theories. In these experiments, researchers directly achieve control comparisons with specific experimental and control groups. We saw the use of control groups in the experiment on the self-fulfilling prophecy. Statistics are important for evaluating the differences in results between the experimental and control groups.

Problems arise for obtaining control comparisons in non-experimental investigations. This is the type of study that typifies most social research. Three basic methods are available to gain control comparisons in non-experimental studies—quasi-experiments, passive control studies, and statistical controls.

Multiple comparisons allow a broad perspective. Strong quasi-experimental and passive research designs provide the control comparisons needed to combat both internal and external threats to validity. Both lack the true experiment's random assignment of subjects to experimental or control conditions. However, researchers keep control of the timing and form of the independent variable in quasi-experimental designs. With passive research designs, they must accept the independent variable as they find it.

Figures 3.5 and 3.6 diagrammed eight commonly used quasi-experimental and passive designs. Many more designs are possible. So investigators can fashion their study to fit with the special features of their problem and research setting. The strongest designs boast such desirable features as pre- and post-measures of the dependent variable, experimental and control conditions, multiple groups for each condition, time sampling of the measures, and time series of the pre- and post-measures.

These features allow researchers to check on the plausible rival hypotheses advanced by the many threats to validity that face non-experimental research. Internal threats are those weaknesses that threaten the accuracy of a study's results and conclusions. We discussed six of them. The history threat occurs when some event exerts an influence on the dependent variable at about the same time as that of the independent variable. The maturation threat refers to changes in the subjects simply from the passage of time. The testing threat occurs when we measure the dependent variable twice, and the first test influences the second. Instrumentation problems result if there is a change in the measures used to gauge the dependent variable at different times. The selection threat refers to the assignment of different types of subjects to the experimental and control groups. Finally, the mortality threat involves different types of subjects dropping out of the study from the experimental and control groups.

Equally important are threats to external validity. Will the study's results apply (generalize) to other situations? If only males were subjects, will the findings also hold for females? Will the findings generalize to other social settings than those used in the study? Many hold field studies to have greater external validity than laboratory experiments. This is a more complex issue, however, than many realize. We must make the distinction between mundane realism and experimental realism. Field studies may have greater mundane realism—the likelihood that events in the study would routinely happen in the subjects' lives. Yet, field and laboratory research may not differ in experimental realism—an interesting situation in which subjects become thoroughly involved.

Many non-experimental studies, however, are unable to attain control comparisons directly. These studies must rely on indirect statistical means for attaining the necessary comparisons. These procedures have their limitations, and they usually involve considerable complexity and simplifying assumptions. The development of new statistical methods and sophisticated computers have greatly benefitted social science in recent decades. Indeed, these advances made modern quantitative social science possible.

We saw how multiple regression analysis provided the necessary controls to allow conclusions about the predictors of European prejudice. These predictors had additive effects—that is, their effects on prejudice added up. Often independent variables involve interactions, and their total effects on the dependent variable are not a simple sum of their separate effects. Such interactions occur when the effect of one independent variable is not the same at every level of another independent variable. We saw how such statistical controls provide an explanation for unexpected results. Sound advice for students planning a career in social science is to gain a solid understanding of modern statistics.

A major problem remains, however, in the use of statistical controls in non-experimental research. In the European prejudice example, the multiple regression analyses made an important, simplifying assumption. These analyses assumed the independent variables had all shaped the dependent variables at the same time. This is a common assumption in social science when we have only cross-sectional data. Investigators collect such data at one point in time, much like a camera's snapshot.

Yet we know that this assumption of simultaneous effects is unrealistic. Many factors influence social life, and their effects occur at different times. Thus, it is more realistic to think of a series of effects unfolding over time. Cross-sectional research can simulate this over-time view of social life with appropriate simplifying assumptions and new statistical procedures (such as path analysis). We gain an over-time perspective best, however, with longitudinal research—with data collected over time. Such data are more like a motion picture than a snapshot. Moreover, we saw in Figure 3.5 that quasi-experimental research designs gain strength by collecting repeated measures over time. We turn in the next chapter to a consideration of longitudinal research designed specifically to collect such data.

ISSUES FOR DISCUSSION AND REVIEW

A> Think of an important public policy question now under debate in the nation. How is the answer to this question shaped by different comparisons? Why is this so?

B> Choose your favorite non-experimental study in social science. Now think of a particular threat to validity in the research design. What is the plausible rival hypothesis that this threat suggests for the findings that is different from that of the researchers? What control group(s) would be necessary to check on your rival possibility? What would be an ideal quasi-experimental design to provide these control groups and comparisons?

C> The author holds that statistics are crucial to modern social science. Some social scientists strongly disagree. They think statistics have their use, but are not a necessary part of how social scientists think. What do you think?

RECOMMENDATIONS FOR FURTHER READING ON ISSUES RAISED IN THIS CHAPTER

On Plausible Rival Hypotheses:

S. W. Huck & H. M. Sandler. 1979. *Rival Hypotheses: Alternative Interpretations of Data-Based Conclusions.* New York: Harper & Row.

On Quasi-Experimental Research Designs:

For readers new to the idea:
C. M. Judd, E. R. Smith & L. H. Kidder. 1991. *Research Methods in Social Relations.* New York: Holt, Rinehart & Winston. Chapter 5.
For readers who wish to read a basic source:
T. D. Cook & D. T. Campbell. 1979. *Quasi-Experimentation: Design and Analysis Issues for Field Settings.* Chicago: Rand McNally.

On Statistics:

For readers with little or no statistical training:
D. Huff. 1982. *How to Lie With Statistics.* New York: Norton. [Or earlier printings.]
For readers with statistical training:
J. H. Dwyer. 1983. *Statistical Models for the Social and Behavioral Sciences.* New York: Oxford University Press.

Chapter
4
—

Searching for Causes
and Changes

L ike cats, social scientists focus on objects that move and change. Static phenomena are difficult to study, because they are difficult to measure. This situation presents few problems for social science. Social life, as discussed in Chapter 1, is always changing and in flux (dynamic).

This dynamic quality of social life allows social science to search for causes. What causes what? Why did that happen? What social policies would help solve a given societal problem? Most of the important questions addressed by social science involve the search for causes, but *cause* is a complicated concept. So the firm establishment of the causes of social phenomena poses a major challenge for social science.

We can glimpse at the complications by reviewing one of the most interesting investigations of college students ever conducted—the longitudinal (over time) study of Bennington College in Vermont. The research began in the 1930s. Theodore Newcomb (1943) collected extensive data on the political attitudes of all 527 students at the private women's college. It was an ideal setting for such research. Bennington was not only small, but in an isolated location and self-contained. The college took public issues seriously and had close faculty-student interaction. If changes in political attitudes take place at college, the Bennington campus would surely reveal them.

Tuition at this exclusive college was high. Most students came from wealthy families. This fact set up the principal tension in this bucolic setting— sharp differences in political views between the students' conservative family backgrounds and a liberal faculty.

The study's initial findings are consistent with the reference group concept described in Chapter 1. Most of the students became increasingly liberal as they progressed through their years at Bennington. There were differences, however, among the women. Those who most strongly identified with the col-

lege revealed the most marked shift toward liberalism. Thos
to identify more strongly with their families than the college
shift toward liberal attitudes. Hence, those students for who
came a major reference group moved to the political left
their family remained as the dominant reference group did

Twenty-five (1959–60) and forty-nine (1984) years later, Newcomb
his colleagues reinterviewed the former Bennington students (Newcomb,
Koenig, Flacks & Warwick, 1967; Alwin, Cohen & Newcomb, 1991). From
our discussion in Chapter 3, this study used a *passive time series design*.
That is, the researchers could not manipulate the dependent variable (the
Bennington experience). They compensated for this by measuring the dependent variable (political attitudes) on four occasions (on entering and leaving
college as well as 25 and 49 years later). This extensive longitudinal research
allows us to find out if the students' liberalism persisted in later life; or, did
their social attitudes shift back toward those of their parents once they left
college?

In general, their liberalism remained remarkably stable from their college
days. Compared to a control group of comparably educated women of the
same age, the Bennington graduates are significantly more liberal in their social attitudes. Figure 4.1 shows the differences between the two groups in
presidential voting over the years. Even as they approach their 70th birthdays,
the Bennington women in 1984 favored the liberal Democratic candidate,

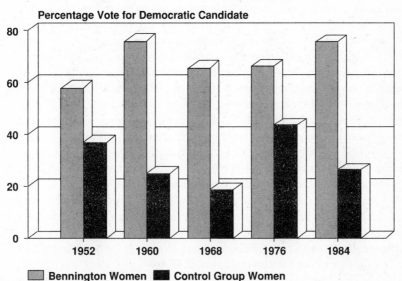

Figure 4.1   Presidential Voting
Bennington Women Vs. Comparable Control

Source: Institute for Social Research, 1991–2.
Note: Control = Same Age College Grads.

alter Mondale, over the conservative Republican candidate, Ronald Reagan, by a three-to-one margin. In sharp contrast, the control group supported the Republican by a three-to-one margin. (Note how the researchers developed a control group without a pre-test of what these women's attitudes were upon entering college a half-century earlier.)

The most interesting result reveals an important life-span principle of social influence. For those women who married liberal men, maintained liberal friends, and led their adult lives in liberal environments, the Bennington changes persisted. For those few women without such supportive settings, the changes of college did not persist. The significant finding is that most of the Bennington women who adopted a liberal political perspective as students went on as adults to shape supportive settings for their liberal views.

Thus, the college influence led to an active selection and shaping of future environments that in turn supported the original influence. It is not simply a matter, then, of "how the twig is bent," but also how the twig itself bends the environment. The women did not just react; the process also involved important proactive considerations. An investigation of students from colleges different from Bennington replicated this important proactive principle. Student attendance at Catholic colleges increases later adult religiosity largely because such attendance makes it more likely that the students will marry a highly-religious spouse (Greeley & Rossi, 1966).

Consider, however, the difficulties of specifying clearly what the causes were in this Bennington College phenomenon that unfolded over two generations. We know considerable change took place from the time these students entered college through their four years of study and into adult life. Yet what actually *caused* these changes? Was it their identification with Bennington that acted as the initial cause? Once the college served as an important reference group, were the women then open to the liberal social attitudes of the Bennington climate? This is the causal sequence suggested by Newcomb. Alternatively, could the liberal atmosphere of the college itself have been the initial cause? In this case, those most affected by the shift in political perspective could then have adopted Bennington as their reference group. Here the issue is causal order—which of the two measured variables came first? Most likely, the two processes acted jointly, each inducing the other as the students progressed through their college training (**reciprocal causation**).

A second causal problem in interpreting this famous study concerns unmeasured variables. No research can measure all the variables that might be important in such a change process. Could there have been key variables that Newcomb did not measure that were the principal causal agents in the change process? Here is where theory becomes essential. As discussed in Chapter 2, we can never measure all possible factors. We need a good theory to guide us in advance as to which variables we should measure. Newcomb chose reference group theory, and it served him well.

A healthy skepticism encourages you to speculate about what unmeasured variables might have been critical in the Bennington situation. Here, too, you should draw on your personal experience for ideas. You have experienced the role of the college student—though probably not in such an intense situation as Bennington's. Can you think of any additional factors that might have been important?

A third set of causal complications involves the general persistence of the changes 25 and 49 years later. Now the women themselves appear as the chief causal agent. They chose and arranged their adult environments to be compatible with their liberal political orientations. These environments in turn fostered and advanced their views further.

The basic causal question, however, is why did the Bennington alumnae do this? Presumably, they did so because they had internalized political liberalism as a central part of their self-definition. These views were no longer simply those of the Bennington faculty. They were now *their* views, and so valued that they influenced their later life choices. Ultimate causes of such a process are difficult to discern without a causal sequence perspective, a type of domino effect. The Bennington atmosphere led the women to adopt, and in time internalize, liberal political attitudes. These attitudes in turn influenced how they shaped their adult environments. And these environments in turn maintained and advanced their liberal attitudes.

One of the interesting ways this continuing process operated involved their children. The third wave of the Bennington study found that the children of these women were important contributors to their mothers' continued liberalism. Most of these children reached political maturity in the Civil Rights era of the 1960s. Their liberalism, shaped in part by their mothers, offered support for their mothers' maintaining their social views. Parents learn from their children just as children learn from their parents. Another longitudinal study, focusing on these activists of the 1960s, found that they, too, maintained their activism into later life (Franz & McClelland, 1994).

These difficulties of assessing causation in the Bennington study introduce us to the complexity of the idea of cause.

4.1 THE COMPLEX CONCEPT OF CAUSE

Thinking like a social scientist entails thinking about what causes social processes. Basic as this task is, it turns out to be difficult. To see why it is not easy to specify causes, we will discuss three aspects of the topic. First, assigning causes in everyday life is typically easy. We shall discuss why this is so, and also how this natural perception of causation features several consistent biases. Second, we turn to the logical complications underlying the concept of cause—a specialty of philosophy. Finally, we shall review the compromise that social science strikes between the rigorous strictures of philosophy's analysis of cause and the practical problems of studying social life.

4.1.1. The Natural Perception of Cause

In everyday life, assigning cause to events happening around us usually presents no problem at all. Take, for instance, when we play pool. As our cue stick hits the cue ball, it moves and hits the ten ball into the left corner pocket.

Determining causation creates no problem for us here. We instantly regard the stick as having *caused* the cue ball to move, and the cue ball in turn having *caused* the ten ball to roll into the pocket. Research by Michotte (1963) shows that the immediacy and naturalness of this process is an integral part of human perception.

We carry over this process into our perception of human beings. With little difficulty, we constantly assign cause to human actions around us. Indeed, it is critical that we do so. Knowing why others act as they do toward us is necessary to understand the situation and react appropriately.

Valuable as it is, however, the human ability to attribute cause is often biased and misleading. In their intensive study of **causal attribution,** social psychologists have discovered consistent biases in the process. Two broad types roughly characterize causal attributions for human actions. With **situational causal attributions,** we explain human actions with special features of the situation. With **dispositional causal attributions,** we explain the actions with special traits of the individual. A principal bias in our perception is that we frequently exaggerate the importance of dispositional causes and disregard situational causes (Ross, 1977). People are salient. They are in the foreground of our visual field, and thus they impress us as causal agents. By contrast, situational factors are usually in the background and out of view. Social psychologists call this phenomenon the **fundamental attribution bias.**

This general preference for dispositional explanations is not the only human bias in causal perception. One study showed that we usually grant those we love the benefit of the causal doubt (Taylor and Koivumaki, 1976). If someone close to us acts negatively, we typically attribute it to a temporary situational cause. "Oh, she just lost her temper, because she's very tired after a frustrating day at work." If, however, the act is positive, we attribute it dispositionally. "What a thoughtful thing to do—she is such a sweet person!"

We are less generous with others (Pettigrew, 1979). At the extreme, with members of disliked outgroups, we often reverse our causal reasoning (the **ultimate attribution bias**). Following a negative act by an outgroup member—such as pushing ahead in line, we attribute it dispositionally. "That's the way those people are—always pushy and aggressive." If the outgroup member commits a positive act—such as holding a door open for us, we maintain our prejudice by denying it, regarding it as a "special case" or explaining it away situationally. We fail to notice the good Samaritan was a member of the disliked outgroup, or we regard it as "the exception that proves the rule." Otherwise we could say, "What else could he do with all those people watching, while I struggled with a big package?"

Such causal reasoning about human behavior has direct effects on how we respond. If we think a person yelled at us angrily for situational reasons, we are likely to understand and remain calm. If we think a person yelled at us as an expression of an obnoxious personality style, we may well act back in kind.

This differential reaction occurs for social action as well. If we think the poor living in wretched housing are not responsible for their condition, we are likely to favor efforts to improve the housing. If we think the slum dwellers brought the bad housing on themselves, we are content "to blame the victim" and take no action. This latter course of blaming the victim may be especially prevalent in Western cultures. Research shows that we typically see victims of accidents and other ill fortune as the causes of their plight. To maintain a "belief in a just world," we are prone to believe that people get what they deserve and deserve what they get (Lerner, 1980).

4.1.2. Philosophical Complications

Immediate and natural as causal attributions are for human beings, logical problems underlie the idea of cause. Philosophers make valuable contributions to scientific thinking on precisely such logical issues. Without reviewing the philosophical analyses of cause in depth, let's look at points of special relevance for social science.

David Hume, the 18th-century Scottish philosopher, raised the basic problem that we can never directly observe causation. Instead, we can only *infer* cause. When we see one pool ball hit another that then moves, we have not actually observed causation. All we have seen is a connection between the two balls in time and space. We then, without hesitation, *infer* that the first ball caused the second ball to roll.

Hume's point is well taken and worth remembering. Causation always involves inference—not direct observation. Yet his insight led him astray. In seeking some observable, objective means to determine causation, he decided that a correlation between two factors was sufficient evidence. If the presumed causal agent preceded and connected with the effect, then a correlation between them established cause.

Think about Hume's argument for a minute. Night always follows day and the correlation is complete ($r = +1.0$), yet day does not *cause* night. A positive correlation exists between weight and height, but genes and nutrition explain the relationship. Similarly, a high correlation exists between wearing jeans and liking rock music. One would doubt, however, that one caused the other. Correlation alone, even when one factor precedes the other, cannot establish cause. There may be additional variables (such as age and conformity to popular norms) that relate both to wearing jeans and liking rock music that account for their correlation. We also should look at error cases—people who wear jeans and abhor rock music, and those who adore rock music and never wear jeans.

Another problem involves the interval between the cause and effect. There is agreement that a causal factor must precede its effect. Yet, how long can this interval between cause and effect extend for us to consider it a causal relationship? In physics, theory can often specify such intervals in advance. Social science can rarely be so precise. The Bennington College effects, for instance, were still evident after a half century (Figure 4.1). In fact, delayed effects are common in social science. Though difficult to predict in advance, such effects demand explanation. A useful explanation of delayed effects must specify when (moderator variables) and how (mediator variables) such effects persisted. In the Bennington study, the mediating variable involved the politically liberal environments the women chose and shaped for themselves after leaving college.

A third complication involves reciprocal causation. This happens when two or more variables mutually influence each other. Such a possibility is more than a concern for philosophers. Reciprocal causation may be the dominant pattern of social life. In economics, for example, what consumers spend depends on their income. It is also true that their income depends in part on their consumption. Such common causal patterns raise complex statistical issues (Ragosa, 1985). Single-equation predictions no longer suffice. Rather, systems of simultaneous equations are necessary, as developed by econometricians.

Reciprocal causation is best studied with longitudinal designs, like the Bennington research, in which the investigation measures the subjects at repeated intervals over time. The liberal political attitudes of the Bennington students and their later liberal environments offer an instance of reciprocal causation revealed by longitudinal research.

On another issue, some philosophers insist that cause and effect must involve perfect correlations. That is, when the cause is present, the effect must *always* follow. When the effect is present, the cause must *always* have preceded it. Such a criterion of cause simply does not reflect the messy nature of social life. Absolute relationships are rare. Instead, probability relationships are the rule. That is, cause A will be present with effect B under some conditions but not others at varying probabilities. Measurement error also will reduce our reading of the relationship between A and B. Correlational statistics measure this relationship, but in practice it can never attain the rigorous standard set by some philosophers. The strict absolutist position on causation is not realistic for social science.

Amidst such causal complications, social science is happy to accept the simplifications of another Scottish philosopher. John Stuart Mill advanced three conditions for inferring cause. The first two are easy to meet: *the cause must precede the effect,* and *the two factors must relate to each other* (though not necessarily perfectly). It is Mill's third criterion that frames the basic task for social research. To establish cause, *one must rule out other explanations for the cause-effect relationship under study.* We discussed this central issue in the last chapter by showing how controlled comparisons exclude plausible rival hypotheses.

Mill helps by proposing three "canons" to meet his third criterion for identifying cause. First, his *Method of Agreement* states that an effect will be present when the cause is present. Second, his *Method of Difference* states that the effect will be absent when the cause is absent. The third canon, the *Method of Concomitant Variation,* implies that when the first two canons hold true the causal inference is stronger. This is so because these canons remove rival explanations for the relationship.

Mill understood, as Hume did not, that mere correlations between variables were not sufficient by themselves to determine causal links. Nor did he require that the correlation coefficients—the *concomitant variation*—be near perfect (r = +1.0). His lasting point was that one must probe the relationship deeply to reach secure causal connections.

To follow Mill's reasoning fully, we would need to test all variables that could possibly provide a rival causal explanation. We saw in the Bennington study how this is impossible in practice. We need theory to guide us to select the most likely variables for testing. Since we can never be sure that we have exhausted all relevant variables or theories, our causal conclusions must remain tentative. For that matter, *all* science is tentative. Social science is as dynamic as its subject matter. New ideas, theories, and research overturn and improve what we call "knowledge" in a never-ending process.

The 20th-century Austrian philosopher Karl Popper (1959; Miller, 1985), best reflects this tentative perspective on science. Though Popper focused on physical science, much of his philosophy is directly useful for the social sciences (Campbell, 1974; Cook & Campbell, 1979; Pettigrew, 1991d). He maintains "truth" is a goal we can never attain. However, we at least can know when we are "getting warm." We know we are approaching "truth" by collecting research evidence that is not inconsistent with our causal theory. In short, we do not *confirm* a theory through research; instead, we *fail to falsify* the theory.

Thus, we do not discover "truth" with research. Instead, we gain confidence in our theory by learning that we have not yet falsified it. Following Mill, we do this by what Cook and Campbell (1979:22) call a *winnowing process*. We continue to test our causal theory repeatedly in ways that remove plausible rival hypotheses. Think back to the Archer and Gartner (1984) example in Chapter 3. Remember how these investigators cast doubt, one by one, on rival ways to explain their finding that homicide rates rise after wars. This emphasis on falsification may sound like "backing into" a causal inference. However, this cautious approach makes good sense when we realize all the logical problems involved.

Moreover, research observations—the *facts* of science—are themselves partly infused and shaped by the very theories they test. That is, scientific observations presuppose a theory and its conditions. "Even a simple reading of a watch presupposes that the hands will move uniformly," and minutes and hours are all constant according to astronomical theory (Von Bertalanffy, 1975:168).

Some modern philosophers go so far as to claim that this "theory-laden" quality of scientific observations means that theory testing is impossible. Social scientists rarely accept this argument. They join Cook and Campbell (1979:23–25) in regarding some observations as "stubborn facts." That is, these observations are often replicated. They recur across many settings by various researchers using different methods and testing different theories. To be sure, theory and methods partly shape facts. Yet not just a single theory or a single research design is usually involved. This overlap allows some degree of theory testing in social science, even if it is not as direct as in physics and chemistry.

Cook and Campbell (1979:25–28) remind us of a further point. Social scientists prefer *manipulable* causal factors. This preference has practical advantages. Causes that we cannot control are obviously of no direct value for applied work. Applying social research to alleviate the world's problems requires causal variables we can alter.

We usually can exercise this preference for manipulable causes. Actually, there is no one cause of a social effect. Since social phenomena operate at multiple levels (Chapters 1 and 6), any particular social effect will have causes at several levels of analysis. In addition, recall from Chapter 1 that many factors cause most social phenomena even at one level of analysis. With so many causal factors, it is likely some will be controllable.

Combatting inflation provides an example. Many factors at many levels of analysis cause goods and services to rise in cost. Such causal factors vary from governmental decisions about interest rates and the money supply to individual decisions on what to buy at what price. Some of these causes are easily altered, others are not. The U.S. Federal Reserve Board can decide to increase interest rates and reduce growth in the money supply to combat inflation throughout the nation. Trying directly to alter the buying patterns of millions of individual Americans is not so readily available.

Furthermore, we usually do not need to have complete information about all causal factors to act effectively. We turn on and off electric lights each day by knowing only that flipping a switch makes it happen. A detailed knowledge of electricity is not necessary. Our limited knowledge catches up with us, however, when the expected effect does not happen. We flip the switch, and the light fails to go on. We go one level deeper. We check the cord and plug and replace the bulb. If these do not work, we call an electrician. Now we need someone whose causal knowledge extends down to more basic levels.

4.1.3. The Social Science Compromise

Picking its way through this thicket of philosophical problems, social science adopts a compromise position to determine causation. This position varies across the various disciplines. Yet social science must strike a compromise between the most severe strictures of philosophy and the practical reality of studying an untidy world. To think like a social scientist, you must keep this compromise in mind.

Our brief sketch of the logical issues involved with causation suggests six major aspects of this compromise.

1. We cannot directly observe causation. We must always infer it.
2. Causes must always precede effects, yet different intervals may occur between them. Moreover, factors can reciprocally cause each other over time.
3. We never know "truth." We can approach it by a winnowing process that invalidates plausible rival hypotheses.

4. All observations partly reflect the theories and methods that led to them. Nevertheless, stubborn facts that replicate across settings, researchers, methods, and theories allow testing of causal theories.
5. Absolutes are not the rule in social life. One must use probabilities. So no findings and theories are final truths. All can and should be challenged in a continuing process of scientific development.
6. Finally, social science prefers manipulable causal factors, since they are of special importance for useful applications.

Several implications flow from this perspective on causation. Obviously, we must be tentative in our causal conclusions. Probabilities, not absolutes, are the rule. Moreover, causal inferences must carefully consider the intervals between cause and effect and the potential for reciprocal causation. We need to spread the net of rival explanations widely, so that we can thoroughly narrow down the most promising causal possibilities. To avoid having our observations become too theory and method laden, we also must measure our basic concepts with multiple indicators and test them from several perspectives. In all this, a healthy skepticism helps again in our approach to social science.

There are, however, two different strategies taken in the social sciences to carry out this causation compromise. We shall label these approaches the *building-block* and *bold strategies*.

The building-block approach comes from an influential school of philosophers of science called the Vienna Circle Positivists. They flourished in Vienna, Austria between World Wars I and II. They held to the view that research should try to *confirm* theory. Their arguments emphasized that research should accumulate in building-block fashion. Each study in a project should maintain the same measures and procedures as earlier studies except the one significant change under test. Then you can be confident that the one change caused any difference in the results. Bit by bit, each investigation provides one more block in the edifice that is the causal theory.

Sharply distinguishing his position from that of the Vienna Circle, Popper (1959) attacks the building-block strategy on two grounds. First, he argues it is not likely to tell us much, because it is too modest in scope. Even if supposedly confirmed, the hypotheses so tested bear little "content" and new information. Second, such a strategy risks having its results shaped by the repeated use of the same limited measures and research designs across many studies. Those who follow the building-block strategy risk having their results influenced by the narrow range of methods they use.

By contrast, Popper (1959; Miller, 1985) calls for a bold strategy. His guiding analogy for testing scientific ideas is Darwin's "survival of the fittest" principle for the development of life forms. He urges the use of the widest range of possible measures and research designs to test broad theories. Such a bold approach leads to bold theories rich in content and new ideas. Hence, *falsification* of these bold efforts is more likely. Such tests, Popper insists, will teach us more, even if falsified, than will the confirmation of timid, incremental tests.

One popular application of the bold strategy is **meta-analysis.** This technique provides statistical analyses of the results of many independent studies of a single phenomenon. Meta-analysis estimates the size of a phenomenon across many studies and conditions. It is most effective when it reviews research that uses diverse types of subjects, measures, and methods. Meta-analysis summarizes all the known research on a given topic with greater precision and objectivity than subjective reviews of the same studies.

How successful have this compromise and these two strategies been in the social sciences? As with most sweeping questions, there are differences of opinion. I believe, however, that there has been considerable progress in the social sciences during the 20th century. The growth of the various knowledge bases reflects this progress. A quick review of published work across this century in any of the social sciences reveals this growth. I was convinced of this by a review I conducted of all research in race relations published in American journals of sociology from 1895 to 1979 (Pettigrew, 1980). It uncovered an enormous development in both methods and theory over these years.

There are many reasons for this progress. We will consider three specific procedures in particular. Evaluative statistics, replication, and longitudinal research designs have all helped social science to meet the terms of its causal compromise.

4.2 STATISTICS EVALUATE CHANGE

Chapter 3 stressed the importance of statistics in modern social science. It showed how statistics help us to achieve controlled comparisons with non-experimental data from the field. Here we see a second vital role for statistics. We have talked about research results that support or falsify hypotheses and theories. But how do we evaluate these results as supporting or falsifying? How do we know if these results are not chance effects? For instance, how do we determine that the attitude changes of the Bennington students were large enough to conclude that a genuine effect had occurred?

These questions require statistics for answers. The various social sciences employ different, though related, approaches. Economics typically uses **effect sizes,** such as correlations, to assess the importance of its results. Effect sizes assess differences largely independent of the number of people (or other units) that make up the sample studied. They are especially useful for applications. They make sense for economics for two reasons. Economists typically deal with data sets that boast large numbers of subjects (or other units). Government agencies prepare many of these data sets. Economists are also often interested in applications of their research to policy.

The disadvantage of effect sizes is that they are unreliable if the research involves only a few subjects or observations. When there are many subjects, they are useful indicators of the strength and importance of effects. Think back to Figure 3.7 on European prejudice. There we had 4,000 subjects across seven samples. So Figure 3.7 used effect sizes to portray the results. With

4,000 observations and robust effect sizes, we can be certain of the **statistical significance** of the findings. That is, such results are unlikely to be due to chance.

If, however, the number of subjects or units is small, then even a large effect size may not be statistically significant. Hence, one must use statistical tests that take sample size directly into account. While needed for small sample studies, tests of significance can be misleading with large samples. Large samples can show a small effect to be statistically significant, even when the effect is too small to be of practical importance.

If you have taken a statistics course, you know that such tests of significance as student's t-test are among the first lessons. You also learned that two benchmarks—the 5% and 1% levels of confidence—mean that the relationship under test would not occur but five times or one time in a hundred by chance. Such tests characterize elementary assessments of data in most of the social sciences. Statisticians choose the 5% and 1% levels of confidence to strike a balance between two kinds of errors we can make using significance tests. **Type I errors** occur when researchers incorrectly accept their hypotheses as supported (the null hypothesis of no effect is true). **Type II errors** occur when researchers incorrectly reject their hypotheses as falsified (the null hypothesis of no effect is false).

There is a close relationship between effect sizes and significance tests. Only the sample size distinguishes them: significance test = effect size + sample size. Hence, studies with large sample sizes aimed at applications find effect sizes to be more useful. For example, meta-analyses, summarizing the results of many investigations, employ effect sizes. Studies with small samples that seek to determine the level of confidence for a result find tests of significance more useful. The point for our purposes is that statistics are essential. Since social life involves probabilities, we need evaluative statistics to assess them.

4.3 THE IMPORTANCE OF REPLICATION

An effective way to increase the power of statistical methods and to establish research findings more solidly is to repeat the study with a fresh sample of subjects (replication). It is surprising how often investigators do not take this straightforward precaution before they publicly announce exciting results. You may have noticed the many times investigators do not replicate pharmaceutical research, and must later withdraw their original claims for a new "wonder drug." This is also true for several celebrated social science studies that originally claimed to be of major significance for public policy. A careful second study before announcing findings of initial work could have prevented these embarrassments.

The complexities of social life cited in Chapter 1 make replication essential for social research. Recall again the study of European prejudice (Pettigrew & Meertens, 1994). Seven independent samples participated in this study—one from Germany, and two each from France, Great Britain, and the

Netherlands. Such multiple samples allow extensive replication of all findings. Special statistics allow researchers to combine the results of such multiple studies into particularly powerful tests of the hypotheses under test. In fact, the data in Figure 3.7 on the correlates of prejudice represent the combined results of the seven samples.

Sometimes repeating social research is not possible. Perhaps the study checked on the effects of a public event, such as the assassination of Dr. Martin Luther King, Jr. described in Chapter 1. It is impossible to repeat the event. Even here a form of replication is available. The researcher can split the sample in half and test each half as if it were a separate study. Though it reduces the sample size, this procedure can exploit the advantages of two separate studies.

The introduction of increasingly sophisticated mathematical models has heightened the importance of replication in social research in recent decades. Often the initial building of these models capitalizes in part on chance. That is, special characteristics of the initial sample inflate the model's "fit" with and prediction of actual data. Thus, replication with new samples is essential to test the model.

In addition to the original researchers, others may also wish to repeat an investigation. Such fresh replication is a major way social science has of correcting itself. This possibility explains why research articles in technical journals use so much space providing the details of the study's methods. Anyone attempting replication would require these details to proceed.

4.4 THE IMPORTANCE OF LONGITUDINAL STUDIES

Longitudinal research studies how social phenomena unfold over time. So, longitudinal data best meet the criteria for inferring causation.

The Bennington College study provides an excellent example of a longitudinal study. Such research collects its data at different times. Usually, like the Bennington study, it involves the same subjects. Social scientists call such research **panel studies,** with the same subjects forming the *panel*. The National Longitudinal Surveys (NLS) of the U.S. Department of Labor are among the most extensive on-going panel studies in the United States (U.S. Bureau of Labor Statistics, 1992). One of these surveys focuses on youth who ranged in age from 14 to 21 in January 1979. It drew a probability sample of 12,686, including a special military sub-sample. Each year the survey reinterviews these respondents about their schooling, jobs, work attitudes, marital history, income and assets, health, and other matters.

Recall the unrealistic assumption underlying the basic form of multiple regression analysis: namely, that all the predictor (independent) variables operate *simultaneously* in influencing the dependent variable. One major advantage of longitudinal studies is that they allow us to investigate how social processes unfold over time. We saw this in the Bennington College study. Many types of research demonstrate this singular asset of longitudinal research. We shall look at a variety of such studies drawn from (1) laboratory experiments, (2) field studies, (3) trend analyses, and (4) investigations using archival data.

4.4.1. A Longitudinal Laboratory Experiment

Most laboratory research is not longitudinal; that is, the experimenter measures the dependent variable only once. Yet over time, research designs with laboratory experiments can be particularly powerful. An interesting investigation of role playing and smoking by Mann and Janis (1968) offers a pointed example.

In July 1963, these investigators had heavy-smoking females play one of two roles. The experimental group played the role of smokers whose doctor had just informed them that they had developed lung cancer. The control group watched the role playing as passive observers. As you can see in Figure 4.2, both groups reported marked declines in cigarette smoking one month later (pre- and post-experiment bars in Figure 4.2). The experimental group, however, showed a statistically significant greater decline. Playing the role of a cancer victim had a marked effect. Even just observing the role playing had some effect.

Six months later, the reduced smoking continued. Despite minor increases in both groups, a large difference remained between the two original groups as well as between them and a second, new and untreated control group (the

**Figure 4.2   Longitudinal Lab Study
Role Playing and Smoking Reduction**

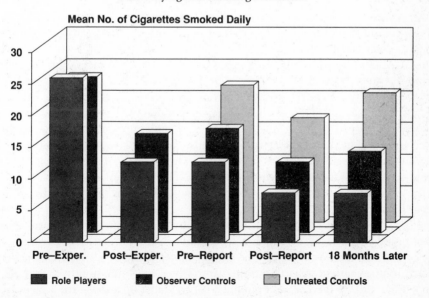

Source: Mann and Janis, 1968.

pre-report bars in Figure 4.2). So both the role playing and observer effects persisted.

Right after this measurement, a significant event occurred. This is a further advantage, as well as a hazard, of longitudinal designs. Often a fortuitous real-world intervention occurs that provides special insight into how the experimental variables operate. Immediately after the third measurement in the study, the U.S. Surgeon General released a highly-publicized report on smoking and health that held cigarettes to be especially dangerous.

The study then tested the smokers again. The three groups were equally aware of the Surgeon General's report and its contents. All three reported similar declines in smoking (the post-report bars in Figure 4.2). Clearly, the Surgeon General's report had its desired effect. Yet this result did not change the differences among the experimental and two control groups. The cumulative effects of the treatments and the new health report simply added together. The groups remained different in their decreased smoking.

Finally, Mann and Janis (1968) tested the subjects 18 months after the experiment. As Figure 4.2 shows, the untreated controls had almost returned to their pre-report cigarette smoking levels. For them, the Surgeon General's report apparently had only a short-lived effect. The two treated groups also reported small average increases in smoking over the year. This increase, however, was particularly minor for the role-playing subjects. They continued after 18 months to reflect on average the additive effects of both the experimental treatment and the Surgeon General's report.

4.4.2. A Longitudinal Field Study

In addition to the Bennington study, another famous longitudinal field study shows how small effects can accumulate over time into large effects. Such effects would go undetected in cross-sectional designs; only longitudinal research can uncover them.

Muzafer Sherif's (1966) Robbers' Cave study at a summer camp began by forming two comparable groups of young boys—called the Eagles and the Rattlers. He first kept the groups apart and unaware of each other in different parts of the camp. They each engaged in popular activities, and soon each group developed a sense of "we-ness" and high morale. Then the second phase of the field study began. Sherif brought the two groups together and had them compete in a series of contests. These contests, such as tug-of-war and softball, all featured **zero-sum** payoffs. That is, one side had to win and the other lose. These contests soon led to intense conflict between the Eagles and Rattlers.

Sherif then set out to reduce the hostility that had arisen between them. He tested the efficacy of cooperative contact in the pursuit of superordinate goals—goals unattainable by one group alone. The two groups engaged in such joint experiences as fixing the camp's broken water supply, working to pay for a motion picture, and pulling a rope to start up a truck for a picnic. In time, Sherif succeeded in sharply reducing the intergroup conflict and prejudice between the Eagles and the Rattlers.

However, these cooperative efforts considered singly did not achieve dramatic change. It was a gradual, additive effect. The attainment of the first superordinate goal, the plumbing repairs, aroused "good spirits" at the time, but "the groups fell back on their old recriminations once the immediate crisis was over" (Sherif, 1966:89). A cross-sectional study would have ended with this one measurement of the dependent variable, and incorrectly concluded that cooperative experiences only temporarily improve intergroup conflict (Pettigrew, 1991c). Sherif persisted, however, with further cooperative experiences. With each new situation, the combined effects added up until little intergroup animosity remained. Only longitudinal research could have uncovered this phenomenon.

4.4.3. Trend Analyses

Political scientists and economists often study long-term societal trends in their primary variables. This work is non-experimental and makes use of various quasi-experimental designs discussed in Chapter 3. This longitudinal perspective focuses attention on sharp deviations that occur from these trends. This non-experimental approach, then, uses past data as control comparisons for interpreting present data.

Some important indicators are surprisingly stable over time. Figure 4.3 provides an example of importance to students of American politics. Over the 30-year period, 1960–1990, political party identifications given by adult Americans to survey interviewers remained remarkably constant (U.S. Bureau

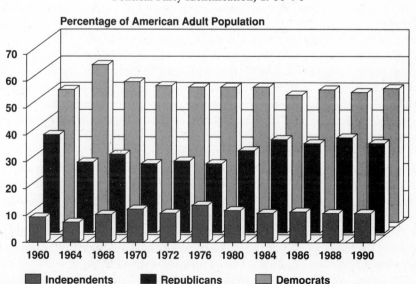

Figure 4.3   Party Trends
Political Party Identification, 1960–90

Source: U.S. Bureau of the Census, 1992a.

Figure 4.4   Consumer Price Index
Inflation Trend for All Items, 1900–1991

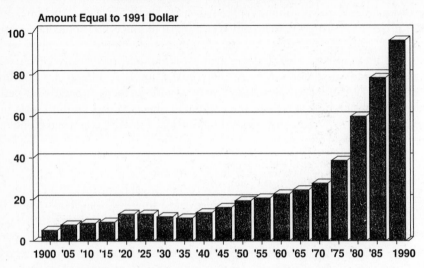

Source: U.S. Bureau of the Census, 1975, 1992a.
Note: All amounts in 1991 dollars.

of the Census, 1992a:270). In 1960, half of the respondents called themselves Democrats of varying strength, two-fifths Republicans, and the remainder Independents. Three decades later, 51% called themselves Democrats, 37% Republicans, and 11% Independents.

Other indicators show considerable variation. Figure 4.4 graphs the cost of living in the United States for all items across the 20th century (U.S. Bureau of the Census, 1975:210; 1992a:469). The benchmark comparison is the U.S. dollar in 1991. We read from Figure 4.4 that what cost one dollar in 1991 cost only 60 cents in 1980, and 28 cents in 1970. These data give a broad picture, though there are technical problems in combining data from the beginning and close of the century. In addition, by using composite averages for all items, Figure 4.4 obscures differences in the trends for various expenditures. Since 1960, for example, housing and medical costs have climbed more rapidly than telephone and transportation costs (U.S. Bureau of the Census, 1992a:469).

While such crude data cannot prove causation, a glimpse at this trend suggests hypotheses for further test. Note the decade of the Depression experienced a drop in prices (1930–1940). Marked increments occurred during decades of major wars (1910–1920, 1940–1950, and 1960–1970). The steep rise in prices during the 1980s suggests additional factors are also important. The 1980s experienced no major war, but it was a time of massive deficit spending on armaments. For those Americans who think their dollar does not buy what it once did, Figure 4.4 shows how right they are.

Observe also that this one indicator of inflation does not chart the economic standard of living. The inflation index improves at a time of economic disaster (the 1930s) and rises during periods of economic prosperity. Obviously, broader indices of economic prosperity need to consider how much money people have to spend, as well as the costs of goods and services.

4.4.4. A Longitudinal Study Using Archival Data

Elder's (1974) sociological study of the effects of the Depression illustrates the use of archival data in longitudinal research. Archival data are records and materials gathered earlier and maintained for later research use. Elder did **secondary analyses** of data from a longitudinal study that earlier researchers had collected for other purposes. Such analyses are "secondary," because he reanalyzed the old data with fresh new hypotheses and methods.

The sweep of Elder's investigation provides a rare perspective on issues normally studied over short periods. With data on 167 families followed from 1932 to 1964, he looked at the effects of unemployment and economic deprivation on family structure and personality. The Depression led to economic loss that generated severe social strains and altered family life. Economic deprivation caused changes in marital relations, parent-child relations, and the division of labor within the family.

For example, the need for girls to take responsibility for home duties and for boys to earn outside income reinforced traditional attitudes about gender roles. Taking early jobs for the boys meant "an accelerated movement toward the adult world." At the personality level, these changes led to a lasting need for stability and security among these Americans who were children in the 1930s. Elder inferred that economic deprivation as children was the cause of these effects. The fact that the effects were greatest for those families whose income loss during the Depression was especially profound strengthens Elder's inference.

With these varied examples, we see the advantages and importance of longitudinal research designs. Now we must review the problems of interpretation that accompany these designs.

4.5 INTERPRETING LONGITUDINAL EFFECTS

Elder's research introduces us to the types of interrelated effects that occur over time. The Depression study revealed **cohort** effects. That is, a particular cluster of Americans who experienced the Depression as children show the effects. That is what a cohort is: *an age cluster of people who experience a significant event at about the same time in their lives* (Ryder, 1968).

One theorist, Karl Mannheim (1952), held that the political events of early life decisively shape every cohort's political orientation. Thus, the events that occur as it reaches voting age (the Depression, a war, the Civil Rights Movement, the Clinton era) have a special influence on each cohort's political perspective throughout life. Americans who entered the electorate during the 1930s provide an example. Their gratitude for President Roosevelt's efforts against the Depression led them to be unusually loyal to the Democratic Party in their voting ever since. So cohort is a useful concept in many fields. We will illustrate its use further in Chapter 5.

Causes of long-term changes are often difficult to untangle. Three overlapping possibilities arise. In addition to cohort effects, there are also **generation** and **life-cycle** effects. The three processes are intertwined, since each relates to age.

Generation is the broadest term. In popular usage generation includes all three effects, yet it has proven helpful in social science to distinguish between them. Social scientists limit generation effects to *the structural and cultural aspects of family lineage and parent-child relationships*. They commonly employ it, for instance, in referring to immigration patterns. They call those American citizens born elsewhere first-generation Americans. The children of immigrants, born in the United States, are second-generation Americans.

Often social scientists use generation in explanations that involve parents passing on cultural values to their children. Hence, Flacks (1967) explained the young political activists of the 1960s as a generation effect. He found these activists typically came from families with liberal, humanitarian values. Their demands for social change, Flacks argued, represented their application of these values to social injustices in American society.

If you are familiar with William Shakespeare's *As You Like It,* you already know the basic idea behind the life-cycle process. Shakespeare provides this most famous of life-cycle theories in his soliloquy about "All the world's a stage, and all the men and women merely players" (Act II, Scene VII). "And one man in his time plays many parts. . . ": the infant, "the whining schoolboy," the lover, the soldier, the middle-aged professional ("the justice"), late-middle age ("with spectacles on nose and pouch on side"), and old age (in "second childishness and mere oblivion, sans teeth, sans eyes, sans taste, sans everything").

Erik Erikson (1963, 1968) advanced today's most popular outline of life stages. He lists eight stages, each with its own "psychosocial crisis": infancy, early childhood, play age, school age, adolescence, young adulthood, adulthood, and old age. Erikson (1968:286) emphasizes two sides of the life cycle. One refers to how an individual's life "round[s] itself out as a coherent experience." The other side is how the life cycle forms "a link in the chain of generations." The life-cycle process, then, is *the course of human life moving through a sequence of developmental stages from birth to death.* All the social sciences make use of the life-cycle idea, but it is a particular specialty of developmental psychology.

To apply these three types of effects, consider a finding from political science. Jennings and Niemi (1975) studied a large national sample of Americans as they developed politically after their high school graduation in 1965. Their longitudinal research followed the respondents for eight years, from the age of 18 until they were 26. Their findings differ from those of the Bennington College women. These young adults changed their political attitudes extensively over this period back toward those of their parents' generation.

All three age effects offer possible explanations for this finding (Smelser & Smelser, 1981). Did this group shift because of their special experience with a particular historical event—such as the return to power of the Republican Party in 1968 under Richard Nixon? This would be a cohort effect. Did they shift back to their parents' more conservative views because their youthful rebelliousness receded? This would be a generation effect. Did they shift because of their passage from adolescence to young adulthood? This would be a life-cycle effect. Most likely, it was a combination of these effects. Obviously, longitudinal data are necessary to grapple with these questions—even then the interpretation of the results can be difficult.

Cohort, generational, and life-cycle effects all involve changes across age groupings. A related set of effects involve the breadth of social changes taking place across a society. Do major shifts in American public opinion, for example, reflect only the replacement of older cohorts by younger cohorts? Or do these shifts represent attitude changes across all cohorts?

These questions involve two separate processes. The first is a demographic cohort replacement process. Younger cohorts reach maturity and replace older cohorts that are dying. Due to educational advances during the 20th century, these younger cohorts are better educated than the older ones they replace. Thus, for this and other reasons, the replacement process has provided a slow but continuous liberalizing trend in American public opinion.

By contrast, the conversion process represents a shift in the cultural norms across all cohorts in varying degrees. Unlike the replacement process, conversion changes are sensitive to immediate events and thus can be rapid and volatile. Davis (1975, 1980, 1992) offers a metaphor using climate and the weather. Climate patterns, like the cohort replacement process, are comparatively stable and change slowly. However, the weather, like the conversion process, can change suddenly.

Sociologists and political scientists extensively analyze shifts in American social attitudes (Chafetz & Ebaugh, 1983; Davis, 1975, 1980, 1992; Kiecolt, 1988; Smith, 1982, 1990). These trend analyses use massive amounts of national survey data and are complex. They would not be possible without the computing and statistical advances mentioned in Chapter 3. There is general agreement in this work on the broad trends of American opinion since World War II. Interestingly, these conclusions differ from popular interpretations by the media of these trends.

As Figure 4.5 (adapted from Smith, 1990) illustrates, there was a marked shift in American public opinion toward liberal beliefs from 1953 until 1973. Though this period covers the Civil Rights era of the 1960s, the shift toward more liberal social attitudes is broader. The trend appears on a range of topics—from abortion to foreign affairs. There are, however, differences among topics. Leading the way were changes toward more liberal positions on individual choice, the treatment of minorities, and civil liberties in general.

Most of the steep liberal climb shown in Figure 4.5 represents a conversion effect. That is, most cohorts and social locations (sex, social class, educational and occupational subtypes) reveal these shifts in varying degrees. This finding suggests a sharp alteration of American cultural norms during this two-decade period. Yet this is not the whole story. As the weather was growing more liberal, so was the climate. Underlying the normative changes was a

Figure 4.5   Social Attitude Trend
Social Attitude Changes, 1937–1985

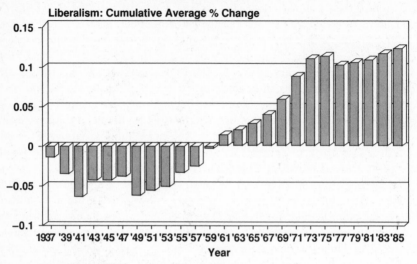

Liberalism: Cumulative Average % Change

Source: Smith (1990).
Note: Positive = Liberal; Negative = Conservative.

smaller but continuous cohort replacement effect. Young cohorts educated after World War II were steadily replacing old cohorts educated at the turn of the century. Thus, a large conversion effect, bolstered by a smaller replacement effect, accounts for the liberalizing trend through this period.

Figure 4.5 also shows that this trend stopped in the mid-1970s. Overall, it did not become a general swing toward conservative positions, for the flat plateau in Figure 4.5 masks different trends in different opinion areas. Attitudes on race, free speech, and gender roles continued to become more liberal, though at a slower rate than before. Two areas, however, reveal conservative trends—opinions about taxation, and crime and the treatment of criminals.

Most of this change in public opinion reflects a definite shift in the conversion effect. Influenced by much publicized rises in crime, drug use, and taxation, cultural norms on these topics moved to the political right. However, the cohort replacement process was also involved. While it still produced a small net shift in the liberal direction, its size markedly decreased from previous years.

Finally, in results only partially shown in Figure 4.5, a rebound back to the liberalizing trend occurred in the mid-1980s (Davis, 1992). This well-documented phenomenon was neither expected nor detected by the mass media in the midst of the Reagan presidency. It represented a shift again in the conversion process, for it occurred among a wide variety of Americans. The cohort replacement effect, however, continued to get smaller and did not account for this liberal shift. Using his metaphor, Davis (1992) called this complicated picture "changeable weather in a cooling climate."

One final point about the replacement effect concerns its value in prediction. Since it is both stable and gradual, one can project its effects into the future with greater confidence than the cross-cutting currents of the conversion effect. Moreover, these effects can be large when there is a marked difference on the dependent variable between the newest and the oldest cohorts.

Consider again the data on political party identification shown in Figure 4.3. Recall that these data revealed overall stability in the percentages identifying with each major party. Additional data not shown in Figure 4.3 exhibit a future shift based on cohort replacement (U.S. Bureau of the Census, 1992a:270). In 1990, 43% of respondents born before 1911 (thus at least 80 years old) identified as "strong" Democrats, another 23% leaned toward the Democrats, only 5% called themselves Independents, and 30% Republicans. This is the cohort who were young adults during the Depression. As predicted by Mannheim, their strong loyalty to the Democratic Party that came from that special experience never waned. The youngest cohort interviewed in 1990 (born after 1958) looks very different. Only 11% regard themselves as "strong" Democrats, 35% leaned toward the Democrats, while 15% are Independents and 39% are Republicans. Not only will cohort replacement cost the Democratic Party support, it will especially cost them ardent followers.

These broad processes—cohort, generation, life-cycle, replacement, and conversion—aid in interpreting longitudinal data. Yet they only suggest, rather than specify precisely, the basic causes of the changes uncovered in longitudinal research. To know that a liberal rebound during the 1980s was a conversion effect suggests that a normative shift occurred in America. That leaves open the causal question of *why* did norms change toward liberalism right when an extremely conservative presidential administration governed the country. Similarly, the decline in the liberalizing cohort replacement effect suggests that those born after 1950 are not much more liberal than the old cohorts they are replacing. Why? These processes narrow and set the causal questions. We need theory to guide us in interpreting these interesting trends in American public opinion.

4.6 SUMMING UP

A primary goal of social science is to measure and explain social change. To achieve this goal, the field must grapple with the complexities of causation.

Assigning cause to events around us is usually natural, immediate, and necessary. To be sure, human perception of causation is biased. We see people as salient, causal agents (dispositional attributions), and neglect the power of situations to influence social behavior (situational attributions). We also typically give those we love the causal benefit of the doubt, while attributing the worst to those we do not like (the ultimate attribution bias).

Establishing cause in social science, however, is not so simple. Indeed, once we consider the logical analyses of causation by philosophers, assigning cause becomes one of the field's most difficult tasks. We have reviewed some complications that underlie the idea of causation. Considering the messy nature of the social world, philosophy's strictest criteria for cause are not possible for social science to meet. For instance, perfect correlations between cause and effect are not realistic in social research.

Thus, a compromise on causation is necessary. This compromise balances the philosophical criteria for identifying causation with the realities of conducting social research. Recall the six interrelated contentions. (1) You cannot directly observe cause; you must always infer it. (2) Causes must precede effects. Widely different intervals between cause and effect can occur, as can reciprocal causation. (3) Since you can never ascertain "truth," you must approach it by winnowing out plausible rival hypotheses. (4) All observations reflect in part the theories and methods that lead to them. Still, stubborn facts exist that replicate widely and allow testing of causal theories. (5) Social life lacks absolutes, so we must take a probability approach to causation. Finally, (6) social science prefers manipulable causal factors, because they are useful in practical applications. These contentions provide further support for the need of a healthy skepticism in social science.

Two contrasting strategies in social science carry out this causal compromise. One strategy believes research and theory should develop in building-block fashion. This strategy maintains the same concepts and measures across studies, so we can more easily trace differences in results to their cause.

The bold approach adopts a different strategy. It uses a broad range of measures and research designs to cast as wide a net as possible. In this way, it tries to avoid overlooking new and rival explanations. This strategy is especially useful for meta-analysis—the procedures for statistically summarizing the results of many studies on a specific topic.

There has been considerable progress in social science over the 20th century in both research sophistication and theoretical rigor. Developments discussed in Chapter 1, such as the surge of computing and statistical capability, fueled this progress. We noted in this chapter the use of statistics in assessing change. Both effect sizes and significance tests effectively assess the importance and reliability of social research results. Replication of research, using new subjects, offers another important tool. It increases the power of statistical methods, and grounds important results more solidly before we apply them to practical problems.

Longitudinal studies are especially important for determining cause. Such research, measuring the dependent variable at two or more times, tracks how social phenomena unfold over time. We reviewed examples of longitudinal research of many types—laboratory and field experiments, trend analyses, and studies using archival data. In each case, we noted how the over-time design uncovered results that cross-sectional research would have missed.

Causal interpretations of longitudinal results are often difficult. For this task, it is useful to distinguish three processes related to age: cohort, generation, and life-cycle effects. A cohort is an age cluster of people who experience a significant event at about the same time in their lives. A generation refers to the structural and cultural aspects of family lineage and parent-child relationships. Finally, the life-cycle process involves the course of human life moving through a sequence of developmental stages from birth to death. While intertwined in practice, these effects have distinctive characteristics that aid analysis of longitudinal data.

Another set of processes gauges the breadth of social change. The cohort replacement process involves younger cohorts replacing older cohorts in society. It introduces slow, continuous change when the young differ from the old in key characteristics other than age.

The rival process entails participation by most cohorts and social locations in social change. This conversion process can be swift and abrupt in its effects. The two processes do not always point in the same direction. In fact, we noted the two form a varied pattern in describing the liberal shift in American social attitudes since World War II. Helpful as these processes are for guiding the interpretation of longitudinal results, more precise causal specification requires theoretical guidance.

ISSUES FOR DISCUSSION AND REVIEW

A> Newcomb's study of Bennington College students is a classic example of longitudinal research. Suppose a social scientist presently conducted a study such as Newcomb's on your campus. What do you think the results would be? Do you think the social attitudes of students at your college change over their years of attendance? If so, how and why? If not, why not? How is campus life at your college different from that of Bennington College's in the 1930s?

B> What makes "cause" such a difficult idea? Are the complications raised by philosophers directly relevant for social science? Why?

C> Choose a cross-sectional study that you know. Suppose it had been a longitudinal study. How might the findings and interpretations have differed with the dependent variable measured more than once? What would be some advantages of the longitudinal study? What are some problems of interpretation introduced by the longitudinal research design?

D> Try to think of further examples of the three principal types of over-time age effects—cohort, generational, and life cycle.

RECOMMENDATIONS FOR FURTHER READING ON ISSUES RAISED IN THIS CHAPTER

On The Logic of Social Research:

For readers new to the subject:

C. M. Judd, E. R. Smith & L. H. Kidder. 1991. *Research Methods in Social Relations.* New York: Holt, Rinehart & Winston. Chapters 3 and 4.

J. A. Davis. 1985. *The Logic of Causal Order.* Beverly Hills, CA: Sage.

On Karl Popper's Philosophy of Science:

For readers new to the subject:
D. Miller. (Ed.) 1985. *Popper Selections*. Princeton, NJ: Princeton University Press.
For readers with a background in the philosophy of science:
K. R. Popper. 1959. *The Logic of Scientific Discovery*. New York: Basic Books.

On Meta-Analysis to Summarize Research Results:

For readers new to the technique:
C. M. Judd, E. R. Smith & L. H. Kidder. 1991. *Research Methods in Social Relations*.
    New York: Holt, Rinehart & Winston. Chapter 18.
For readers with statistical and methodological training:
R. Rosenthal. 1991. *Meta-Analytic Procedures for Social Research*. Rev. Ed. Newbury
    Park, CA: Sage.

Chapter
5

Sampling, Selecting, and Socializing

For many years, the *New York Daily News* conducted large pre-election polls with thousands of participants. The results regularly covered the paper's front pages. The problem, however, was that these polls did not allow for differences between those who responded and the voters on election day. Everyone was welcome to join the fun and list the candidates they favored. Thus, the *Daily News* did not conduct a survey with a **probability sample** that carefully mirrored the voters.

The paper's editors argued that their rough-and-ready polls compensated for their lack of sampling sophistication with their massive size. In truth, these polls were many times larger than any probability survey of New York voters that any agency could afford. Sometimes the *Daily News* polls correctly picked the election winners. Sometimes they failed miserably. Surveys using far smaller probability samples of respondents did much better.

Why? What was wrong with these enormous *Daily News* polls? Just what are probability samples, and why do they perform better? These are the questions we will consider in this chapter. Then we will show that sampling is a general social science issue, not one confined to election surveys. In fact, concern for sampling issues is an integral part of how social scientists think.

5.1 WHY ELECTION POLLS GO WRONG

The "everybody is welcome" technique of the *New York Daily News* results in massive constant errors. That is, such polls attract only particular types of people. These types are different in many ways from the total voting population. The target population to which you wish to generalize the results of a political poll are those who will vote.

Those who went to the trouble to respond to the *Daily News* polls were undoubtedly more politically active and interested than others. This difference suggests that they were more highly partisan. Hence, the poll's participants underrepresent the many voters who consider themselves political independents and decide how they will vote late in campaigns.

Those polled also apparently found participating more convenient than others. For state elections, New York City area residents are only a part of the electorate. In addition, those polled were more likely to be *Daily News* readers. In these and other ways, the poll's respondents differed from voters who did not participate. When these differences relate to diverse voting preferences, the poll will be inaccurate (**biased**).

The newspaper editors' hope that the large number of people taking part would compensate for these biases is unjustified. It exposes a misunderstanding of constant error. Recall from Chapter 1 that increasing the number of respondents will simply magnify, not correct for, constant errors.

It would be different if the electorate consisted of only 2,000 people, and the *Daily News* secured the voting choices of 1,900 of them. Then the editors would have a point. Here a sample is not necessary to generalize about a large population, since the poll includes 95% of all voters. The New York State electorate, however, involves millions of people. Not even the large *New York Daily News* poll can reach more than a tiny fraction of this total. There is a clear need for a probability sample. The accuracy of the sample, not the proportion of the total, is what determines a poll's validity.

Political surveys with probability samples do better than those with haphazard sampling, because they more closely reflect the voting population. They manage this by providing *each person of voting age with an equal (or known) chance of being selected*—the definition of a probability sample.

Even these surveys often miss in their political predictions. Worse, rival surveys sometimes advance conflicting results. Why? There are three basic reasons.

5.1.1 Not Precise Enough for Close Elections

The broadest reason why survey results sometimes conflict is that even probability surveys are not ideal instruments for predicting elections. This is surprising when one considers their widespread use and popularity for precisely this purpose. Even the best of sample surveys can provide only "order of magnitude" estimates, not the precision required by close elections. For close races, the shrewd politician's best guess may be as accurate.

Part of this imprecision can be due to not asking the right questions. Designing effective survey questions is an important part of accurate surveys. Queries about salient political issues are helpful in addition to direct inquiries about voting. Badly worded, confusing questions yield distorted results (Schuman & Presser, 1981). For example, a national survey in 1992 asked Americans: "Does it seem possible or does it seem impossible to you that the Nazi extermination of the Jews never happened?" When 22% responded that it was possible the Holocaust never happened, a furor arose (Associated Press,

1994). The question posed a double negative. To affirm belief in the Holocaust, respondents had to agree that it was *im*possible it *never* happened.
Later a simpler question asked: "Do you doubt that the Holocaust actually
happened, or not?" Now only 9% expressed doubt and 4% were unsure—a
markedly different result.

5.1.2. Two Predictions at Once: The Problem of Differential Turnout

In addition, pre-election polls err because they must make several com-
pounded predictions at once. That is, they must predict *who* will vote as well
as *how* they will vote. Differential **turnout** has often reversed the results of
close races. In general, registered Republicans, being on average richer and
better able to vote on a working day, typically vote in larger percentages than
registered Democrats.

The Gallup Poll organization has developed a useful set of questions to
predict turnout. It asks whether you have voted in recent elections and the location of your voting place. Yet, predicting voter turnout remains such a problem for pollsters that they sought another method to bypass it.

Exit polls question only known voters. They do so by sampling voters as
they leave the voting place on election day. They are also useful in gaining in-
stant information about the social characteristics of particular types of voters.
Television reporters use exit poll data to state on election day that most Ital-
ian-American voters in Newark are voting for candidate X.

Yet even exit polls do not solve the problem of predicting the vote. The recent rise in absentee ballots in such states as California presents new difficulties. These mail-in voters do not go to any voting place, so no exit poll can
sample them. In California's razor-close gubernatorial race in 1982, Field's
(1983) exit poll correctly showed the Democratic Party candidate had won by
a slim margin of the votes cast in person. The Republican candidate won the
contest, however, because of his large lead in absentee ballots.

5.1.3. Bias from Selective Non-Response

The third reason for election poll error involves **selective non-response**. This
problem refers to particular types of people selected for the sample who do
not respond to the survey. This is the selection threat to internal validity we
discussed in Chapter 3. When these drop-outs from the sample differ in voting
preferences from those who participate, they introduce bias (constant error) in
the results.

Selective non-response is a more serious problem than recognized by
many political pollsters and the mass media (Pettigrew, Coltrane & Archer,
1995). In fact, it is a major reason for conflicting poll results. Unfortunately,
most survey agencies do not release their data on non-response. This practice
makes it impossible to estimate the full extent of the problem.

The growing use of "tracking polls" adds to this problem. These quickie polls, often conducted overnight in the heat of a contest, use telephone interviews to *track* shifts in voter sentiment as they occur. Done over a brief time, such a rough-and-ready technique typically suffers serious **non-response bias.** The brief time span restricts the number of call-backs that can be made—the chief method for reducing non-response.

Two major types of non-response plague political surveys in general, and tracking polls in particular. *The not-at-home sample members* are often busy, younger people. *The refusals* are older and at home when the survey calls, but they refuse to participate. Maybe they cannot be bothered, or they fear the survey is an advertising ploy. They may resent the interruption in the middle of their dinner or favorite television program. These two types of non-respondents create different biases. Yet, both types usually differ in their voting preferences from those who respond, and are likely to add to the bias of the survey's results.

Non-response rates for all types of surveys in both North America and western Europe have been rising in recent years. They reach unacceptable levels in many political polls. This is especially true of the tracking polls that receive so much attention in the mass media. The usual research standard is a *maximum* non-response rate of 30%. Political polls often attain as high as 85% non-response rates—with five in six of the original probability sample not responding to the survey.

If you read newspaper stories on political polls, this fact may surprise you. You have probably seen the reassuring statement that the results are accurate within such a narrow range as +3% to −3%. This statement represents false advertising. It refers to statistical sampling error. This is random (or variable) error that an increase in the sample size will reduce. This so-called accuracy range commonly appears in newspapers and on television, but unrealistically assumes a 100% response rate. Moreover, the reporting of poll results rarely tells you what the non-response rate was and how this problem could drastically affect the error range.

Is this, as some critics scoff, merely an "academic" point? Decide for yourself. A leading American newspaper regularly reports results from its own sponsored surveys with response rates as low as 15%. It does not report this fact. I only found out when the newspaper asked me to consult on its surveys.

An example shows what a 15% response rate means in practical (not "academic") terms. Suppose 40% of the many non-respondents support issue X, but 60% of the few respondents do so. In this situation, the actual percentage supporting the issue would be only 43% ([.85 non-respondents × .40] + [.15 respondents × .60]). Yet the newspaper, depending on the unrepresentative respondents, would report that a solid majority favors issue X. Simple arithmetic shows that a response rate of at least 55% would be necessary in this case to determine correctly that a majority opposes issue X.

Some defenders of political polls admit to the non-response problem, but argue that it is not a serious difficulty in practice. Their contention is that non-respondents are rarely different from respondents on the principal items of interest—such as voting preferences. Moreover, even if they are different, the poll defenders hope that the constant errors introduced by various types of non-respondents will cancel themselves out. Recent research with data from other sources on non-respondents casts doubt on these claims (Pettigrew, Coltrane & Archer, 1995).

Another way to deal with non-response bias is by "weighting." This method counts the data from underrepresented types of respondents as more important than those from overrepresented types. This technique eases the problem in many instances. It is of little use, however, when there is only a 15% response rate. And it does not always operate as optimally as assumed (Pettigrew, Coltrane & Archer, 1995).

5.2 SELECTION BIASES ARE A GENERAL PROBLEM

Surveys are not the only method plagued by selection biases. Both social and medical research suffer from underrepresentation of women and minorities among their subjects. That is, studies often fail to sample subject populations appropriate to their problems. Gaps abound in medical knowledge because of the exclusion of major groups in medical research (Cotton, 1990). Research on heart disease, for example, has largely used male subjects, leaving open whether its results hold for (generalize to) females (Gurwitz, Col & Avorn, 1992). Selection biases, then, are a general problem, so general that the issue shapes the way social scientists think.

Most social science research involves sampling—at least implicitly. Consider two types of social scientists who rarely think explicitly in sampling terms—social psychologists and cultural anthropologists. Experimental social psychologists do their laboratory studies largely with North American and western European college students. Yet they generalize their results widely—to adults, to other social classes, and cultures. Is this justified? Some observers, noting that these students are overwhelmingly of European origin, middle-class, and young, question whether such generalizations should be made (Sears, 1986). Others show biases that are introduced by using volunteer subjects in psychological experiments (Rosenthal & Rosnow, 1975).

Consider the study of attitude change—a major focus of social psychology. College students may be inappropriate subjects for research on this and similar topics. College years are a time of major alterations in students' lives. Many are living away from home for the first time. They are learning new ideas in a new environment; they are expecting to change and "grow up." Thus, college students, like the Bennington College women, are especially susceptible to changing their attitudes. This highly non-random slice of humanity may not provide attitude change experiments with typical results. Worried about this selection bias, some social psychologists have taken care to conduct their attitude change studies with adults and in field experiments.

Similarly, when cultural anthropologists spend years studying one African tribe, they are implicitly sampling humankind with this single group. To what larger universe can these researchers generalize their results from this one group? Cultural anthropologists have an informative answer to this query. They maintain they are not trying to generalize their results to all humankind. Rather they wish to expand our understanding of humanity by revealing cultural patterns that contrast sharply with dominant patterns elsewhere. It is precisely the group's uniqueness, not its representativeness, that is the anthropological focus. For such a purpose, the sampling perspective is not germane.

There is, however, another sampling issue facing cultural anthropologists. Even years of work will not allow them to interview everyone in the tribe or all situations in tribal life. They are implicitly sampling interviewees and situations within the tribe. Informal sampling in cultural anthropology can lead to serious selection biases when the researcher does not know the language or otherwise must depend on a guide. Such assistants may provide a biased sampling of their choosing. They show you what they want you to see—not unlike a guide on a package tour.

Once I went to a remote village in South Africa's Zululand to conduct social perception experiments (Allport & Pettigrew, 1957). Kate Mdlala, a cheerful Zulu woman, greeted me as I arrived. She spoke fluent English as well as Zulu. She announced she was "the official guide" for visiting researchers and listed off the many scholars she had helped. Mdlala was a warm, intelligent person in the best Zulu tradition. Yet, I wondered if she had provided all the social scientists with the same tour that emphasized certain elements of Zulu culture and ignored others.

Longitudinal studies are especially subject to problems of non-response and the mortality bias mentioned in Chapter 3. We have noted the importance of longitudinal research. Yet, because it is longitudinal, the drop-out rates of these studies over their duration are typically high. In addition, the subjects who drop-out are not a random group. You can easily imagine who are the most likely to drop-out of longitudinal research—such as those who die young or often change their residence. Such people are likely to differ from those who remain in the study on a wide range of other variables of interest.

There is, however, one major advantage that longitudinal panel studies have to correct for this problem. Recall that panel studies repeatedly interview the same respondents. So, unlike political polls, panel studies already know a lot about their missing members. Since the study interviewed drop-outs in a previous wave, one can easily check these earlier data to see what selection biases may be operating.

Imagine a health survey that interviewed the same people when they were 50, 60, and 70 years of age. Suppose the data show that between 60 and 70 the entire sample on average got much *healthier!* They report as a group fewer symptoms and health complaints at 70 than they did at 60. An initial possibility is this finding results from a selection bias among the drop-outs between 60 and 70 years of age—the mortality threat to validity described in the previous chapter. When you think like a social scientist, you would test for this explanation before concluding the panel members are getting increasingly healthier as they grow older.

Thus, a plausible explanation is that the less-healthy people in the panel died younger or were otherwise less available for the interview at age 70. This selecting out of the least healthy could account for the apparent improvement during the panel's seventh decade of life. Since there are data on the drop-outs when they were younger, you can easily test for this **artifact** (*an erroneous result due to a problem in the method*). You can check to see if the drop-outs at 70 had more health problems when they were younger and still in the investigation. In addition, you can check the health changes of only those respondents for whom you have data when they were 60 and 70 years of age.

Similar selection bias examples appear regularly in newspapers. For instance, the Scripps-Howard News Service (1993) did a national poll on attitudes toward marriage. It found only 6% of men and 8% of women said "they would not marry the same person again." Unless you think in selection terms, these data suggest the nation's marriages are overwhelmingly happy. However, we know the nation's divorce rate is extremely high—with almost one in every two marriages ending in divorce (U.S. Bureau of the Census, 1992a). The poll's data reflect the answers of only those still married. The many Americans who have experienced divorce and have not remarried are missing. Moreover, those divorced who have remarried are only responding about their present spouses. Therefore, the data reflect a biased sample of successful marriages.

Selection bias operates in all the social sciences. In economics, the term **underground** (or informal) **economy** refers to this problem. It consists of the economic activity that takes place in every economy but goes unrecorded in official data. Such unrecorded activity is different from that which is recorded. Some of it is illegal activity—drug and other criminal activities and tax evasion efforts. Much of it is just barter and other informal arrangements that never surface in the banking and taxation systems. Some observers may exaggerate the size and importance of the underground economy (Harding & Jenkins, 1989). Whatever its size, however, the data used to measure the economy are selectively biased and represent an underestimate of "true" economic activity.

Similar problems arise for the U.S. Census. Over recent decades, the Census has seriously undercounted the population (Allen, 1989; Johnson, 1994; Williams, 1980; Williams, 1989). The Census estimates that it did not count 5.3 million people in 1970 and 3.2 million in 1980. Despite special efforts to reduce this figure, the Census estimates the 1990 undercount between 4.3 and 5.3 million people—roughly two percent of the population.

Like most non-response, these undercounts are not randomly distributed across the population. The Census is far more likely to omit minorities in large cities. Thus, estimates of the undercount of blacks are four times greater than that of whites in 1970, and six times greater in 1980. Hispanics as well as blacks are more often left out of the counts. Black men are the largest missing group. In 1980, the Census calculates that almost a fifth of all black men between 35 and 54 years old went uncounted.

Census undercounting is a critical issue. State and federal governments use these counts to calculate political representation. The bias in 1990, for example, probably cost southern California and Arizona one seat each in the U.S. House of Representatives.

In addition, population size is a basis for 60 federal programs that award over $73 billion annually. Undercounting means that cities with large minority populations will unjustly receive reduced funding. Baltimore officials, for instance, figure their city's undercount of 29,000 people in 1980 resulted in the loss of $232 million in federal funds during the 1980s. San Jose's undercount of 19,000 people in 1990 cost the city almost two million dollars in grants in 1991 alone. Little wonder, many cities have brought court suits to have adjustments applied to the population estimates of the Census.

How, you might ask, does the Census know it is undercounting minorities in general and black males in particular? The Census does the job with large computers, sophisticated statistical methods, and massive amounts of data from birth, death, immigration, emigration, and other records. In 1990, the Census also conducted a Post-Enumeration Survey that sampled 17,390 households to estimate its undercount. With these methods, the Census can adjust for much of their undercounting. The political sensitivity of this phenomenon, however, has turned the problem into more of a legal and political issue than a demographic one.

Political scientists study an intriguing selection issue. Who votes in American elections is a dual selection process. First, one must register to vote. This initial barrier is a major reason that American voting percentages, even for presidential elections, are low compared with those of other democracies. Not only are convicted felons barred, but so are many who are recent residents and late registrants. Twenty-five states require you to be a state resident for at least four weeks. Twenty-eight states require that you register at least four weeks in advance of an election.

Then there are those who select themselves out of the process by not registering for any number of reasons. These barriers, both state- and self-imposed, combine to keep between a fourth to a third of the nation's voting age population unregistered (U.S. Bureau of the Census, 1992a:271). It will be interesting to see if present efforts to make it easier to register will prove effective.

The second selection process involves who actually votes. Obviously, only those who have passed the first barrier of registration can actually come out and vote. Turnout voting percentages vary widely across the United States and between different types of elections. Local races for minor offices typically attract only small percentages of the registered voters to the voting booths. Presidential elections attract the largest turnouts. Yet just over a half of the total potential vote cast their ballots in even presidential contests in recent years. Since 1932, the percentage of voting-age Americans casting a presidential ballot has varied from 50.1% (in 1988) to 61.9% (in 1964) (U.S. Bureau of the Census, 1992a:270). For candidates for the U.S. House of Representatives, the voting percentages ranged from only 33.1% (in 1990) to 57.8% (in 1964). On average, then, about seven of every ten Americans register to vote, and about three out of four of these registrants actually vote for president.

Structural barriers to voting also exist at the turnout stage. For example, Tuesday is the traditional American voting day. Why Tuesday? It is a work day, and therefore inconvenient for people who work long hours. Many other democracies hold their elections on Sundays, a time that better accommodates most voters in predominantly Christian countries. If the U.S. is serious about increasing political participation, why does it not shift its elections to Sunday?

The research literature in political science is replete with incisive analyses of this dual selection process of American voting. It shows how the various barriers all contribute to the low political participation of Americans. Considering this dual selection process, each with its own barriers, it is remarkable that as many Americans vote as they do.

5.3 SELECTING OUR POSITIONS IN SOCIETY

The voting selection process offers a simple analogy for thinking about the uneven distribution of opportunities and other resources in society. Just as some people are far more likely to vote than others, some people have far greater access to resources than others. Sociologists deal with this question, and ideas drawn from sampling issues shape how they view the problem.

How people are selected (or **allocated**) and how they select themselves into various positions in society is as non-random as the *New York Daily News* election polls. Though we rarely think about it, we occupy our present roles through a series of selection processes more complicated than those for voting.

First, we all start at birth with certain ascribed statuses—race, ethnicity, and sex. As noted before, these statuses are ascribed, as opposed to **achieved status,** because they are bestowed upon us at birth without our choosing or earning them. These ascribed statuses affect where we will end up in society.

There has been wide discussion of how race and gender shape opportunities. Although less discussed, social class also shapes our destinies. Our family structure, our home environments, the schools we attend—each shapes and selects us in our development through the stages of life.

For example, suppose you are born an African American and grow up in a virtually all-black area of a large city. Unless the city has an effective school desegregation program, this location means that you will attend virtually all-black public schools. Research conducted at Johns Hopkins University shows what this start in life is likely to mean for your future. Compared with a black American similar in talent and family social class who attends interracial schools, you are less likely to go to college and later to gain a well-paid job, and more likely to hold a job with largely black co-workers (Braddock, 1989; Braddock, Crain & McPartland, 1984; Braddock & McPartland, 1987).

Figure 5.1 shows part of this chain of interlocking events. Both black males and females who have attended predominantly white high schools later tend to work in predominantly white situations. Those who attended predominantly black high schools later tend to work in predominantly black situations. Since predominantly black work situations have poorer pay and less

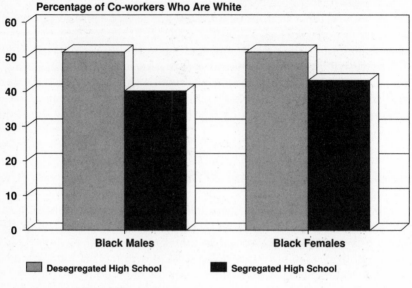

Figure 5.1   We Live What We Learn
High School Desegregation Leads to Employment Desegregation

Source: Braddock & McPartland, 1989.
Note: Only full-time workers included.

promotional opportunities, this difference in co-workers has both income and advancement implications for African Americans.

This example suggests how social processes accumulate over time to influence your future. We discussed one of these processes in Chapter 1. Recall how job information flows through loose social networks of "weak ties."

Different social sciences emphasize different allocation (selection) processes. Anthropology focuses on kinship structure, political science on power, economics on financial structures, and sociology on race, ethnicity, gender, and social class. When several social sciences focus on the same institution, such as the family, they study it from different perspectives. Anthropology views the family largely as a unit within a kinship system that transmits culture through the generations. Demography considers the family as a reproductive unit and economics as an income unit. Such diversity is healthy, for together the various approaches provide a rounded view. The problem is there are few who can span and bridge the disciplines and synthesize the multiple, but complementary, perspectives.

The emphasis of demography on cohort opportunities is especially interesting. Recall from Chapter 3 that a cohort is an age cluster of people who experience a significant event at about the same time in their lives. A particular event, then, will affect various cohorts at different times in their lives. So the same event may have contrasting effects on various cohorts. These cohort effects set the background for opportunities for each age grouping.

Take the writer's cohort, for instance. I was born just after the collapse of the stock market and the start of the nation's deep economic Depression of the 1930s. Not surprisingly, this was a time of few births. Hence, I belong to the small Depression cohort of Americans born during the 1930s.

The post-World War II "baby boom" came next. Suddenly, there was a need to educate millions of young Americans. The need for teachers combined with the small size of the Depression cohort to provide many opportunities for those in my cohort who desired teaching careers. Thus, many of us found good jobs and later received rapid promotions. Naturally, human vanity being what it is, we would each like to think we did well because of our individual efforts and talents. Less obvious are the benefits my cohort received from the expanding opportunities of an unusually open selection system created by the differential birth rates of two adjoining cohorts.

The "baby boom" following World War II is one cohort that has received considerable attention. "Boomers," as the media call them, have commanded attention, because they are such a large market for goods and services. As they proceed through their life-cycle stages, marketing efforts and the media have centered on the Boomers' current concerns—crowded schools, then college attendance, newly married life, having children, and recently the angst of middle age. It is always stale news to my cohort. Each concern was always a decade or more behind my age group's life-cycle stages. Now the children of the Boomers form a large cohort. Demographers call this an **echo effect.** This term refers to a large cohort providing a new large cohort at child-bearing age.

However, people are not just corks in the ocean, drifting where the structural tides push them. We also constantly make choices throughout life. These choices also shape the positions we end up occupying. To be sure, our choices are themselves narrowed and channeled by the societal allocation processes to which we have been subjected. Growing up poor in a tough slum with bad schools severely limits individual choice. Growing up in advantaged circumstances, however, allows considerable freedom to self-select your future.

Hence, where we end up in society is a complicated mixture of societal selection processes combined with self-selection. In social science thinking, we do not find ourselves in particular occupations and statuses by chance.

5.4 BEING SOCIALIZED INTO OUR POSITIONS IN SOCIETY

The plot thickens further when we consider what happens to us once we attain particular positions in society. We are then *socialized* into our societal roles. That is, we learn how we should act in our new roles and what others expect of us. This helps to explain why people with the same job, from janitors to medical doctors, act much the same despite their individual differences. Socialized into our occupational roles, we *become* janitors or doctors.

We learn new roles both formally and informally. First, we often **presocialize** for a role. That is, we prepare ourselves for a new role before we occupy it. You imagine years in advance what it must be like and how you should act in roles ranging from a rock star to a lawyer. Then, you formally learn how to behave and think like a lawyer in law school. You learn legal ethics and your professional responsibilities as a lawyer. You also learn how to be a lawyer in countless informal ways. Clients and other lawyers start treating you as if you were a lawyer. They expect you to act like a lawyer. Very shortly, you meet their expectations. You begin to act like a lawyer and think of yourself as a lawyer. You have become socialized into the role.

Medical and law schools provide pointed examples of how selection and socialization operate together. Since they can accommodate only limited numbers, rigorous selection processes determine who get the valued positions in these schools. Moreover, their degrees are a critical part of the larger selection process of who gets to be a doctor or lawyer. Put bluntly, degrees from many of these schools are licenses to later wealth and prestige.

An attractive feature of both the law and medicine is the wide variety of sub-specialties each offers. There is some specialty within these broad professions to fit almost any personality type. Here we see how individual choice and personality differences play a part in determining our positions in society.

In the law, only a minority actually practice in court as portrayed on television. A wide variety of non-court roles are available, not the least of which is politics. American legislatures, state and federal, have lawyers as large majorities of their elected members. In fact, America has the highest percentages of lawyers as elected legislators of any major democracy.

In medicine, you can choose specialties that deal only with the dead (pathology), or those that deal directly with the daily problems of the living (intensive care medicine and psychiatry). You can specialize in treating everything from skin conditions (dermatology) to the eyes (ophthalmology). You can practice medicine, teach it, administer it, do research in it, or various combinations of these options. Medical schools provide their students a chance to try out these specialties. They introduce the sub-fields in formal classes; then, during the clinical years, you rotate through various hospital and clinical services.

When my wife attended medical school, we watched with interest as her classmates selected their specialties. Knowing them and their personalities, we guessed which specialties they would choose. We were correct for most of them. An informal matching process took place while these medical students sampled the possibilities. They carefully matched their talents, interests, and personality preferences with the contrasting demands of the wide-ranging specialties.

Once in the specialties, a more specified form of socialization takes place. Already socialized into the general role of medical doctor, the new doctors get additional socialization as specialists during their internship and residency training following graduation from medical school. Now they learn directly what being a surgeon, internist, pediatrician, or public health specialist entails. All told, this series of selection and socialization processes of medical school, internship, and residency training typically requires almost a decade.

5.5 SUMMING UP

This chapter has covered a broad range of topics—from political surveys to medical school training. Yet a few fundamental, interlocking ideas underlie the discussion. These ideas are basic ways of thinking about society from a social science perspective.

The basic ideas involve sampling, selection, and socialization. Political polls present a well-known example of probability sampling. Serious selection biases that arise from such problems as non-response from sample members can invalidate poll results. When reviewing data sampled from a large population, the healthy skepticism of social scientists leads them first to seek information about the adequacy of the sample. Did each member of the studied population enjoy an equal (or known) chance of selection into the sample? Was the sample size large enough? Was the response rate from the sample high enough to generalize the sample's results to the larger population with confidence?

Selection biases pose problems for all social research. Even those social sciences, such as cultural anthropology and social psychology, that do not usually employ sampling still face selection biases. Longitudinal studies are especially prone to the related problems of non-response and selection biases. Fortunately, since these studies have prior data on the non-respondents, they can usually correct for these biases.

Other examples of selection bias occur in economics, demography, and political science. Such issues as the underground economy and the minority undercount by the U.S. Census offer striking illustrations of selection bias. So does the dual selection process of voting in America studied by political scientists. First, there are barriers to registering to vote. There are further barriers for those registered to vote. These two sets of barriers cause the United States to have one of the lowest voting percentages among democracies.

This selection process of voting provides an analogy for thinking about the uneven distribution of opportunities and other resources in society. Selection biases describe how societies work. It is not a random matter how various people end up in different positions. From this view, life is a series of selection processes, each biased, that accumulate into a final allocation of who gets what. These processes can vary from those that affect individuals (such as the Scholastic Achievement Test to get into college) to those that affect whole age groups (such as the baby boomer cohort).

Once in our institutional positions, socialization takes place both formally and informally. We learn directly in school and on the job how to fit into our new role. We also learn at least as much by simply being in the role and having others treat us as a lawyer or medical doctor. The final mark of socialization comes when we fully internalize the role. Now we think of ourselves as a lawyer or doctor.

Law schools and medical schools illustrate how these processes combine. Only a selected subset of Americans get the opportunity to attend these entrance tickets to wealth and prestige. Once in, socialization processes shape this non-random sample of citizens into lawyers and doctors. Then, further selection and socialization take place between specialties within the law and medicine.

Once you see this complex web of events as the result of sampling, selection, and socialization, you readily understand why members of a particular job or position resemble each other in backgrounds, behavior, and beliefs.

ISSUES FOR DISCUSSION AND REVIEW

A> Select a report of a recent political poll from the local newspaper. Analyze and discuss it. Does it report sampling error? Does it report its non-response rate? How might the results be different if the non-response rate were high?

B> How did you get to college? Consider the various factors that may have been involved—from society's allocation (selection) processes to your choices.

C> Have you decided what career you wish to pursue? If so, are you already socializing for such a career? Have you started to presocialize—thinking about what it would be like in the future to be in that career? Have you had a summer job or any other opportunity related to your career choice? If so, did socialization processes begin to shape you into the career role?

RECOMMENDATIONS FOR FURTHER READING ON ISSUES RAISED IN THIS CHAPTER

On Probability Sampling for Surveys:

For readers new to the idea:

C. M. Judd, E. R. Smith & L. H. Kidder. 1991. *Research Methods in Social Relations.* New York: Holt, Rinehart & Winston. Chapters 6 and 9.

R. L. Scheaffer, W. Mendenhall & L. Ott. 1986. *Elementary Survey Sampling.* 4th ed. Boston: PWS–Kent.

For readers who wish to read a basic source:

A. Chaudhuri & H. Stenger. 1992. *Survey Sampling: Theory and Methods.* New York: Dekker.

On How Cumulative Barriers Operate Against Black Americans:

For readers who wish to read a basic source:

G. D. Jaynes & R. M. Williams, Jr. (Eds.). 1989. *A Common Destiny: Blacks and American Society.* Washington, DC: National Academy Press.

Chapter
6
—
Keeping Our Levels Straight

A merican society suffers from widespread violence. It endures high rates of both homicide and suicide—a rare occurrence among the world's nations. National violence is a *societal* problem, so social scientists look to the *societal* level of analysis to explain this dark side of American life. The nation's frontier history, massive gun sales, widespread use of drugs, and maldistribution of wealth are all proposed contributors to this pattern of violence.

By contrast, popular analyses typically debate this societal issue as if it were simply a problem of disturbed *individuals*. The National Rifle Association, the gun manufacturers' lobby, typifies this tendency with its slogan—"guns don't kill people; people kill people." Even trained observers are prone to reducing this societal problem to a personality issue. In doing so, they mix their levels of analysis.

Consider one such analysis by a psychoanalyst. *Our Violent Society* (Abrahamsen, 1970) casts the national problem almost completely in personal terms. It views society as simply the source of stress that triggers sick individuals. The argument is that "[t]he roots of our violence thus lie in unresolved hostile aggression . . . " (Abrahamsen, 1970:128). Such personal conditions as loneliness, frustration, and a desire to dominate are all implicated. Society must recognize and treat these sick people who are prone to act out their hostility.

Such an argument vividly illustrates how *not* to think like a social scientist. Were the analysis limited to a discussion of violent *individuals,* it would be an interesting treatise. As an analysis of national violence, however, the healthy skepticism of social science raises a host of questions. Is violence due only to sick, frustrated people? If so, why is there a higher percentage of such people in the U.S. than in the many societies with far less violence? How can this analysis explain the sharply different rates of violence within the U.S. by time, region, and ethnicity?

What major remedy does this analysis advance? Do Americans need thousands of hours of treatment on the psychoanalytic couch so each citizen can resolve her or his "hostile aggression?" Such questions underscore the difficulties of such analyses. By confusing levels of analysis, both the explanation and the remedy prove inadequate.

A similar confusion of levels gained currency in 1954, when the U.S. Supreme Court handed down its historic ruling that racial segregation of public schools was unconstitutional. Many wondered how white Southerners would accept this decision. After all, the ruling threatened to end their region's rigid system of racial segregation. Pessimists claimed that mass psychiatric therapy for millions of white Southerners was the only way the Court ruling could win acceptance, and anti-black racism would be reduced. This represents another naive misuse of personality explanations for a societal problem. It was actually a not-so-subtle way of saying that racial change in the South was impossible.

I argued the opposite sequence for remedy (Pettigrew, 1961, 1991a). The popular argument held personality change to be necessary to trigger social change. Social science evidence shows that structural change to which individuals (even highly prejudiced people) must adapt is both more practical and effective. Altered social structure leads to altered attitudes.

This case is an example of the greater effectiveness of **top-down** rather than **bottom-up** approaches to social change—an emphasis of this chapter. That is, structural change in society's laws and norms leads to behavioral and then attitude changes at the individual level. The rival model holds that the attitudes of individuals must first change before structural change is possible. The old saying for this belief is "laws cannot change the hearts and minds of men."

Four decades later we can assess the two theories. Without psychotherapy being necessary for white Southerners, the slow but relentless destruction of racially segregated institutions in the South has had major effects. Deep racial problems remain in the region, but consider the changes since 1954. Racially desegregated schools and workplaces led to new interracial situations. These new situations required new interracial behavior that led to more tolerant racial attitudes. Indeed, white Southerners' racial attitudes have improved more over these years than those of other Americans (Schuman, Steeh and Bobo, 1985). And, as predicted by the institutional-change-first model, these changes in behavior and attitudes *followed* the desegregation of public facilities. The institutional alterations were wrought by court decisions and black American protest, and were initially unpopular in the white South. Yet white Southerners in time not only came to accept the changes, but have had their racial views altered by these institutional changes.

Laws *did* change the hearts and minds of many white Southerners. They did so by first changing the institutional arrangements in which black and white Southerners interacted with each other. These altered situations shaped new behavior that in turn began to erode the racist beliefs that have burdened the South for centuries.

This structural way of thinking not only keeps the levels of analysis straight, but differs from popular thought. Many maintain that such sweeping societal alterations as ending racial segregation cannot happen without widespread support from individual citizens. Yet a far higher percentage of black children now attend desegregated public schools in the southern United States than any other region of the nation (Farley, 1984).

6.1 THE COMPOSITIONAL FALLACY: CONFUSING MICRO WITH MACRO LEVELS

Both examples illustrate the **compositional fallacy.** This fallacy is a special case of Aristotle's famous dictum—"the whole is greater than the sum of its parts." We shall consider the theoretical implications of this dictum in the next chapter. Gerald Weinberg neatly captures the logical problem involved.

> I stand on a bridge and spit in the river. Seeing that it makes no noticeable difference in the purity of the water, I go to the polls and vote against the municipal bonds for a new water-treatment plant. (Weinberg, 1975:42)

In social research, the compositional fallacy occurs when an analyst considers only individual people, but draws conclusions about the entire society. This procedure is a fallacy, because the **micro-level** units are too small to represent phenomena and processes at the societal level.

To reduce societal-level (**macro-level**) issues to individual-level (micro-level) terms is to ignore that each level of analysis has its own unique processes and properties. Societies and institutions are not simply the sum of the individuals who comprise them. These macro-level entities have their own properties, and these properties are a primary focus of social science. Societies and institutions are more than mere collections of people. By their very structures and functions they are different in kind from micro-level entities.

When you think like a social scientist, you are wary of drawing simple analogies between levels. In popular language, you will observe the compositional fallacy when people use individual terms to describe societies and institutions. Japanese society is "anal retentive" (Gorer, 1943); South African society is bigoted. *Some individual* Japanese are anal-retentive, and *some individual* South Africans are bigoted. Societies require terms that correspond with their macro-level status.

The compositional fallacy is more than an interesting point for social scientific thinking. It can lead to serious mistakes in interpretations and policy recommendations. Consider the two examples we have just discussed. By using only individual terms, *Our Violent Society* ignores the structural issues that the U.S. must address if it is to reduce its violence. Similarly, those who saw implementing racial change in only individual terms would have prevented the Supreme Court from acting decisively in outlawing racial segregation.

6.2 THE ECOLOGICAL FALLACY: CONFUSING MACRO WITH MICRO LEVELS

The **ecological fallacy** also involves a confusion of levels. It presents precisely the opposite problem, however, from that of the compositional fallacy. Some call it the **decompositional fallacy.** It maintains "the part is more than a fraction of the whole." Weinberg captures the illogic here with another story.

> I stand on the bridge and notice that the river is clean, so I conclude that nobody spits in it. (Weinberg, 1975:43)

The ecological fallacy occurs in social analysis when only data from large macro-units are available, with no data from individual people. Nevertheless, the analyst draws conclusions about individuals. This procedure is a fallacy in so much as the macro-units are too large to represent individual differences within the unit (Robinson, 1950).

The classic illustration of the ecological fallacy occurred in Emile Durkheim's (1951) famous study of suicide. This 19th-century investigation is an early example of non-experimental research on a major societal phenomenon. Durkheim had data on religion (the independent variable) and suicide (the dependent variable) from various nations and regions of Europe. He uncovered a striking relationship between the two variables. Heavily-populated Protestant areas had high suicide rates, while heavily-populated Catholic areas had low rates.

Durkheim concluded that Protestants were individually far more likely to commit suicide than Catholics, but there is a problem with this conclusion. Durkheim had not kept his levels straight. His conclusion involved *individual* Protestants and Catholics (the micro-level of analysis), but his data involved nations and regions (the macro-level of analysis).

The rareness of suicide heightens the ecological fallacy. Few people, fortunately, commit such a drastic act. Here, a plausible rival hypothesis presents itself. Maybe the Catholic minorities living in mostly Protestant areas commit most of the suicides. This would explain the macro-level finding, but it leads to precisely the opposite conclusion at the micro-level. Even though the Protestant areas had high suicide rates, the individual Catholics living in them could have been responsible for these high rates. A possible explanation leaps to mind for this rival interpretation. Perhaps, Catholics in largely Protestant regions were victims of religious persecution, and this situation led to committing suicide.

Durkheim, however, was a careful researcher and aware of the problem. Since he could obtain only fragments of individual data on suicide to strengthen his conclusion, he did the next best thing. He checked on his finding in increasingly smaller and smaller regions—thus getting closer and closer to the micro-level of individuals. His initial hypothesis continued to hold true:

even small Protestant areas had higher suicide rates than comparable Catholic areas. Thus, Durkheim did not eliminate the ecological fallacy, but he did narrow the problem as much as his data allowed. By the way, Durkheim *was* right. Later research with individual data established that suicide *is* more prevalent among Protestants.

We need not look back to 19th-century research to uncover instances of the ecological fallacy. As with the compositional fallacy, examples of this confusion of levels regularly occur. One illustration of the fallacy occurred during the 1964 presidential election. George Wallace, then Governor of Alabama, ran for President on a third-party ticket. As a racial segregationist, he sought northern votes with a campaign that combined racism with a social class appeal to white workers. In parts of the industrial Midwest, Wallace received sizeable support.

The southern governor's ability to attract northern votes surprised the mass media. In trying to explain this unexpected phenomenon, media analysts committed the ecological fallacy. The data available were largely macro-level data—voting percentages from various areas. The popular explanations, however, involved micro-level, individual phenomena. The analysts described northern voters for Wallace as angry white workers who left the Democratic Party to engage in a "racial backlash" against black Americans. Note the problem here is the same as Durkheim's in analyzing suicide. The media drew inappropriate conclusions about individual people from macro-level data.

What these analysts overlooked was that the *total* vote increased in areas where Wallace ran well in the North. As with Durkheim's case, the ecological fallacy allows another hypothesis. The increased vote suggests that *new* white voters had entered the electorate, people so alienated that they had seldom voted in the past. Wallace's message induced them to vote in 1964. Thus, according to this interpretation, no "racial backlash" had occurred. These new voters had long been racially prejudiced, but only Wallace expressed their views and attracted them into the electorate. Closer examination of both voting and survey data showed that this rival interpretation accounted for much of the northern voting for Wallace (Pettigrew, 1964).

A similar phenomenon of new voters occurred in 1990 when David Duke, a former Ku Klux Klan leader, ran for the U.S. Senate in Louisiana (Giles & Buckner, 1993:708). Duke lost this race, his 1991 contest for Governor, and his bid for the Republican presidential nomination in 1992. Yet, like Wallace, he won large votes in selected areas in part because of new white voters.

6.3 DIFFERENT LEVELS OF SOCIAL ANALYSIS

Figure 6.1 presents a simplified diagram of three levels of analysis. The broadest level is the macro-level. It includes an array of expansive entities that all evolved from human efforts—societies, nations, cultures, economic and political systems, institutions and organizations. To speak of Canada, Mexican culture, Arizona, your high school, or the Girl Scouts is to refer to the macro-level. Obviously, this broad sweep covers a wide variety of social structures.

Figure 6.1   Six Causal Paths

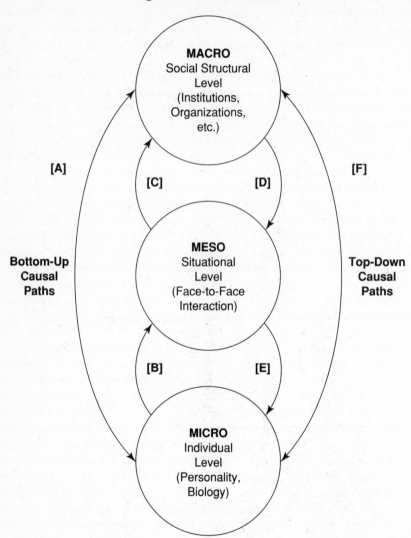

We could complicate Figure 6.1 by separating the macro-level into many structures of varying size. For our purposes, however, we will consider them one level, as they are all macro compared to Figure 6.1's other levels.

The macro-level of analysis is the major focus of social science. It is this level where the central concept of social structure is essential in social science analysis. Recall from Chapter 1 that social structure refers to relatively persistent social patterns of many types. While popular thought centers on individuals and the micro-level, thinking like a social scientist entails concern for such structural entities as nations, societies, and institutions.

The various social science disciplines, as their names suggest, carve out for study different slices of this macro terrain. Cultural anthropology specializes in cultures. Political science studies political systems, nations, other political units, and political parties. Economics focuses on economic systems, while sociology concentrates on societies as a whole as well as on institutions and organizations. There is, of course, overlap among the disciplines in their various interests, yet there is not as much interdisciplinary work on common problems as one might wish. Each discipline acts like a fiefdom in the Middle Ages, complete with a moat around its intellectual castle. Students who take courses in several social sciences must develop their own syntheses.

The middle level of analysis in Figure 6.1, the **meso-level**, involves face-to-face situations. Unlike the macro-level above it, it is small enough for the participants to interact with each other. Unlike the micro-level below it, it involves more than one person. Sandwiched between the broadest and narrowest of the levels, the situational level mediates the effects between the macro- and micro-levels. For example, we noted how changed interracial situations, wrought by Supreme Court rulings at the macro-level, led many white Southerners to alter their attitudes toward black Southerners at the micro-level.

Many social sciences have interests at this intermediate level, too. For example, cultural anthropologists, demographers, sociologists, and developmental psychologists all study the family—a meso-level unit of analysis. One discipline, social psychology, centers its attention primarily at this level. We have described several studies from this field in earlier chapters. Recall the laboratory study that induced hostile behavior through a self-fulfilling prophecy, and the Robbers' Cave field study of intergroup prejudice. Notice how social psychological research focuses on the face-to-face level of individuals interacting with each other.

Figure 6.1's third level of analysis is the most familiar. The micro-level considers human beings one at a time. We could elaborate on this level, too, with smaller biological units down to the gene. Again, we choose to keep Figure 6.1 as uncluttered as possible. Yet we need to remind ourselves that the figure is a schematic presentation of a highly-complicated picture.

The study of personality in psychology concentrates completely on this level. Other disciplines also have components that are primarily micro-level in scope. Micro-economics, in contrast with macro-economics, centers on this level, as does much of behavioral political science and its attention to the individual voter. Social psychologists and sociologists also study individual phenomena.

Thus, social science thinking does not overlook the micro-level in spite of its primary focus on social structures at the macro-level. It differs from popular thought by insisting on placing micro concerns in their larger social structural contexts. The chief problem at this level of analysis becomes: "How can the individual be both a cause and a consequence of society?" (Allport, 1968:9) To show how social science tackles this question, Figure 6.1 traces the various causal paths between the levels.

6.4 DIFFERENT CAUSAL PATHS: BOTTOM-UP AND TOP-DOWN

Social scientists usually answer questions of what causes what within levels of analysis. Hence, macro processes explain macro phenomena, and micro processes explain micro phenomena. The most interesting causal questions span levels. Figure 6.1 traces six cross-level paths of causation (A through F).

The three paths on the left (A, B, and C) are all bottom-up paths that extend from the narrower micro- and meso-levels *up* to the macro-level. The three top-down paths on the right (D, E, and F) extend from the broadest macro- and meso-levels *down* to the micro-level. These terms—bottom-up and top-down—are useful for classifying causal theories. Popular analyses favor bottom-up arguments, while social science favors top-down ones. We can gain a better sense of what these cross-level causal paths entail by reviewing theories and research that typify each.

6.4.1. Individuals Shape Social Structure Directly

(Path A) Sweepingly global "great man" theories of history put in disrepute the contention that a single individual can change history. Had Napoleon not lived, goes the counter, the zeitgeist might well have produced another charismatic French leader with little change on history. At this gross level of abstraction, of course, such popular arguments are of little value. Yet personality *can* shape social structure once there is careful specification of the measures and the effect.

Max Weber's (1930) theory of the rise of capitalism is the classic Path A linkage between individuals and social structure. In his *Protestant Ethic and the Spirit of Capitalism,* Weber held that such micro-phenomena as beliefs, motives, and values independently shape macro-structure. Focusing on the 17th-century Dutch, Weber explained why ascetic Protestant sects often meet with economic success. These austere Protestants frequently became rich, although they viewed wealth as dangerous for the soul. His theory maintained the *Protestant ethic,* epitomized in the stern religious doctrine of John Calvin, explained the puzzle. This doctrine had its believers follow a frugal, work-oriented routine in preparation for God's final judgment of salvation. This rigorous routine frequently led to wealth.

Weber also held that social structure, once established, shaped personality in a reciprocal cycle. He understood that family, work, and other face-to-face situations (Paths B and C) partly mediated the Protestant ethic's influence on capitalism. Yet his famous theory remains the prototype of a Path A causal theory involving personality and social structure.

Building on Weber's theory, David McClelland (1961) advanced the theory that one particular human motive at the micro-level is critical to this process. He held that such Protestant ethic values as frugality and hard work create child-training practices that develop in children a high need for personal achievement. This *achievement motive,* McClelland argues, is the important causal link underlying Weber's observation that the Protestant ethic and capitalistic success occur together.

McClelland, a personality psychologist, shows that the need for achievement is both challenged and satisfied by operating small businesses. This activity characterizes capitalism in its early stages. Both high-need achievers and small-business people are independent strivers for success. They like situations where they feel personally responsible for clearly measurable results of their efforts (Atkinson & Hoselitz, 1958).

Carrying his analysis to the macro-level, McClelland (1961) attempts to show that the micro-level achievement motive played a part in the economic growth of the West. He emphasizes cross-national and longitudinal relationships between levels of achievement and several measures of technological growth.

Psychohistorical studies, from biographies of Luther and Gandhi (Erikson, 1958, 1969) to analyses of racism (Kovel, 1970), offer further examples of sweepingly broad Path A theories. More recently, however, research and theory in this area are more limited in scope. For example, Gluckstern and Packard (1977) studied change in a prison. In viewing change agents, they noted that different personality styles are important at different times in the process of organizational change in the prison. Such results suggest the interactive nature of personality and social structural relationships.

6.4.2. Individuals Shape Social Structure Indirectly

(Paths B and C) Individuals also indirectly influence social structures by first changing situations (Path B in Figure 6.1). These changes in turn cause changes at the macro-level (Path C). In short, the situational level *mediates* the micro causes of macro changes.

The importance of Path B can be dramatic. Many studies show how a single disruptive person (a mental patient, an untreated alcoholic, a schoolroom deviant) can radically alter a family or classroom (Yarrow, Clausen, & Robbins, 1955; Jackson, 1956; Gnagey, 1960). Relevant social psychological work studies small groups in the laboratory. One impressive model anticipates from personality variables alone what behavior is likely to occur in small, task-oriented groups. Freed Bales (1970) accurately predicts which members of a group are likely to form coalitions, and which are likely to assume *task-oriented* and *socio-emotional* (joker) roles.

Path B often involves subjective interpretations of the social environment. For example, people widely vary in how much control they think they have over events in their lives (Rotter, 1966). Some see most events as under their personal control (*internals*). Others see most events as beyond their control and caused by external agents (*externals*). These different types of people are obviously going to perceive the same situations in contrasting ways and respond differently.

Applied social psychology's remedies for problems using this bottom-up direction involve special training. The critically ill, the shy, the elderly, job burnouts, rape victims, and those facing major surgery learn how to reconceptualize their situation. Often these people blame themselves for their difficulties in life, and this self-blame adds to their problems. Special training converts such maladaptive dispositional causal attributions to situational attributions when appropriate.

Path C from face-to-face situations to social structures is of special interest to sociologists and organizational specialists. Often these studies involve give-and-take negotiation over the way the organization informally operates. Such informal communication at the situational level can cause continual changes in how highly-structured governmental agencies work (Blau, 1955). Similar negotiation even occurs in prisons. Sykes (1958) showed how prisoners, working collectively at the situational level, altered the structure of a maximum-security prison. Unpopular rules went unenforced, and prisoners wrested considerable control over their lives while neither escaping nor rebelling.

6.4.3. Social Structure Shapes Individuals Directly

(Path F) The top-down causal links are the most studied in social science. Instead of being the initial causal agent, personality and other micro-level factors are now the dependent variables. Two paths are possible—the direct, unmediated route (Path F) and the mediated route (Paths D and E). In the latter, structural changes shape personality by first altering face-to-face interaction in situations.

Path F examples are rare in social research. One famous political science study comes closest. Almond and Verba (1965) studied five democratic nations with varying political cultures. They used surveys to measure the political attitudes in each nation, then they compared these data with each nation's political institutions.

Their Path F contentions advance structural explanations for the extensive attitudinal differences they found across the five populations. These differences in political views remained even after the investigators controlled for such variables as education. Thus, British respondents evinced considerable confidence in both their administrative and legislative officials. Germans showed particular confidence in administrative officials, Americans in legislative officials, and Italians and Mexicans in neither.

Almond and Verba explain these individual differences as reflections of the contrasting structural histories across the countries. Germany established an early and stable bureaucracy, but had a late and unstable political development. The United States had the reverse history, with a late-developing civil service but an early foundation of its political structure. The United Kingdom experienced early development of both institutions, while Italy and Mexico had late development of both.

Note the top-down form of this causal theory. The independent variables are the depth and time of the political entity's establishment—macro-level variables. The theory holds them to be the major *causes* of the wide variance across the nations in the micro-level dependent variable—the public's confidence in different political entities.

6.4.4. Social Structure Shapes Individuals Indirectly

(Paths D and E) Social science prefers mediated causal theories, because they more precisely specify the links between levels. Direct effect theories (Paths A and F) usually signal a failure to specify how the causal sequence carries through the face-to-face interaction stage. Most top-down theories in social science are Path D and E contentions. So social science is rich with studies that specify all three levels of Figure 6.1.

Many of the best examples of Paths D and E focus on social class. The longitudinal research of Sewell and Hauser (1975), for instance, shows the strong influence of socioeconomic status on educational aspirations and attainments. Middle-class children typically develop more ambitious goals than working-class children. In predominantly middle-class schools, the question is usually *which* college are you going to attend? In predominantly working-class schools, the question is often *are* you going to college? Chapter 5 mentioned how such situational contexts as neighborhoods and schools *mediate* social class effects. Sewell and Hauser show these strong effects of social class remain even after they control for sex and measured achievement.

Two research projects have helped to define top-down analyses of the structural and cultural shaping of personality. Melvin Kohn and his colleagues emphasize how the situational demands of parents' jobs (macro- and meso-levels) influence the way parents raise their children (meso-level—Path D). Then, Kohn checked on how parents shape their children's self-direction versus conformity (micro-level—Path E).

First, Kohn (1969; Pearlin & Kohn, 1966) showed that in both the U.S. and Italy middle-class parents stress self-direction, while working-class parents stress obedience to external authority. Next, he and Schooler (1969, 1973) found links between self-direction values and occupational position. Those in higher-status positions that allow self-direction on the job value self-direction for their children. Those in lower-status positions, who must obey orders on the job, value obedience to authority for their children. Thus, the demands of the work place generalize to the home and the preferred parental means of socializing children.

Thus, Kohn provides a three-level, top-down answer to a broad causal question: How do different jobs translate into different values? He shows the relationship between class and values derives from conditions of life, especially the work situation, that reflect social class differences. "It is chiefly by shaping the everyday realities people must face," he writes, "that social structure exerts its psychological impact" (Kohn, 1977:xlviii).

The second famous project using causal Paths D and E extends this analysis of occupational effects. Alex Inkeles (1969, 1978; Inkeles & Smith, 1974) surveyed 6,000 industrial and agricultural male workers in six developing countries—Argentina, Bangladesh, Chile, India, Israel, and Nigeria. He carefully specified his independent variables at the macro- and meso-levels (the structural positions of the workers in society) and the dependent variable at the micro-level (modern man).

By *modern man,* Inkeles means people who are open to new experiences and ambitious for themselves and their children. These people follow modern leaders, plan ahead, and take an interest in local politics and news of the world. In all six nations, educated young people with factory experience, exposure to the mass media, and urban residence are more likely to exhibit this personality syndrome. From these results, Inkeles concludes that industrialization leads to similar forms of social organization across societies with contrasting cultures. These modern organizations in turn shape face-to-face situations (Path D) that produce similar patterns of modern beliefs, perceptions, and values (Path E).

Social psychology's Path E focus uses situational variables that are easily manipulated (Pettigrew, 1988). Chapter 4 noted that this is a big advantage when dealing with practical problems. It is both easier and more ethical to alter situations than to alter people. The Path E, top-down approach searches for features of situations that elicit specific behavior from individuals. When pressed for advice in solving practical problems, social psychologists typically advance top-down, situation-to-individual recommendations. Change the situation (increase choice, stop labeling people, allow more participation), and individual changes will result (improved morale, higher self-esteem, greater involvement).

Elliot Aronson's Jigsaw cooperative learning design for classrooms offers a superb example (Aronson, Blaney, Stephan, Sikes & Snapp, 1978). The city of Austin, Texas asked Aronson to help improve learning at their newly desegregated schools. After analyzing the classroom situation, he decided that intense individual competition hurt learning and interracial attitudes. He and his colleagues designed a classroom teaching method that requires students to work cooperatively in teams. Competition is now between teams, not individuals. Each team puts the parts of a lesson together, like a jigsaw puzzle. Each team member contains a needed part for the lesson, a device that encourages cooperation within the teams.

The student effects of this Path E, situational remedy are positive (Aronson, 1988:280–282). Compared to similar students in regular classrooms, the examination performance of minority children improves. In addition, children in the jigsaw classroom grow to like each other more, and this crosses racial and ethnic boundaries. They gain greater self-esteem, as well as an improved ability to see the world through other people's eyes. Thus, an extensive alteration in the classroom situation leads to a host of benefits for individual students.

Often the links invoked to explain Path E relationships involve family expectations or role playing. The double bind theory of schizophrenia provides an example of family involvement. This theory contends that children who later become schizophrenics are often caught in the midst of conflicting parental expectations (Bateson, Jackson, Haley & Weakland, 1956).

Lieberman (1950) showed how attitude changes followed role changes among industrial plant foremen and union stewards. Newly-appointed plant foremen soon became more pro-company in their attitudes, while newly-appointed union stewards became more pro-union. Within three years, the two groups had established almost "diametrically opposed sets of attitudinal positions." Moreover, foremen and stewards who later returned to the production line as regular workers frequently reverted to their earlier attitudes.

6.5 SUMMING UP

Thinking "straight" in social science means keeping your levels of analysis clearly in mind. Popular social analyses often confuse the micro- and macro-levels. They try to explain such societal problems as widespread violence in purely personal terms. This mistake results in remedial proposals, such as individual therapy, that are inappropriate for structural problems.

Two types of level confusion commonly occur. The compositional fallacy involves drawing conclusions at the macro-level of analysis from individual data alone. This is a fallacy, because organizations and societies are more than the sum of their individual members. They are social systems, as Chapter 7 will stress, not mere collections of individual people. Macro-level units have unique properties of their own—properties that social science specializes in studying.

The ecological fallacy involves the opposite confusion of levels. Here we draw conclusions about individuals from macro-level data alone. It is a fallacy, because the macro-units of analysis are too broad to determine individual data. Moreover, individuals, too, boast unique properties that we cannot infer from macro data. Hence, ecological fallacies allow plausible rival hypotheses to explain the results. We saw examples of this in studies of suicide and voting. The possibility that Roman Catholics in heavily-populated Protestant areas could have accounted for the high suicide rates of these areas undermined Durkheim's conclusion that Protestants committed suicide more than Catholics. In the political example, new, not "backlash," voters were largely responsible for Wallace's northern support in 1964. A similar increase in voters took place more recently in the election races in Louisiana of the former Ku Klux Klan leader, David Duke.

Figure 6.1 outlines the basic contentions of the chapter. Three levels of analysis are delineated—the macro-, meso-, and micro-levels. Each level has its own properties, but each influences the others. Many causal social science explanations remain within one level. The most interesting ones, however, cross levels. Six such cross-level causal paths emerge in Figure 6.1. Three are bottom-up paths: the initial causes are lower-level phenomena that effect higher-level phenomena. Three are top-down paths: the initial causes are higher-level phenomena that effect lower-level phenomena. Usually, popular analyses offer bottom-up arguments, while social science analyses offer top-down arguments.

The chapter reviewed examples of all six causal paths. Weber's thesis of Protestant ethic values leading to capitalism is a model bottom-up theory. Mc-Clelland shows how individual motivation for achievement serves as a personality link for Weber's theory.

Top-down analyses are more plentiful. In political science, the age and stability of political institutions helps to explain widely-varying attitudes toward these institutions across five democracies. In sociology, social class experiences help to explain widely-varying aspirations, values, and personalities at the micro-level. In social psychology, carefully altered situations cause helpful changes for individuals.

You may have asked yourself at this point if there is not a contradiction in the chapter's contentions. Are these cross-level causal paths not examples of the compositional and ecological fallacies? This is a good question that deserves an answer. The fallacies occur when the data come from only one level, and we apply their results to another level. All the examples described of cross-level causal path research carefully had their theories and data from each level involved.

In Chapter 7, we shall consider **social dilemmas.** These dilemmas occur when many actions of individuals acting at the micro-level cause problems at the societal macro-level. Once we begin to think of major social issues in multiple level terms, we need the concept of system. This concept introduces us to thinking in wholes and not in parts. Going beyond the search for simple relationships between variables and their effects, systems thinking encourages us to consider complex social processes. The idea of systems is basic to social science thought at all levels.

ISSUES FOR DISCUSSION AND REVIEW

A> Find an example in the local newspaper of either a compositional or an ecological fallacy. Offer a rival explanation for the phenomenon that the fallacy caused the writer to overlook.

B> Select a major study in social science not mentioned in this book. What level or levels of analysis is the research using? Trace the causal path that the author(s) uses. Does the causal argument remain at one level of analysis? If not, how is the cross-level causal path described in Figure 6.1?

C> Consider several of the major problems facing the nation today, and the types of remedies often advocated to address them. Are the forms of these remedies bottom-up, top-down, or both? Which types do you prefer? Why?

RECOMMENDATIONS FOR FURTHER READING ON ISSUES RAISED IN THIS CHAPTER

On Compositional and Ecological Fallacies:

For readers new to the idea:

C. M. Judd, E. R. Smith & L. H. Kidder. 1991. *Research Methods in Social Relations.* New York: Holt, Rinehart & Winston. Chapter 16.

For readers who wish to read a basic source:

W. S. Robinson. 1950. Ecological correlations and the behavior of individuals. *American Sociological Review, 15,* 351–357.

On Causal Order in Explanations:

J. A. Davis. 1985. *The Logic of Causal Order.* Beverly Hills, CA: Sage.

Chapter
7

Thinking in Systems Terms

Imagine that a severe drought grips your region. The resulting water shortage leads officials to call for voluntary water conservation. If you follow this request, you will suffer a bit—shorter showers, no car washing, and the destruction of your garden. These problems tempt you not to obey the call. Besides, a little water for your dirty car and thirsty garden will not make a noticeable difference in the region's total water supply.

But if everybody follows your reasoning, it would completely deplete the region's water. What would you do? Take the *defecting* choice—clean your car and save your garden? Or would you take the *cooperative* choice—let your car stay dirty, lose your garden, and do your bit for the good of the whole community?

Such social dilemmas are common in modern life. We must adopt a systems view to understand them. This requires thinking like a social scientist at the macro-level of analysis in order to see "the big picture." Only then can we design effective remedies for these problems.

Many of these dilemmas revolve around three major problems—resource depletion, overpopulation, and pollution. No one wants Los Angeles or Mexico City to be smothered in smog and pollution, but each motorist adds to the problem daily. No one wants the earth's atmosphere warmed by a blanket of carbon dioxide, but we each contribute to this growing problem.

These dilemmas share two features. First, each individual benefits more from making the selfish, defecting choice than for the socially cooperative choice regardless of what others do. Plausible excuses are readily available for the anti-social choice. "The small amount of water I use will not make any difference." "The authorities are exaggerating the problem." "They couldn't have meant for me to let my garden die." "Most people will use all the water they want, so why shouldn't I?"

The second feature of social dilemmas is that everyone is better off if *all* cooperate than if all defect. The danger is that many people will seek their short-term personal gain at the expense of the usually longer-term collective gain. Everybody's business becomes nobody's business. Individually, we gain by continuing to use up scarce resources, have many children, and pollute. Collectively, we lose as a member of society and humanity by the depletion of resources, overpopulation, and pollution.

The *commons problem* is the classic social dilemma. Hardin (1968) draws his overpopulation analogy from the old English village practice of setting aside land for common grazing. Farmers can graze their animals on this land for free. Yet, the commons can accommodate only a certain number of animals and still replenish its grass. Farmers who enlarge their herds will gain individually. Once they surpass "the carrying capacity" of the commons, however, all farmers who use the commons stand to lose. The collective good—free grazing pasture—will be depleted for use by everyone. "Virtue may be its own reward," observes Thomas Schelling (1971:96), "but the reward is too often a collective good."

Social dilemmas often involve a time lag. The individual gain comes now and the collective loss occurs in the distant future. I save my parched garden now, and the total exhaustion of the region's water supply will not happen for years. The farmers make more money from their larger herds now, but total depletion of the commons takes years. This time lag is similar to many traps we get into as individuals. Cigarettes and alcohol relax addicts now; the throat cancer and liver cirrhosis that can follow take years to develop. Warnings on the packages may unnerve us, but they describe a long-term risk. We know the problem, and we plan to combat our addiction "soon"—just not right now.

This time delay feature of social dilemmas makes it difficult to enlist cooperative efforts. We may realize the officials who call for changes are right, but the immediacy of the benefits makes it hard to comply. Besides, old habits resist change. Compliance also can involve large amounts of money. Manufacturing companies save millions of dollars by polluting nearby ground and water. Preventive measures are expensive, and government may pay for the expensive clean-up if detection occurs after the plant has closed.

Not all social dilemmas involve time lags. Thomas Schelling (1971), an economist, provides an example that may be familiar. Suppose you are living on a tight budget and agree to go to a restaurant with nine friends. If there are separate checks, you choose the least expensive dinner on the menu—the hamburger plate for $10. If there is only one check, however, you may reconsider your choice. You would love to have the $20 filet mignon. You could not consider it if there were to be separate checks, but the single check alters matters. Having the filet mignon instead of the hamburger will now cost you only one dollar more ($20 − $10 = $10/ten people = $1). The individual gain spread over the collective cost creates the dilemma. Of course, the same situation holds for your friends. So the total bill may well hurt your tight budget.

Restaurant managers know this social dilemma and often discourage separate checks.

7.1 THE INVISIBLE HAND VERSUS THE INVISIBLE FIST

Not all individual actions lead to harmful collective results. A **market,** a core concept of economics, involves situations where individual acts have positive societal effects. Pure markets entail buyers and sellers determining prices by a series of uncontrolled individual exchanges. Such unfettered exchanges stabilize prices at their "true" value through supply and demand processes. Producers of goods supply their products in response to the demand for them. Sellers compete with each other to attract buyers, and buyers seek the lowest prices. The desirable result is stable, reasonable prices with products in supply as wanted by consumers.

Pure markets, operating without interference, occur more in economic theory than real life. Producers and sellers form monopolies to restrict competition and control pricing in their favor. Buyers form cooperatives to drive down prices with larger orders. Governments limit open markets with restrictions, tariffs on foreign goods, and other means. Markets require governmental protection—as with anti-monopoly legislation. People of different political persuasions, however, argue endlessly over what governmental actions are in fact *necessary.* Conservatives want little if any interference, while liberals see the need for considerable governmental control. Though neither magical nor unproblematic, largely open markets for many products and services typically work reasonably well. The North American Free Trade Agreement (NAFTA) between Canada, Mexico, and the U.S. expands the market for all three countries. Such markets look especially effective when compared with central economic planning of totalitarian regimes.

Adam Smith, the 18th-century Scottish economist, focused on these benefits of effective markets. He argued for lowering British tariffs against cheaper foreign goods to free and broaden markets. Smith (1952 [1776]:194) wrote of an *invisible hand* that leads individuals acting only in their self-interest to promote unwittingly the public interest. The careful Scot knew that this beneficent process was not inevitable. Smith wrote that self-interested actions are *not* ". . . *always the worse* for the society" (Smith, 1952 [1776]:194, italics added). Thus, he realized that individual choices often lead to negative societal results. His point was open markets were an important *exception.*

Conservative economists and politicians, however, are often not so careful. In misinterpreting Adam Smith, they maintain the collective self-interests of individuals will *always* be consistent with the best interests of the economic system. Yet, we have seen in the many social dilemmas that lurk in the modern world that such a contention is untenable. Many areas of social life do not operate as markets, and individual actions cumulate into massive social problems.

A useful concept in economics makes the point. **Externalities** are *the social benefits or costs of an economic activity that occur without the explicit agreement of those affected*. Smith's markets, guided as if by an invisible hand, have *positive* externalities. Hardin's overgrazing of the commons has *negative* externalities. The political argument for near-total individual freedom because negative externalities do not exist is unrealistic. It ignores the fact that individual needs and system needs frequently conflict.

Is this merely an abstract point of interest? Or is it important for modern public policy? Consider the use of the invisible hand contention in the 1980s under President Ronald Reagan. He based his economic policies in large part on a supply-side theory that holds you should cut taxes—especially on the wealthy. This would stimulate business activity so strongly that governmental revenues would actually rise from the tax reduction. We could have our cake and eat it, too. It would serve the self-interests of the richest Americans, as well as the best interests of the American economy and government. The invisible hand would make it all possible; only positive externalities would flow from letting the most wealthy Americans pay less taxes.

Economics widely repudiates this theory. In the self-interests of their wealthy constituents, however, conservative politicians adopted it as gospel truth and enacted it into law during the 1980s. The nation also began to borrow massively to afford a major build-up of the military, while reducing the taxes of the rich. Now the economic results from this experiment are in. The United States is now the world's leading debtor nation. Reagan's eight years in office saw the national debt soar more than it had ever increased under any three previous presidents. Where was the *invisible hand?*

Social dilemmas, with their negative externalities, form an *invisible fist* instead of Smith's invisible hand (Platt, 1973). The unfettered expression of individual self-interest often does not serve society's interests. The competition of individuals in many situations does not reach a median value or "fair price"—as in effective markets. Instead, the process

> "... runs away from the median, with either escalation or elimination past some point of no return. . . . Several of our current crises have this characteristic, as with the escalation of arms races or unrestrained pollution . . . ." (Platt, 1973:647)

The prevalence of the invisible fist in modern society raises our next question. What can we do to prevent these widespread and difficult social dilemmas?

7.2 REMEDIES FOR SOCIAL DILEMMAS

There are six interrelated ways to combat social dilemmas. (1) We can have government *regulate* the problems in a variety of ways. (2) We can *change the payoffs for individuals* so people will see it in their own interest to be socially responsible. (3) We can *strengthen and appeal to the societal norms of altruism, social responsibility, and equity.* (4) We can *change the long-term social results* of the dilemma. (5) We can *increase communication* between people about the dilemmas. Finally, (6) we can *keep the situations small.* Let's briefly discuss each of these remedies.

7.2.1 Regulation

Usually administered by government, regulations of many types are commonly accepted as a major means of restricting the operation of social dilemmas. Government can simply signal the desired behavior (one-way street signs). It can regulate administratively (traffic police and safety inspectors). It can ration (fish and game quotas on fisherman and hunters) and charge user fees (parking meters and toll roads).

Government also can facilitate legal arrangements (patents, copyrights, and licenses for radio and television stations). It can flatly prohibit (firearms on airplanes) as well as command (required vaccinations). It also can provide needed services that cannot be marketed (weather information and street lights). Governments also can participate in multinational agreements to confront worldwide social dilemmas (stopping the spread of nuclear weapons and controlling the killing of whales).

Such regulatory methods use both incentives and penalties to influence individual behavior in ways that benefit the collective whole. These incentives and penalties, Schelling (1971:94) points out, also convey important information. To know an action carries with it a large penalty forcefully makes the point that such action violates what society regards as the public good.

Regulation bears costs, of course. It increases bureaucratic control, diminishes freedom, and costs tax dollars to administer and enforce. Well-designed regulatory devices, however, can be lean as well as effective. Behold the traffic light! Invented in 1923, the traffic light exemplifies the minimal solution to a social dilemma. As automobile traffic increased, urban intersections posed a special problem. It was to the advantage of each driver to come charging across. Life-threatening accidents were the result of this invisible fist. The traffic light solves the dilemma. As Schelling (1971:61–62) observes, "with magnificent simplicity" it divides the traffic into two groups—those going east-west and those going north-south. It uses a simple three-way system of lights—red, yellow, and green. It ignores differences among vehicles and drivers, while instituting an alternating pattern of conspicuous fairness. It requires no tickets, schedules, reservations, or extensive enforcement. Many dilemmas cannot be so simply resolved. Nonetheless, the traffic light offers a model for lean and effective regulatory approaches to combatting social dilemmas.

7.2.2 Change the Payoffs for Individuals

Since an essential ingredient of social dilemmas is a positive outcome for individual actions, one can try to change the payoff. Many regulatory remedies do this, at least indirectly. Here we consider direct attempts at altering the payoffs. Returning to the commons problem, one could divide the commons into small plots of grazing land for each farmer's animals. Now overgrazing will directly hurt those who unduly increase the size of their herds. The problem arises, however, that many resources involved in these dilemmas are not so easily divided among users—air, highways, and public parks.

Platt (1973:648) argues the commons farmers were not as dumb as Hardin's example implies. The key issue ". . . is not a problem of thoughtless competition, but rather the problem of setting up a superordinate authority to handle the reinforcement mechanisms . . . for getting out of these traps." Hence, the core problem lies less with the people involved in social dilemmas than with macro-level management. This explains why government is so often the authority of last resort for tackling these difficult problems.

Government uses many means for distributing scarce resources—tickets, auctions, licenses, even administration of the principle of first-come-first-served. Recent remedies for traffic gridlock, another social dilemma, stress creative incentives. Many bridges now charge tolls in only the one direction where planners wish to discourage traffic (such as into major cities). Total collections remain much the same by simply doubling the toll. Similarly, cars carrying more than one or two passengers use fast lanes reserved for them. Carpooling is also encouraged by not charging such cars tolls, thus offering these cooperative citizens the incentive of saving both time and money. Since incentives are both more popular and more effective than penalties, such efforts are likely to increase in the future.

There is another approach to changing the payoff structures involved in social dilemmas (Dawes, 1980:175–178). Here economic concepts again are useful. From value theory in economics, the idea of **utility** is broad. It refers to *the satisfaction a person gets from a particular good or service*. **Marginal utility** refers to *the additional satisfaction that a person gets from consuming one more unit of that good or service*. The principle of diminishing marginal utility holds that the value of anything eventually declines as you have more of it. Several thousand dollars can bring great satisfaction to a poor person, yet mean little to a millionaire.

In our examples of incentives, we have mentioned only time, money, and other resources directly involved in the dilemma. Yet, many things bring people satisfaction—that is, have utility for individuals. So other types of incentives also can be effective in changing payoffs. If these incentives bring satisfaction because they are scarce (that is, have marginal utility), they should be effective. Many incentives involve psychological satisfaction. Thus, most human beings value the idea that they are good people who "try to do the right thing." This leads us to a third general means for combatting social dilemmas.

7.2.3 Strengthen and Appeal to Societal Norms of Altruism, Social Responsibility, and Equity

Human societies value pro-social behavior. We admire generous, altruistic people who sacrifice personal gain for the benefit of others. Moreover, social norms support socially responsible behavior.

The prevalence of social dilemmas despite these values and norms, however, suggest the ineffectiveness of these principles. This does not mean that persuasive appeals to these values and norms for socially responsible behavior are doomed to fail. To be sure, vague appeals that do not specify alternatives are ineffective. President Jimmy Carter's call for conservation in 1977 by describing the energy crisis as "the moral equivalent of war" went unheeded. The next summer, Americans used more gasoline than ever before (Myers, 1993:552).

Specific local appeals from people who are important to you are more likely to succeed. It also helps if the new behavior is public and others can monitor it. My town has a successful recycling program. In Santa Cruz, California, citizens are urged to put their salvageable paper, metal, and glass out each week in front of their homes with their trash barrels. The voluntary cooperation on my residential block reaches almost 100%. I know because I can observe each week who is and is not participating. Once a program reaches this level, *not* to join in becomes a conspicuous violation of the new neighborhood norm of recycling.

7.2.4 Change the Long-Term Social Consequences

We also can change the other side of social dilemmas—the negative social results (Platt, 1973:649). Often new inventions accomplish this remedy. Air pollution is a major negative externality of massive individual car use. Electric cars would sharply reduce the problem, though there would be some air pollution from the generation of electricity to power the new vehicles.

7.2.5 Increase Communication

Several thousand laboratory studies have simulated social dilemmas (Dawes, 1980). One can question how well these dilemma games in the laboratory generalize to the social world. Yet their findings are interesting and suggestive. Two conclusions from these experiments suggest the last two potential remedies—communication and group size.

Forthright communication is necessary for subjects to avoid the dilemmas of the laboratory. The same is true in the social world. Obviously, people have to understand the social dilemmas they collectively face before they change their behavior. Communication is also important beyond mere information. It helps to forge a sense of group identity—"*we* are all in this together." Communication also builds trust. If I am the only one who puts out recyclable materials, I may come to feel like it is a meaningless effort. I must trust that my neighbors are also cooperating with the program before my efforts make sense. Newspaper articles about the recycling program's success are both informative and reassuring.

7.2.6 Keeping the Relevant Situations Small

Another finding from laboratory research on social dilemmas is that the smaller the group, the greater the cooperation and avoidance of negative system results. Small groups typically have a stronger sense of group identity, of *we-ness*. They also have a stronger sense of *common fate* where the group's welfare is more immediately salient to each member. In addition, small groups create a situation where the monitoring of everyone's behavior is possible. It becomes difficult in the small group *not* to cooperate.

Look back at these six types of remedies for social dilemmas. All require a broad view of social dilemmas as systems problems. That is, we cannot just focus on the behavior of individuals that cause the dilemmas. Governmental regulation, changing the payoffs, appealing to societal values, altering the social results, achieving greater communication, and keeping the situation small—each requires a systems perspective.

7.3 A SYSTEMS PERSPECTIVE

Thinking in systems terms is a special way of thinking about social life. At its simplest, a system is just an *"ensemble of components and the relations existing between them"* (Von Bertalanffy, 1975:153). Systems theory takes Aristotle's dictum seriously: "The whole is greater than the sum of its parts." What the whole has in addition to its separate parts are the complex relationships *between* the parts. The essential point, then, is the cohesion of a system's components, their interaction, and interrelationships.

While many social scientists do not endorse formal versions of systems theory, most think broadly in systems terms. In truth, systems thinking is more of a loose perspective than a tight theory. One critic contends it only "illuminates at low wattage" (Berlinski, 1976). Yet the systems perspective pervades social science. The macro-level focuses on cultural systems, political systems, economic systems, and social systems. The micro-level focuses on the personality system. Applied fields also use a systems perspective. Specialized work in management, organizations, and communication centers on the concept.

Mathematics and the physical sciences also widely employ systems thinking. Biology, with the living organism as the model, principally started and advocated the systems perspective. The intriguing feature is that such a broad idea has proven useful in such diverse fields. Moreover, particular characteristics emerge that are common to systems in all their variety.

Before we review these common features, we must make a sharp distinction between closed and open systems. Closed systems are self-contained. They are internally self-sufficient and do not interact with the environment. By contrast, open systems are in constant communication with the environment. Every living system exchanges matter with its environment, as do social systems. Hence, both living and social systems are open systems.

7.3.1. Eight Characteristics of Open Systems

Katz and Kahn (1966:14–29) list eight characteristics shared by all open systems. Each deserves discussion.

(1) *Open systems import energy from the environment.* Personality and social systems need environmental inputs just as the human body requires food and air. Human beings deprived of light and sound can develop stress symptoms. Deprivation of social stimulation can cause mental illness. Similarly, social systems deprived of external inputs wither. Factories need raw materials; universities need new students, scholars, and ideas. The almost continuous flow of immigrants throughout American history has invigorated the nation's life and purpose. Look at any social system, and you will see its dependence on external imports.

(2) *Open systems convert the energy into products.* Open systems work and produce. Just as the body converts sugar and starch into heat and action, personality and social systems convert their inputs into products. Individuals change information into thought patterns. Organizations process materials, train people, or provide a service. Nations protect and support their citizens.

When open systems no longer effectively produce their needed products, they decay. Systems, then, are functional; they exist because they provide needed products. The collapse of Communist nations in the 1980s and 1990s offers a striking demonstration. They did not explode from revolution or succumb to invasion. Rather, they *imploded*—they simply collapsed from within as failed regimes that could no longer function as effective systems.

(3) *Open systems export their products to the environment.* Once they have produced their products, open systems export them. By being open, social systems compensate for their energy intake by returning their products back to the environment. Often these products are beneficial; even humans' carbon dioxide helps to maintain plant life. Yet, as we noted, exported products also can be harmful. Toxic wastes are now a global problem.

(4) *The patterned activities of an open system's energy exchange are cyclical.* The previous three characteristics of open systems—energy intake, energy conversion, and the exportation of products—form *a patterned cycle* of system activity. The open system gets its needed energy through this cycle in one of two ways. The product itself can earn the energy. Hence, a factory's finished goods earn money that pays for more raw materials and labor to renew the cycle. Sometimes the patterned activity itself furnishes the renewal. Katz and Kahn (1966) give the example of a voluntary organization for charitable activities. Here the activities provide satisfaction to its members directly, and this satisfaction motivates the continuation of the system's cycle.

This description may seem obvious, but its implications are subtle and important. First, this patterned cycle helps to define the structure of systems. Recall from Chapter 1 that we defined social structure as relatively persistent social patterning. This definition begs the question: *What* is it that is patterned? Now we can answer from a systems perspective. It does *not* consist of physical entities with fixed boundaries. Rather, *structure* consists of the interrelated set of events that repeat themselves in a patterned way to complete the system's cycle of activities (Allport, 1962).

A second implication follows from this view. Since it involves events and not things, social structure is dynamic and not static. That is, social structure is always in motion at any point in the system's cyclical patterning. Recall from Chapter 1 that continuing change is a fundamental feature of social life.

The systems perspective on continuing change underlines what is *not* social structure. Any system component or any one phase of the system cycle is not in itself structure. It requires the full cycle to constitute structure, not just energy intake, product building, or product exporting by itself. By definition, then, social structure is always in motion, always changing.

(5) *Open systems survive by importing more energy than they consume.* **Entropy** is the universal process in which all forms of organization move toward destruction. People die, organizations dissolve, and nations perish. Systems survive by managing **negative entropy**—resistance to this natural tendency to run down and expire. Open systems do this by importing more energy from the environment than they use in maintenance and production. Social systems are less immediately dependent on their environments than living systems. Therefore, social systems can, under optimal conditions, achieve negative entropy for centuries and survive in ever-changing forms.

(6) *Open systems can self-correct through negative feedback.* The most studied characteristic of systems is their self-regulation through **negative feedback.** This feature is the primary concern of cybernetics, a spin-off of systems theory. Feedback mechanisms play a central role in automation, missiles, and many other examples of applied science.

Feedback is information on the system's operations. Negative feedback is information *fed back* to a central mechanism that reports disturbances and deviations in the system. Then, the central mechanism triggers corrective adjustments in the system's processes. The room thermostat that controls temperature typifies a regulatory mechanism that uses negative feedback.

Such informational input is as critical to a system's effectiveness as its intake of energy. Yet, leaders often resist the bad news about the social systems they govern and fail to act. The failure of Communist governments to act on the negative feedback they received on their systems led to their recent collapse. I vividly recall a young Russian sociologist telling me in the 1970s how the Soviet Union's ethnic relations were about to boil over. He accurately predicted the tragic ethnic conflicts that have erupted in recent years. The Soviet government at the time would neither hear nor act on his advice. As we shall see, it is a major task of social science to provide society with negative feedback.

(7) *Open systems can attain a steady state through dynamic equilibrium.* The stability of open systems is also important. Many writers use "steady state" to describe system stability; this term is misleading in its implication that such systems are static and unchanging. Talcott Parsons' (1951) term is more apt—a **dynamic equilibrium.** The system is always in motion, but we regard it as stable when its various components and processes reach a delicate, if ever-changing, balance. This dynamic balance usually means that the energy exchanges and the interrelations of the system's parts remain fairly constant. In short, the basic *character* of the system remains about the same.

The human body offers a pertinent example. The body's temperature remains roughly constant despite rapid changes in temperature and humidity in the environment. Catabolic and anabolic processes of tissue breakdown and restoration within the body maintain a dynamic equilibrium. The underlying theme is that the system preserves its character even as its components, their interrelations, and the environment are constantly changing.

Large social systems typically maintain a dynamic equilibrium through growth and expansion. In time, of course, this growth slowly alters the character and operation of systems. The Santa Cruz campus of the University of California has doubled in size since I joined it. Its distinctive character compared with the University's other eight campuses has not drastically changed. Yet, the rapid expansion has altered the way the campus operates. It is now more formal and bureaucratic; the trade-off entails more efficiency for a less flexible system.

(8) *Expanding open systems differentiate further components with increasingly specialized functions.* When social systems expand, they develop more components. Specialized functions replace diffuse patterns. Cell division in developing organisms illustrates the process. You have undoubtedly noticed this feature in systems that were rapidly growing. In Chapter 5, we saw how both the law and medicine have increasingly divided their fields into narrower specialties. You can see the same development on college campuses. At small colleges, one administrative office can handle all aspects of student financial aid. As a campus grows, so does the number of offices handling student aid. You go to one office for scholarships, another for loans, and still another for work. Sociologists call this process **structural differentiation.**

The differentiation process also leads to a hierarchical arrangement of the components within systems. The college's scholarship, loan, and work offices require an additional office to oversee and integrate them. As this process evolves, the relationships between components become increasingly organized in a top-down, hierarchical fashion. Similar hierarchical arrangements develop among systems themselves. Hence, political and economic systems become components of larger societal systems. National systems in western Europe become part of the larger European Community system.

7.3.2 Practical Implications of Systems Thinking

Popular thought rarely uses a systems perspective. It is another difference between how social scientists and others think about the social world. What are the practical implications of this perspective? What does systems thinking lead you to consider that you might otherwise overlook?

We have already discussed several points. First, the chapter's discussion of social dilemmas underscores one major consideration. A systems perspective questions the comfortable assumption that what is good for particular individuals is good for society. Individual and system needs often conflict. An invisible fist instead of an invisible hand can mediate between individual interests and the public interest. The many social dilemmas we reviewed suggest how widespread such conflict is.

A second point concerns the constantly changing character of social structure. Popular thought often views change as a disturbance from the present, static situation. To think of open systems, with their constant cycle of exchange with the environment, is to view change as a perpetual process. You cannot stop social change; at most, you can slow it and shape it.

A third point involves a favored social science strategy. When social scientists learn of a change in one part of a social system, they ask what implications this change has for other parts and relationships of the system. This application of systems thinking leads to an important contribution of the social sciences—the search for unintended consequences of social policies and social change.

7.4 UNINTENDED CONSEQUENCES OF SOCIAL CHANGE

The focus on the unintended consequences of social change is an intriguing aspect of the systems perspective. Since any change affects all aspects of a system, there is a high probability that changes in one part of a system will have unexpected effects on other parts. Computer simulations reveal the counterintuitive nature of system changes caused by only minor alterations in its components (Waddington, 1977:104). Chaos theory, although disseminating slowly into social science, demonstrates the same point in dramatic fashion (Gleick, 1987).

Put differently, social systems are so complex that human beings rarely foresee all the consequences of any given change, planned or unplanned. Unintended consequences involve structural changes that result from other structural changes. While they overlap with social dilemmas, they result from broad social changes and policies rather than the cumulated actions of individuals.

Social science's emphasis on unintended consequences also differentiates its thinking from popular thought. Conventional wisdom views bad events as having bad effects, and good events as having good effects. Social life, however, is rarely so simple. Unintended consequences can be positive or negative. Negative social phenomena will, from this perspective, create unexpected positive effects. We shall call this process the silver lining principle. If this sounds too sanguine, consider the opposite type of unintended consequence. Positive social phenomena will create unexpected negative effects. We shall label this process the dark cloud principle.

7.4.1 The Silver Lining Principle

War and totalitarian governments are surely negative social phenomena. Yet, clearly positive effects can develop from them as instances of the silver lining principle in operation.

Heavy Allied bombing destroyed Japanese and German industry by the close of World War II. In the late 1940s, it was difficult to see how this shattered scene held any positive effects for these countries. Yet it did. After enormous effort over the next two decades, both Japan and Germany rebuilt their entire industrial systems.

By the 1960s, the plants and machinery of the rest of the industrial world were aging. As wartime winners, the industrial systems of the Allies had not had to adapt. The Japanese and Germans suddenly found themselves with major technical and system advantages in world trade. Their modern plants were more efficient and capable of turning out superior products at lower costs. To be sure, other factors were involved. The major entry of their automobiles into the huge American market in the 1960s offers conspicuous evidence of this advantage.

Even the totalitarian regime that sternly ruled East Germany from 1948 until 1990 illustrates the silver lining principle. As protection against the regime's tyranny, many East Germans informally developed tight little groups of close friends who supported each other. The collapse of East Germany's Communist government reduced the need for these small groups. Friends began to drift away, seeking their fortunes in the new and open society. Only then did East Germans fully realize the value of their intimate friendship networks—a direct and unintended consequence of totalitarianism. They did not wish to return to the old Communist state, but they missed their close friends.

7.4.2 The Dark Cloud Principle

Once you start to look for unintended consequences, instances of the dark cloud principle readily come to mind. Negative results of positive events are upsetting, receive mass media attention, and cause politicians to lose elections. It offers a special case of Murphy's Law—if anything can go wrong, it will go wrong.

The dark cloud principle operates even for the most successful examples of medical and social systems. Take, for instance, antibiotics—an impressive system of defense against infections. Yet, the success of this effort led to the development of new drug-resistant micro-organisms. Similarly, the 20th century's elaborate system of automotive transportation is also impressive. Yet its success led to such unanticipated negative effects as air pollution and widespread accidents with premature deaths.

Consider, too, an educational act passed by the U.S. Congress in 1965. The Elementary and Secondary Education Act used federal monies to improve American public schools—especially those serving the economically poorest sectors of American society. Being a worthy cause, the Act did successfully aid the nation's schools. However, the way Congress structured the Act had the unintended negative consequence of deterring the racial desegregation of the public schools.

How this unintended effect came about is a case study of how a well-intended structural feature can harm other aims. It provides a structural version of the old saying, "no good deed goes *unpunished*." Congress fashioned the Act to provide extra money for schools with a high percentage of impoverished children. To assure this money would go where most needed, the Act established a fixed percentage of children from poor families that a school must have to receive the funds.

Unfortunately, the dark cloud principle arose in a way Congress did not foresee. Given racial discrimination throughout American history, a larger percentage of black children come from poor families than white children. Thus, racial desegregation programs carry a double benefit. They decrease social class segregation as well as racial segregation across schools. So school systems, such as the one in Berkeley, California, that were racially desegregating their schools, suddenly found their federal funds sharply reduced. Their successful desegregation programs had lowered the concentrations of economically-deprived children in particular schools as required by the Act. In a Catch-22 situation, these school systems lost federal funds for carrying out their legal duty to desegregate their schools racially. Later, federal educational officials restored the funds. They also began to administer the Act so this unintended negative consequence would not recur.

Europe also supplies an ironic example of the dark cloud principle. Unity is the central theme of the European Community (the EC). Since the EC formed in 1957, old dreams of a United States of Europe seemed to be coming true. A growing number of Europeans think of themselves primarily as Europeans—not as Germans, French, Dutch, etc. Nation states grow weaker as the EC gains in strength and effectiveness. Individual countries increasingly become components of a larger economic and political system.

Yet within this unity framework, the EC has had the unintended effect of strengthening *disunity* through regional nationalisms. The Basques and Catalons in Spain, Bretons in France, Scots in Great Britain, and others now boast strengthened nationalist movements demanding various forms of autonomy from their national governments. These movements all existed before the EC, but their regions lack the size and resources to form viable nations. This fact restrained the movements. Now these regional ethnicities view a strong EC as making possible their viability as small parts of a larger whole. A unifying system at a level above nation states inadvertently triggered separatist aspirations for regions at a level below nation states.

One final point on unintended consequences concerns conspiracy theories. Some observers ascribe negative effects of ostensibly positive actions to deep, dark plots hatched by conspirators. Many view the dark cloud principle in operation as intended events carefully thought out in advance.

Once you think like a social scientist, you rarely pay attention to such theories. No social scientist would deny that conspiracies exist, but their success is highly doubtful. Conspiracy theories typically oversimplify social life and fail to understand its systems character. Worse, such theories assume an unrealistic ability of human beings to foresee the future and to plan particular outcomes in complex social settings. Hence, conspiracy theories give the presumed plotters far too much credit. From the systems perspective, then, there may or may not be many plotters of foul schemes in this world. Few of them are so clever that they can carry out their schemes as planned.

7.5 WHEN SOCIAL SCIENCE IS DOING ITS JOB

We have seen that social science considers the complexity of social life in part by studying social dilemmas and unintended consequences. This raises the next question. Once social scientists gain some understanding of these phenomena, what should they do with this knowledge? Not all social scientists agree on the answer to this applied query. Disagreement on this issue relates closely to the division among social scientists about the role of values in science—as discussed in Chapter 1.

The author contends, however, that it is a professional duty of social scientists to make their insights widely available to society. This means providing insights not only to government and others with power, but also to the public at large and to those without power.

Pointing out social dilemmas and unintended consequences usually means providing negative feedback about society. It means adopting a critical stance about the society to which social scientists themselves belong. As messengers of bad tidings, social scientists find this an unpopular role to play. It sometimes requires the courage of a resident of 17th-century Salem, Massachusetts who publicly doubted the reality of witches. Some people even regard such criticism of the nation as "unAmerican." Negative feedback remains a professional duty of social scientists, however, even if the advice is ignored and the scientist is abused.

Besides being unpopular, such a critical stance for social science raises two additional problems. First, there is an inherent conflict between social science as a critic of society and as a beneficiary of society. That is, social science subsists on the support of the society that is the target of its critique. This conflict creates tension. As dependents of society, social scientists may think twice about meeting their obligations as societal critics. Yet, as is true for all systems, societies flourish best when they receive and act on a steady flow of negative feedback. Thus, when social scientists withhold their insights on social dilemmas and the negative effects of social policies, they are failing to aid the society that supports them.

A second issue raised by the critical stance of social science concerns the nature of the advice. It will appear to many as being unbalanced or even inconsistent. This is true in part because social scientists may disagree with each other. It is also true for a deeper reason. Social science is doing its job best when it is countering the fads and fashions of the day. In addition to sensitizing the society to unnoticed relationships, it must challenge the popular assumptions and beliefs of the time. This characteristic keeps most social science insights out of step with the rest of society (Williams, 1976).

This counter-the-fashion quality of social science work will anger almost everyone. A liberal President Johnson regularly became upset during the 1960s with social science when it showed some of his programs were not working as intended. Two decades later, conservative President Reagan viewed social science as "the enemy" and tried to end federal funding for much of its research. You know social science is doing its job when those of the political left, center, and right are all unhappy with having their cherished dogmas held up to scrutiny.

Why should this difficult role of societal critic be a professional duty of social science? The basic reason is to be useful, to help alleviate problems and improve social life. The role of critic is a major way that thinking like a social scientist can be helpful to society. Popular thinking about social life swings in wide sweeps of the pendulum. The mass media, dramatizing the present, amplify these pendulum swings—as, for example, between the "idealism" of the 1960s and "cynicism" of the 1990s. The aims for social science is to achieve the opposite—a balance that narrows the pendulum swings of interpreting social life.

7.6 SUMMING UP

Social dilemmas are part of modern life. They share two features whether they involve resource depletion, overpopulation, pollution, or other problems. First, individuals gain more from making selfish, defecting choices than cooperative choices regardless of what others do. Second, everyone is better off if all cooperate than if all defect. In short, individual benefits add up to collective costs. To make matters worse, most social dilemmas have a time dimension. Usually, individual gains are short-term, and collective costs long-term.

Not all individual actions accumulate into social problems. Open markets allow individual economic transactions that have positive societal effects. Market exchanges stabilize prices through supply-and-demand processes. Producers, sellers, and buyers act in their self-interest, yet their acts establish a stable market that is beneficial to society.

Pure markets, operating without interference, are rare. Monopolies form to control pricing, and governments set tariffs and other impediments to unfettered exchange. Some governmental restrictions are necessary, though the political right and left disagree about what is necessary. Effective markets are far more successful than the closed, centrally planned economies of totalitarian states.

Two centuries ago, Adam Smith argued that open economic markets are an important *exception* to the rule that self-interested actions of individuals lead to the "worse for the society." He wrote of individual acts working effectively in a market as if guided by an invisible hand. By contrast, individual acts that lead to social dilemmas act as if guided by an invisible fist.

The useful concept of externalities refers to the social benefits or costs of economic activities that occur without the explicit agreement of those affected. Effective markets have positive externalities; social dilemmas have negative externalities.

Six interrelated types of remedies combat social dilemmas. (1) Government can regulate individual choices with a variety of measures. Such regulation brings costs—bureaucratic control, taxes, and diminished freedom. Yet, well-designed measures can be lean and effective. Traffic lights, for example, solve the traffic intersection problem with elegant simplicity.

(2) Government also can change the payoffs for individuals. It can punish socially harmful behavior and reward pro-social behavior. Thus, it can encourage car-pooling with reserved highway lanes and no tolls. Such incentives can be anything that brings psychological satisfaction. (3) Hence, appeals to societal norms of altruism, social responsibility, and equity can be useful. These appeals are most effective when they call for public behavior, and people important to us make them.

(4) Inventions can change the long-term effects of social dilemmas. If electric cars replace gasoline cars, it would reduce the automotive externality of air pollution. Laboratory experiments suggest two additional remedies. (5) Increased communication not only provides needed information, but it also furthers trust and a sense of group identity. (6) Keeping the situations small furthers group identity, too. Small groups also allow a situation where the monitoring of behavior is more likely.

These remedies require a systems, rather than individual, approach to social dilemmas. A system is an ensemble of components and the relations existing between them. While more a general perspective than a theory, systems thinking pervades social science. The distinction between closed and open systems is vital to this thinking. Closed systems are self-contained; they do not interact with the environment. Open systems are in constant communication with their environments. Both living and social systems are open systems.

Open systems share common characteristics. First, they import energy from the environment. Then, they convert this energy into products that they return to the environment. Open systems are functional; they exist to serve needs. These operations—energy intake, conversion, and return of the products—form a patterned cycle of activity. It is this patterned cycle that defines social structure. It refers not to physical entities, but to this patterned cycle of a system's activities. This characteristic of social systems helps to account for the dynamic, ever-changing nature of social life.

Open systems survive by importing more energy than they consume. In this way they resist the natural process of entropy in which everything runs down toward destruction. Open systems also survive by responding to negative feedback. Such feedback is information sent to a central mechanism about any disturbances in the system's operations. These data then trigger corrective adjustments. Room thermostats use negative feedback to maintain stable temperature.

Open systems also maintain a dynamic equilibrium—a delicate, if everchanging, balance. Social systems typically attain this through growth and expansion. Such growth produces additional system components with increasingly specialized functions—like cell division in living systems. This structural differentiation leads to hierarchical arrangements among a system's components.

Systems thinking has three implications for thinking like a social scientist. First, it suggests that what is good for individuals can be harmful for social systems. Thus, systems thinking puts social dilemmas in a broad context. Second, the perspective reminds us that social change is a perpetual process. You might slow and shape social change, but you cannot stop it. Third, systems thinking leads to a favored social science strategy. Any change in one part of a system will affect all other aspects of the system. This insight causes social scientists to seek the unintended consequences of social policy. We labeled unexpected positive effects of negative events the silver lining principle. Even war and totalitarian rule provide examples of this principle. The dark cloud principle involves unintended negative effects that result from otherwise positive events.

The chapter closed with the contention that social science has a duty to make its insights widely available. It is not, however, popular to convey negative feedback for society. The critical role of emphasizing social dilemmas and unintended consequences is important, if unappreciated. The advice will usually be out of step with current popular thought. But popularity is not the aim of social science.

ISSUES FOR DISCUSSION AND REVIEW

A> Think of a social dilemma that has involved you. Be sure it is a clear instance of where individuals, acting in their self-interests, behave in ways that harm the larger system (group, organization, nation, humankind). What might you recommend to avert the problem? Try to think of positive incentives for individuals to behave in ways that would help to resolve the dilemma.

B> Select an organization to which you belong. Now, analyze it in systems terms. Consider each of the eight characteristics of open systems and apply them to your organization. Does the analysis "fit" well? Are there problems in applying these characteristics to your organization? Does your analysis suggest altering or adding to the list of open system characteristics?

C> Think of an example of an unintended consequence of a current social policy. It can be either a positive silver lining or a negative dark cloud result. Why do you think this unintended effect was not foreseen by those who planned and carried out the policy?

D> The author holds that social science is doing its job best when it counters whatever are the popular contentions of the day. Others disagree. They point out that society pays the bill for social science. So, they argue, social scientists should support current thought and efforts. What do you think?

RECOMMENDATIONS FOR FURTHER READING ON ISSUES RAISED IN THIS CHAPTER

On Social Dilemmas:

For readers new to the idea:
G. Hardin. 1968. The tragedy of the commons. *Science,* 162 (Dec. 13), 1243–1248.
T. Schelling. 1971. The ecology of micromotives. *Public Interest,* No. 25, 61–98.

For readers who wish to read basic sources:

R. M. Dawes. 1980. Social dilemmas. *Annual Review of Psychology*, 31, 169–193.

J. Platt. 1973. Social traps. *American Psychologist, 28*, 641–651.

T. Schelling. 1978. *Micromotives and Macrobehavior.* New York: Norton.

On Systems Thinking:

For readers new to the idea:

G. M. Weinberg. 1975. *An Introduction to General Systems Thinking.* New York: Wiley.

F. E. Emery. (Ed.). 1976. *Systems Thinking.* Baltimore, MD: Penguin Books.

For readers who wish to read a basic source:

L. von Bertalanffy. 1975. *Perspectives on General Systems Theory.* New York: Braziller.

For readers wishing to read a critique of systems theory:

D. Berlinski.   1976. *On Systems Analysis.* Cambridge, MA: M.I.T. Press.

Chapter
8

Try Out Your Healthy Skepticism!

U.S. REPORTS RISE IN DRUG EMERGENCIES. POVERTY IN U.S. GREW FASTER THAN POPULATION LAST YEAR. POLL: MORE FEAR BEING MURDERED. FAMILY LIFE ON DECLINE, POLL FINDS. GUN IN HOME? STUDY FINDS IT A DEADLY MIX. WORKING MOMS' SONS MORE LIKELY TO HAVE SEX EARLY. CAUTIOUS, DOUR PEOPLE LIVE LONGER, STUDY FINDS.

Headlines blare out bottom-line conclusions of social science research in our newspapers every day. You cannot avoid being a consumer of its work. Since this work may affect your daily life, you need to evaluate it. Are the conclusions of the reported research justified? Has the newspaper provided enough information about the research to assess it adequately? Are there alternative explanations for the findings?

This final chapter invites you to use what you have learned by asking these and similar questions of seven newspaper stories. They are not a random sample, but they present a range of social science reports that appear in our newspapers. The leading social science reporters in the nation wrote several of them. Others are of dubious quality, but typical of much reporting in the press. The point is not to criticize newspaper coverage by highlighting the problems raised by these articles. These problems are as much the responsibility of social scientists as they are of the journalists who wrote them (Pettigrew, 1985, 1988). This exercise offers you a chance to flex your new social science muscles.

Before starting, let us first review the principal contentions the book has outlined for how to think like a social scientist.

8.1 COMPONENTS OF A HEALTHY SKEPTICISM

Social science allows more than *one* type of thinking. There are multiple routes to follow across the various specialities. Among these routes, an author's preferences, training, and experience influence any book. Therefore, some social scientists might well object to particular points advanced in this book.

If one considers the complete book, however, I believe most social scientists would agree with the basic points emphasized. Problems of omission, rather than commission, are a more serious risk for a volume of this limited length. That is, what the book leaves out is likely to be more important than problems with what it includes. In addition, this book has focused upon the most basic and widely-accepted aspects of "thinking like a social scientist." By way of quick review, refresh your memory with the following thumbnail sketches of the preceding chapters.

Chapter 1. Social life is complex. Social events are typically multiply determined, systemic, and operate at several levels at once. Social life is also reactive; human beings react back on their environment. In addition, social science must work with high levels of error in its measurements. The lesson is clear. Use a modest, cautious approach in your analyses of these newspaper accounts of social research.

Chapter 2. Theories are important for many reasons. They classify, predict, and explain events; they help us to understand causes and guide research. Concepts are the building blocks of theories, while relational statements form their structure. These statements usually involve causal predictions. They also often include moderators (variables that determine *when* the effect will take place) and mediators (variables that explain the *how* and *why* of the causal process).

In addition to looking for moderators and mediators in the following articles, watch for error cases. Recall that error cases do not fit the expected pattern of results, and thus suggest improvements for the theory. Also note the paradigm—the overall perspective—within which the researchers conducted their work. Sometimes the power of the paradigm blinds the researchers and discussants in the article to their unstated assumptions. Watch carefully for these unstated, but important, assumptions.

Chapter 3. Different comparisons can lead to different conclusions. Check carefully in each article on the comparisons involved. Check also on the controls used. Can you think of plausible rival hypotheses that could explain the results that the controls do not exclude? Recall that effective controls are hardest to achieve in non-experimental research conducted in the field. All the research reported in these newspaper accounts involves precisely such studies.

Chapter 4. Determining causation is one of the most difficult tasks facing social science. Look for causal statements and assumptions in these articles, especially in the last three that explicitly claim causal relationships. Remember the minimal requirements for inferring causation. Causes must precede effects; controls must exclude rival causal explanations. Causal inferences are strengthened by replication and longitudinal research designs. Look, too, for cohort, generation, and life-cycle effects in longitudinal studies. Remember also the difference between cohort replacement and conversion effects in long-term trends.

Chapter 5. In analyzing two reports of public opinion surveys, do not forget the importance of solid probability samples with high response rates. Keep in mind also the problems raised by selection biases. Do these reports give enough information to assess the sampling procedures and response rates?

Chapter 6. We should not confuse levels of analysis. This occurs when researchers draw societal conclusions from only individual data (the compositional fallacy); or draw conclusions about individuals from only macro-data (the ecological fallacy). Watch for these fallacies, for they typically leave open plausible rival hypotheses.

Chapter 7. The accumulation of individual actions can produce either positive social benefits (as in markets) or negative social effects (as in social dilemmas). Remedies for social dilemmas require a systems approach. Systems thinking is central to social science thought and contrasts with much popular thought. Both living and social systems are open systems, in constant communication with their environments.

Three key insights derive from systems thinking. Look for their operation in the following articles. (1) What is good for individuals is not necessarily good for societies. (2) Social change is a perpetual process. (3) Any change in one part of a system will affect all other parts of the system. This last insight leads to the common occurrence in social life of societal change having unanticipated consequences. Recall the two types of unanticipated consequences: the silver lining principle (positive effects of negative events) and the dark cloud principle (negative effects of positive events).

Keep these basic points in mind as you analyze the following social science news stories from leading newspapers.

8.2 NOW THINK LIKE A SOCIAL SCIENTIST!

For each story, ask yourself such basic questions as: What is the principal contention? How well is this conclusion supported by the results reported? What additional features of the study would you like to know? Are there any plausible rival explanations to explain these results? What about error cases—those results that differ from the main contention?

8.2.1 Reports of Social Trends

Many popular reports of social science work do not involve rigorous research designed to test causal theories. Rather, they describe social trends. Often governmental agencies issue these documents, imply causal relations, and draw policy conclusions. Consider two such reports published during October 1993.

(1) Analyze two stories that appeared about the same U.S. Census report on growing poverty in the United States.

Poverty in U.S. Grew Faster Than Population Last Year

By Robert Pear

Special to the *New York Times*

Washington, Oct. 4—Despite the end of the recession, the number of poor people in the United States increased last year by 1.2 million, to 36.9 million, increasing three times as fast as the overall population, the Census Bureau reported today.

The number of poor people was higher than in any year since 1962, when John F. Kennedy was President. In that year, of course, the nation's population was much smaller, and the poor accounted for a larger proportion of the total population: 21 percent in 1962, as against 14.5 percent last year.

Census Bureau officials and economists said the rise in poverty last year reflected lingering unemployment and a slow recovery from the last recession, which ran from July 1990 to March 1991.

The poverty rate last year was three-tenths of a percentage point higher than in 1991, and it was the highest since the 15.2 percent level recorded in 1983.

Many Parallel Data

At the same time, the Census Bureau reported that the number of Americans without health insurance rose 2 million last year, to 37.4 million. President Clinton has repeatedly cited such statistics in asserting that the Federal Government should guarantee health insurance coverage for all Americans.

The new poverty data reflect trends already evident in other statistics. Unemployment last year averaged 7.4 percent, up from 6.7 percent in 1991, the year the recession ended. The number of people receiving food stamps climbed steadily, to 26.6 million in December 1992, from 24.9 million in December 1991. And the number of people on welfare, in the program known as Aid to Families with Dependent Children, rose to 14 million in December 1992, from 13.4 million in December 1991.

Daniel H. Weinberg, chief of income and poverty statistics at the Census Bureau, said many analysts had predicted a drop in poverty last year after the recession ended.

Household income, after adjusting for inflation, declined last year in the Northeast, but was virtually unchanged in other regions and in the nation as a whole. But nationwide, a series of small declines from 1989 to 1992, cut the real purchasing power of the typical household's income by $2,000, to $30,786 in 1992.

Black Couples Not Immune

Overall, the number of poor Americans rose 3.3 percent last year, while the total population rose just 1.1 percent.

For years, the Census Bureau has been saying that the high poverty rates for blacks resulted, in part, from the breakup of many black families. But last year the bureau also found a significant increase in the poverty rate for black married couples, to 13 percent from 11 percent.

A family of four was classified as poor if it had cash income less than $14,335 last year. A family of three was poor if its income was less than $11,186. The official poverty levels are updated each year to reflect changes in the Consumer Price Index. Though living costs vary widely across the country, the poverty level is the same nationwide.

As defined by the Government, income includes wages and salaries, Social Security and welfare payments, but does not include the value of food stamps, Medicare, Medicaid or health insurance provided by employers. Counting these noncash benefits would make the poverty rate seem lower but would not change the trends in poverty observed in recent years, Census Bureau officials said.

Household income declined last year in 14 states, including New York, New Jersey and Connecticut. The poverty rate rose in 33 states, including Connecticut and New Jersey; in New York it was unchanged at 15.3 percent.

More Poor Children

Mississippi, Louisiana, West Virginia and New Mexico had the highest poverty

Poverty in the United States

Americans in poverty each year as defined by the Government. The poverty level for a family of four in 1992 was $14,335.

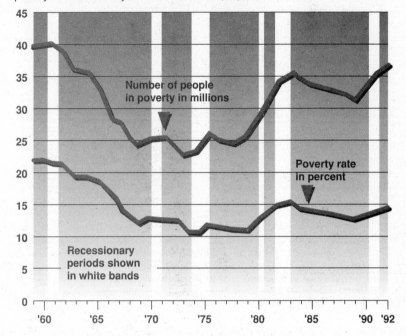

Source: Census Bureau, National Bureau of Economic Research

rates. Delaware, New Hampshire, Utah, Connecticut and Virginia had the lowest.

The Census Bureau found a slight increase in poverty among young children. Twenty-five percent of those under 6, and 21.9 percent of those under 18, were poor last year. Nearly half of black children under 18 were poor.

Clifford M. Johnson, policy director at the Children's Defense Fund, said the new data showed that "poor children are more likely to suffer extreme poverty than ever before."

Last year, 47 percent of all poor children—6.8 million of the 14.6 million poor people under 18—lived in households where incomes were less than half of the official poverty level.

"The rich clearly did get richer from 1967 to 1992," Mr. Weinberg said. But he found some preliminary evidence to suggest that the trend toward greater inequality in the distribution of income, after accelerating in the early 1980's, had begun to slow.

Offering historical perspective, the Census Bureau said that the poverty rate fluctuated between 11.1 percent and 14.2 percent from 1967 to 1981. It peaked at 15.2 percent in 1983—the highest since the 17.3 percent recorded in 1965—and then declined to 12 percent in 1989. It has risen each year since then, to 13.5 percent in 1990, 14 percent in 1991 and 14.5 percent in 1992.

'Safety Net' Is Credited

Wendell E. Primus, a deputy assistant secretary of health and human services, said the new data "show that Government programs are helping reduce poverty."

Poverty rates, excluding the value of Government assistance, increased significantly from 1991 to 1992, Mr. Primus said.

"But after taking into account Government programs like Social Security and Aid to Families with Dependent Children, the poverty rate was not significantly higher in 1992 than 1991," he said.

"The rate did not go up nearly as much in the latest recession as in the 1980–82 recession, partly because safety-net programs were better used, and we didn't cut benefits as much under President Bush as under President Reagan," Mr. Primus said.

The data in the report are drawn from interviews with 60,000 households chosen to be representative of the entire population.

In its report, the Census Bureau made these points:

• The poverty rate for children under 18, listed at 21.9 percent last year, was the highest since 1983 and was nearly as high as in 1964, when it stood at 23 percent. It was in 1964 that President Lyndon B. Johnson declared his War on Poverty.

• In 1992, only 47.2 percent of poor people were covered by Medicaid, the Federal-state program for low-income people. In many states, the income limit for those seeking Medicaid is substantially below the official poverty level. In some states, it is difficult for poor people to get Medicaid if they have no children.

• Among poor people 16 years old and over, 40 percent worked in 1992, and 9.2 percent had full-time jobs throughout the year.

And the Rich Got Richer

Using a new measure of economic well-being, the Census Bureau reported that the condition of the most affluent families improved substantially in the last 25 years, while the condition of the least affluent families appeared to stagnate.

The most affluent one-fifth of all families had incomes averaging 8.4 times the poverty level in 1992, as against six times the poverty level in 1967. By contrast, the least affluent one-fifth of all families had incomes averaging 91 percent of the poverty level in 1992, down from 97 percent in 1967.

The 33.3 percent poverty rate for blacks last year was nearly three times the 11.6 percent rate for whites, the Census Bureau said. The rate for Hispanic people, who may be of any race, was 29.3 percent last year. For Asian Americans, it was 12.5 percent.

The South, which has for years had a higher poverty rate than other parts of the nation, was the only region in which the rate increased significantly last year. The poverty rate was 16.9 percent in the South, 14.4 percent in the West, 13.1 percent in the Middle West and 12.3 percent in the Northeast. Forty percent of all poor people live in the South.

Ranks of Poor, Uninsured Americans Swelled in '92, Census Bureau Says

By Christopher Scanlan
Mercury News Washington Bureau

Suitland, Md.—The number of poor Americans increased for the third straight year in 1992 to 37 million, the highest figure since Lyndon Johnson launched the War on Poverty nearly three decades ago, the Census Bureau said Monday.

An increase also was reported for Americans without health insurance. Their ranks climbed by 2 million from 1991 to 1992, up to 37.4 million. About 15 percent of Americans—including 19.3 percent of Californians—reported that they had no health insurance in 1992.

"We can clearly reject the view that the recovery is turning things around for those at the bottom," said Sheldon Danziger, a professor of social work and public policy at the University of Michigan. "To the extent that anybody talks about the great economic boom of the 1980s and how we were all made better off, it just hasn't trickled down."

Analysts said the increasing number of poor in the United States can be traced in part to a "jobless recovery" from the recent recession. That appears to be especially true in California, where defense-industry cutbacks have contributed to unemployment that remains stubbornly high.

State Poverty Rate

The poverty rate in the Golden State climbed to 15.8 percent last year, up from 15.7 percent the year before and far more than the national average of 14.5 percent.

Only three other states—Nevada, North Carolina and Rhode Island—showed increases in poverty rates last year, and no state reported a decrease.

The 14.5 percent national average was up from 14.2 percent in 1991, an increase census officials said was statistically insignificant. But the bureau said 1.2 million more Americans were living in poverty in 1992 than the year before.

For a family of four, the poverty line is a yearly income of $14,335, census officials said. For a single person, it is $7,143.

Supporters of health care reform said the increase in the number of medically uninsured provides strong evidence of the need for universal access to health care and should help the Clinton administration get its reform plan through Congress.

"Regardless of how well or poorly the economy does, this number just keeps going up, and that's likely to continue until we reform the health care system," said Robert Greenstein, executive director of the Center on Budget and Policy Priorities.

Statistical Snapshot

The census reports were based on a survey of 60,000 households asked in March about their economic status during the year

Poverty in a rich nation

A new Census Bureau report gives the latest figures on U.S. poverty:

The poverty line

■ One Person: $7,100
■ Couple: $9,100
■ Four people: $14,300

Poverty rates by ethnic group

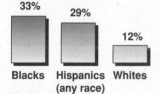

33%   29%

12%

Blacks Hispanics Whites
        (any race)

The health insurance crunch

Uninsured

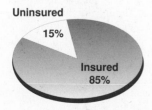

15%

Insured
85%

Percentage of Americans in poverty

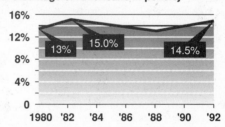

16%

12%   13%   15.0%   14.5%

8%

4%

0
  1980 '82 '84 '86 '88 '90 '92

Youth poverty: The new plague
Percentage of group below poverty line

65 or older ——— 17 or younger ———

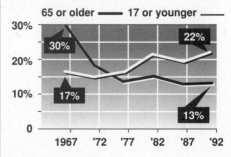

30%   30%   22%

20%

10%   17%

                              13%
0
  1967 '72 '77 '82 '87 '92

Source: Census Bureau

before. They provide a statistical snapshot of income, poverty and health insurance coverage as the country slowly emerged from the recession of 1990 and 1991.

Liberal and conservative analysts offered dramatically different interpretations of the figures.

"We have gotten richer as a nation, but the benefits of that growing wealth have been all but invisible to a growing number of our families," said Clifford Johnson, a spokesman for the Children's Defense Fund.

The advocacy group noted that 21.9 percent of American children—14.6 million—lived in poverty in 1992, up by 276,000 from 1991.

Greenstein said more Americans are poor because of persistent unemployment, widespread cuts in social services by the states and a failure by the federal government to close gaps in the safety net of aid.

Had it not been for federal benefits for long-term unemployed available during 1992, "the increase in poverty probably would have been much larger," Greenstein said. The jobless benefits expired Sunday.

But Robert Rector, a welfare policy analyst for the conservative Heritage Foundation, dismissed the report "as a deliberate political effort to exaggerate the amount of poverty in the United States in order to promote additional welfare spending."

Rector and other conservative critics argue that the government's official definition of poverty is skewed because it is based only on cash income and does not include assets, such as home ownership, or non-cash welfare benefits, such as food stamps, Medicaid and housing assistance.

(2) Now consider a story from the *New York Times* concerning a rise in drug emergencies.

U.S. Reports Rise in Drug Emergencies

By Joseph E. Treaster

Federal health officials in Washington yesterday reported sharp increases in the number of medical emergencies resulting from drug use. They said the numbers underscored the need for more rehabilitation programs and more effective prevention efforts.

While casual drug use has continued to decline, heavy users of cocaine, heroin and marijuana have been streaming into hospital emergency rooms in unprecedented numbers, the officials said.

The number of those seeking help for adverse reactions to cocaine in 1992 increased 18 percent over the previous year, to 119,800. At the same time, heroin overdoses and other reactions to the drug rose 34 percent, to 48,000, and casualties of marijuana jumped 48 percent, to 24,000.

"These are the highest levels ever," said Daniel Melnick, a senior official in the Substance Abuse and Mental Health Services Administration, which released the data yesterday.

'Desperation of Use'

Dr. Mitchell S. Rosenthal, the president of Phoenix House, the largest residential treatment organization in the country, said: "These kinds of big rises suggest a desperation of use and a kind of hopelessness among users. They think they are trapped and can see no alternative but to keep using."

The emergency-room cases resulting from heroin and marijuana use included people of all ages, from adolescence up. But cases among cocaine users 12 to 17 years old declined, the data showed.

While the emergency-room visits were attributed mainly to chronic drug users, Mark A. R. Kleiman, a drug expert who teaches public policy at Harvard University, said the data appeared to reinforce the notion "that heroin is coming back in a serious way and that marijuana may also be coming back."

The unrelenting rise in drug cases in hospital emergency rooms from the mid-1980's goes to the heart of the national health crisis, many drug experts said.

Emergency-room treatment is among the most expensive kinds of care, the experts pointed out, and it has little effect in reversing chronic drug use.

Drugs and Emergency Room Visits

THE NUMBER OF PATIENTS HAS RISEN...

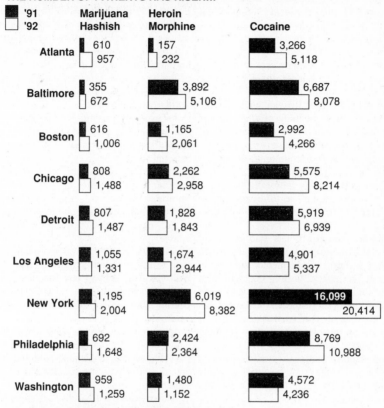

	Marijuana Hashish	Heroin Morphine	Cocaine
	■ '91 □ '92		
Atlanta	610 / 957	157 / 232	3,266 / 5,118
Baltimore	355 / 672	3,892 / 5,106	6,687 / 8,078
Boston	616 / 1,006	1,165 / 2,061	2,992 / 4,266
Chicago	808 / 1,488	2,262 / 2,958	5,575 / 8,214
Detroit	807 / 1,487	1,828 / 1,843	5,919 / 6,939
Los Angeles	1,055 / 1,331	1,674 / 2,944	4,901 / 5,337
New York	1,195 / 2,004	6,019 / 8,382	16,099 / 20,414
Philadelphia	692 / 1,648	2,424 / 2,364	8,769 / 10,988
Washington	959 / 1,259	1,480 / 1,152	4,572 / 4,236

...AND HAS BECOME A LARGER PERCENTAGE OF ALL EMERGENCY ROOM PATIENTS

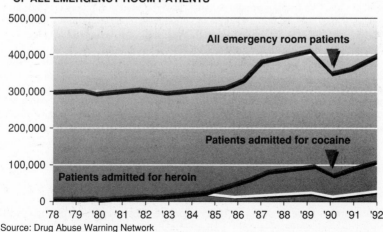

All emergency room patients

Patients admitted for cocaine

Patients admitted for heroin

Source: Drug Abuse Warning Network

151

Cry for More Treatment

Both Donna E. Shalala, the Secretary of Health and Human Services, the parent organization of the substance abuse agency, and Lee P. Brown, President Clinton's chief anti-drug aide, said the soaring drug casualties cried out for more spending on treatment and anti-drug education.

But President Clinton's proposed $13 billion anti-drug budget for the coming year sticks with the pattern established by Presidents Ronald Reagan and George Bush, in which the biggest share of the money goes to trying to stop the flow of drugs rather than to programs aimed at rehabilitation and discouraging drug use. With the President's consent, Congress trimmed from his proposal $100 million that had been earmarked for treatment and $143 million designated for anti-drug education.

White House officials had promised that the Administration's national health system overhaul would include substantial increases in money for drug treatment. But the proposals include no provisions for the kind of long-term residential treatment that most experts say is needed to deal with the kind of chronic drug users now flooding emergency rooms. Instead, Mr. Clinton's health insurance proposal would cover two periods of 30 days of hospital or clinic treatment in any year, along with 30 days of outpatient care.

"We're not talking about people who can use 30 days of inpatient treatment," Dr. Rosenthal said. "We're talking about people here who, if they are not in the emergency room, they are likely to be getting into all kinds of anti-social behavior that can lead to prisons, courts and everything else."

Many experts say that curtailing heavy drug use would sharply cut national health costs. The Center on Addiction and Substance Abuse at Columbia University, for example, recently found that 20 percent of all Medicaid costs were related to drug abuse. Medicaid is the Federal-state program for the poor.

'Feeling of Being Left Out'

"Trying to cut health care costs without solving the drug crisis is like trying to sail a sinking ship without fixing the hole on the bottom," said Paul Samuels, the president of the legal Action Center, a national drug policy organization based in New York.

Many experts said Mr. Clinton appeared to be avoiding the drug issue. The President has seldom addressed the issue in public and has not presented a comprehensive national strategy.

Herbert D. Kleber, the executive vice president of the Center on Addiction and Substance Abuse, said, "the President is so concerned about health care reform that he is not paying enough attention to drug abuse."

Dr. Kleber added: "And it is going to be hard to reform health care in a cost-effective way if he doesn't pay adequate attention to this group of heavy users that we're hearing about today. It's also going to be hard to stop violence."

A number of studies have shown that heavy drug users consume most of the illegal drugs sold in this country, and that they are often involved in property crimes and violence.

Representative Charles B. Rangel, the Manhattan Democrat who heads the House Caucus on Narcotics Abuse, said there was clearly a relationship between the steep increases in emergency-room cases due to drugs and "the feeling of being left out economically."

"If you plot the hospitals where the highest amounts of casualties are coming from," Mr. Rangel said, "you will also find the highest concentrations of AIDS, of unemployment, of people going off to jail, of teen-age pregnancies, and of violent crime."

8.2.2 Survey Results

Another common type of social science story in newspapers cites the results of public opinion surveys—usually called "polls." We discussed problems of such survey reports in Chapter 5. Now test out these points on the following reports on two surveys, (3) starting with one on fear of crime.

Poll: More Fear Being Murdered

By Robert Davis
USA Today

Nearly twice as many Americans worry about being murdered now than in 1981, and many are arming themselves.

A USA TODAY/CNN/Gallup Poll shows 30% have bought a gun for protection and only 33% feel safe alone at night on public transportation.

More than 20,000 people are slain in the USA annually.

"If that happened all at once, maybe we

Many taking precautions as fear of crime increases

A USA TODAY/CNN/Gallup Poll shows that more people are worried about being crime victims than were in a 1981 poll. People's crime fears and what they are doing about them:

Percent who worry often about being...

■ 1981   ☐ Now

	1981	Now
Sexually assaulted	31%	38%
Burglarized when not there	35%	35%
Beaten up, shot, stabbed	19%	23%
Killed	11%	19%

Percent who feel safe alone at night...

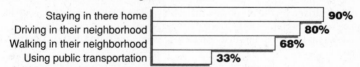

Staying in there home	90%
Driving in their neighborhood	80%
Walking in their neighborhood	68%
Using public transportation	33%

How people are protecting themselves:

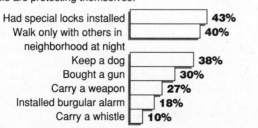

Had special locks installed	43%
Walk only with others in neighborhood at night	40%
Keep a dog	38%
Bought a gun	30%
Carry a weapon	27%
Installed burgular alarm	18%
Carry a whistle	10%

Source: A USA TODAY/CNN/Gallup national telephone poll of 1,244 adults, conducted Oct. 13–18. Margin of error ± 3 pecentage points.

would put the effort into solving the problem," says Christine Edmunds of the National Victim Center.

A Justice Department survey says crime cost $19.1 billion in 1991. Contributing: saving the kids who are shot. Their advanced care averages $14,434, says a survey by the National Association of Children's Hospitals and Related Institutions.

Fifteen youths a day were killed by gunfire in 1991.

Mental costs also are high. Survivors are haunted by losses, especially when the holidays bring "an empty plate, and empty place," says Lula M. Redmond, author of *Surviving When Someone You Love Was Murdered.*

"You go crazy," says Genelle Reilley, 55, a Laguna Beach, Calif., homemaker whose 23-year-old daughter was stabbed to death in 1986. "We will never really be happy again."

In Largo, Fla. Teri Peters, 38, still lights a holiday candle for her father, who was shot and killed 18 years ago.

Trauma lingers for victims of other types of violent crime.

Audrey Tucker, a training specialist for the Navy, says she was treated "like a leper" after she was abducted on a Baltimore sidewalk by a masked, gun-wielding rapist. It's "still devastating" 11 years later. Her attacker has not been caught.

"Life is exhausting because I have to put out two or three times more energy," she says. "I'm very suspicious of everyone, asking: 'Is this the real personality of the person?'"

(4) Now analyze another survey report from the Gannett News Service.

Family Life on Decline Poll Finds

Gannett News Service

Washington—A poll measuring changes in American family life found that middle-income college graduates are the group most likely to believe that family life has worsened.

That is proof that problems with the family are driven by factors other than economics, says the Family Research Council, the conservative think tank that conducted the poll.

"This sense of discontent, that something is wrong, that it's tough to raise children—our sense is these concerns are held not only in the inner cities but in suburbs as well," said Gary Bauer, a former aide to President Reagan and president of the council.

The survey asked a broad range of questions about the American family, touching on day care, education reform, out-of-wedlock births and "traditional values" themes.

The trend in family life over the past three decades has been "generally for the worse," said 72 percent of those surveyed. Among middle-class college graduates, 91 percent thought family life had worsened.

The telephone survey, which has a margin of error of plus or minus 3 percentage points, included 1,100 Americans ages 18 and over.

On a question asking whether children were worse off today, it was black Americans who as a group stood out. While 60 percent of all those surveyed thought children were worse off today than when they were children, 77 percent of black Americans felt life had worsened for children.

Poor schools may be one reason black Americans answered that way, said Bauer. While 51 percent of all those surveyed supported vouchers, 61 percent of blacks supported choice.

Some of the findings of the survey:

• 83 percent said children do best in two-parent families. "Dan Quayle was right," said the report.

• Nine of 10 dual-earner couples said children are better off with their mothers than in day care.

• Supporters of 1992 independent presidential candidate Ross Perot could be key on the education "choice" issue: 64 percent of Perot voters favored choice, compared with 51 percent of the total.

• 66 percent said children "are no longer safe at their school or at play in their neighborhood."

Changes in family life

Responses to the survey question:
Do you think changes in family life over the past three decades have been generally for the better or the worse?

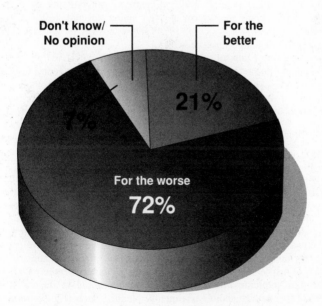

Don't know/ No opinion

For the better

21%

7%

For the worse
72%

Source: Family Research Council

8.2.3 Causal Research

Other newspaper stories focus on specific research that makes causal claims. Frequently, these stories center on issues of crime, sex, or health—always topics of interest. Sophisticated media follow leading research journals and report on their studies of general interest. This allows us to compare the popular and journal publications. Then we can see if the newspaper article omits information essential to an informed evaluation of the research.

(5) Critique the following *New York Times* story about the effect of guns kept in the home.

Gun in Home? Study Finds It a Deadly Mix

By Warren E. Leary
Special to the *New York Times*

Washington, Oct. 6—Instead of increasing protection, a handgun in a home almost triples the chances that someone will be killed there, a study of homicides in three metropolitan areas has found.

The conclusions of the study contradict the popular notion that keeping a gun at home increases personal safety, the researchers said today.

"This study is the first to clearly link the risk of homicide to the immediate availability of a gun," said Dr. Arthur L. Kellermann of Emory University in Atlanta, the lead researcher.

"In light of these results, people who are considering buying a gun for protection should think again," he said in an interview, "and families who keep guns in their homes should strongly consider getting them out of the house."

Findings From 3 States

In a report in Thursday's issue of *The New England Journal of Medicine,* the researchers said they looked at homicides from August 1987 to August 1992 in Shelby County, Tenn., which includes Memphis, and in King County, Wash., which includes Seattle. Another team looked at murders in Cuyahoga County, Ohio, which includes Cleveland, from January 1990 to August 1992.

Studying 420 homicides that occurred in the homes of the victims, about a quarter of the total, the researchers found that a majority of victims, 76.7 percent, were killed by a spouse, family member or someone they knew, and that in 85 percent of cases there was no forced entry into the home.

Documented homicides by a stranger accounted for only 3.6 percent of the cases, although in 17.4 percent of the cases the identity of the killer was not known.

Gunshot wounds were by far the most common cause of death, killing half, or 49.8 percent, of the victims killed at home. Even in the 14 percent of cases involving forced entry, which often involved a spouse or other family member, a gun in the home offered little protection, Dr. Kellermann said at a news briefing here.

Variety of Sources

"Guns were not found to be associated with decreased risk of homicide in any subset, or subgroup, that we studied," Dr. Kellermann said, "even when we just looked at cases involving forced entry or cases in which the victim actively resisted the assailant."

To get a detailed picture of each household where a homicide occurred, the researchers said they not only examined reports by the police and medical examiners, but also interviewed surviving family members or others who knew the victim well. In addition, they developed a matching control group for comparison by interviewing an adult member of a randomly selected household in the neighborhood of the victim. Such a household included a person of the same age range, sex, race and economic circumstance as the victim.

Dr. Kellermann and colleagues at the University of Tennessee, the University of

Washington and Case Western Reserve University in Cleveland found six risk factors for homicide in the home: living alone, having a household member who was ever arrested or who used illicit drugs, living in rental housing, having someone who was ever hit or hurt in a family fight, and keeping one or more guns.

Domestic violence and the use of illegal drugs were the strongest risk factors for domestic homicide. But even when these were factored out, the researchers said, they found that the risk of being killed was 2.7 times higher, or nearly triple, in homes with guns than in homes without them.

The National Rifle Association criticized the findings, saying that a study of homicides could not reflect the effectiveness of guns for personal protection. That is because "99.8 percent of the protective uses of guns do not involve homicides," said Paul H. Blackman, research coordinator for the group. Such uses, he said, would include brandishing a weapon to deter assault, holding an assailant at bay or firing a weapon to wound or frighten off an attacker.

(6) Now analyze a report on working mothers and teenage sex.

Working Moms' Sons More Likely to Have Sex Early

By Christopher Scanlan
Mercury News Washington Bureau

Washington—As if working mothers didn't have enough to worry about, now comes word that their sons are more likely to lose their virginity at a younger age than teens whose mothers don't work outside the home.

A new analysis of 1988 federal data estimates that the sons of mothers who worked full-time were 45 percent more likely to have sex at an earlier age than those whose mothers were not working. The odds were 25 percent higher if the mothers worked part-time.

The report did not give ages of first intercourse for all 1,880 single males aged 15 to 19 surveyed. But in 42 instances, the reported age at first intercourse was 10.

The study, conducted by researchers at the Urban Institute, a Washington think tank, and Wellesley College in Massachusetts, appears in the upcoming issue of Public Health Reports, a journal published by the federal government's U.S. Public Health Service.

Analysts familiar with the study said they were concerned that working mothers will consider—wrongly—that the findings are an attack on them.

"There's so much stress on working mothers, and they feel so guilty so often, that I think that they might see this and think, 'Oh no, not another thing for which I'm responsible,' " said Kristin Moore, executive director of Child Trends, a Washington research firm that focuses on teen sexuality.

"I wouldn't say this proves mothers shouldn't work outside the home," said Gary Bauer, president of the conservative Family Research Council in Washington. "I would say the government needs to wake up and start developing policies that make it possible for more families to provide more time with their children."

Among the options, Bauer said, would be lower tax burdens on families with children by raising the personal exemption.

Leighton Ku, a public health expert at the Urban Institute and one of the authors of the study, said the findings suggest that sons of working mothers could benefit from sex-education programs, perhaps linked with afterschool activities. The study found that teen-age boys who were taught about AIDS and ways to say "no" to sex begin to have sex later than other boys.

Moore said the study should send a message to parents that boys need as much attention as girls.

Supervision, Moore said, "doesn't just mean watching them every minute, but talking to them, explaining risks. There are lots of things that working parents can—and do—do to lower the risks for their kids.

Sons of working moms have sex earlier

A new survey says sons of working mothers are more likely to have sex at an earlier age. Here are some figures on trends in male teen sex and working mothers.

Boys starting sex earlier

Percent of teen boys in metropolitan areas who have had sex

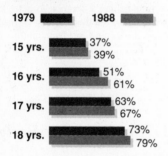

1979   1988

15 yrs.   37%
39%

16 yrs.   51%
61%

17 yrs.   63%
67%

18 yrs.   73%
79%

More mothers are working

Full-time and part-time working mothers of children 18 years and under, in millions

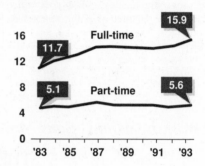

16   Full-time   15.9

11.7

12

8   5.1   Part-time   5.6

4

0

'83   '85   '87   '89   '91   '93

Source: Bureau of Labor Statistics, Urban Institute

And that's really the issue. It's not employment per se."

And, Moore said, it's not just an issue for mothers.

"I think we want to ask what are the fathers doing in these families and what could they be doing, whether they live in the home or not. They could be doing something to protect their sons. We're beyond the time where there's a clap on the back and 'Way to go.' We're at a point where this is risky," she said.

The study did not look at the father's employment: in many cases, the fathers did not live at home. Nor did it examine the sexual history of teen-age girls.

(7) Finally, analyze a social psychological study that links personality characteristics with longevity.

Cautious, Dour People Live Longer, Study Finds

Cheerfulness Can be Liability in Longevity

By Daniel Goleman
New York Times

Score one for those pious voices of prudence: Being cautious and somewhat dour is a key to longevity, according to a 60-year study of more than 1,000 men and women.

Those who were conscientious as children were 30 percent less likely to die in any given year of adulthood than their more free-wheeling peers. But those who were ebullient in childhood fared less well in life's roulette wheel; they were about 6 percent more likely to die in any given year than the least cheerful children.

"We don't really know why conscientious people live longer—it's not as simple as wearing your sweater when it's cold outside," said Dr. Howard Friedman, a psychologist at the University of California, Riverside who did the research. "And despite assertions that optimism and a sense of humor are healthy, we found no evidence for this claim. Cheerfulness predicted a shorter life, perhaps because it indicated an unrealistic optimism, which led people to ignore risks to their health."

The findings were based on research with 1,178 California boys and girls who in the early 1920s, at an average age of 11, were first studied by Lewis Terman, an inventor of the IQ test. All the children were bright.

Terman and later psychologists interviewed them at regular intervals throughout their adult lives, from the 1920s until the 1980s, when most were in their 70s. Friedman's research, supported by the National Institute on Aging, was published in the October issue of the *Journal of Personality and Social Psychology.*

At age 11, the children were evaluated by their parents and teachers on measures that Friedman summarized into five personality traits: sociability and extroversion; self-esteem and confidence; physical energy and activity level; conscientiousness; and "cheerfulness," a combination of optimism and sense of humor.

To his surprise, Friedman found that traits such as sociability and self-esteem had no relationship to how long people lived.

8.3 COMMENTARY ON THE NEWSPAPER STORIES

Unlike the answers to Chapter 1's quiz, this section offers *commentary* on the articles—*not answers.* Undoubtedly, you found many points not mentioned here. Good! Think for yourself—that's a critical part of a healthy skepticism.

8.3.1. Comments on Story 1: Poverty Increases

Policy interpretations of the data dominate these two articles that describe the same Census report. Yet they are careful to show that many different indicators support the chief contention—that U.S. poverty rose during 1992. In addition to the Census income data, increases in unemployment and those receiving food stamps and welfare payments all reveal the same distressing trend. This use of *multiple indicators,* then, firmly establishes the headlined conclusion: POVERTY IN U.S. GREW FASTER THAN POPULATION LAST YEAR.

Nonetheless, the various commentators put contrasting "spins" on the results. Whether from the political left, government, or political right, the conflicting interpretations focus on the Census definition of poverty. Thus, these stories provide an instructive example of how important operational definitions are in such politically-sensitive topics as poverty.

Different definitions suggest different comparisons and policy conclusions. We can expect the political left, wishing to highlight social problems, to regard the Census definition as too severe, thus leading to an undercount of the "real" poverty problem. Government officials are likely to interpret the data as showing how well their programs are working. We can expect the political right, wishing to restrict taxes and governmental spending on the poor, to claim the Census definition is too generous, thus leading to an exaggeration of the "real" problem.

So the Census definition of what constitutes poverty becomes pivotal. Both articles clearly present this definition. In 1992, the Census counted a family of four with less cash income than $14,335 as poor. It also counted as poor a family of three with less than $11,186 cash income, a family of two with less than $9,100, and single people with less than $7,100. These income levels rise each year to reflect inflation in consumer prices. Note the Census includes only *cash* income in their calculations (wages, salaries, and government payments). This omits such items of value as food stamps and various medical payments.

From this definition, the commentators (called "spin-doctors") play their roles as expected. Liberals see the results as a mandate to "reform the health care system," and an indictment of cuts in state and federal services. They emphasize the growing numbers of young children in poverty—21.9% (and almost half of all African American children). Robert Reno (1993), a *Newsday* columnist, attacks the Census definition as too harsh. He invites his readers to try living as a family of three on $11,186.01 (not poor by the Census definition). A *New York Times* (1993) editorial uses Canada as a comparison to show "humane social welfare programs" can reduce poverty even in bad economic times.

Wendell Primus, an official overseeing federal welfare programs, sees it differently. He rejoices that the new data "show that Government Programs are helping reduce poverty." To reach this conclusion, Primus evokes two arguments. First, he stresses that the poverty percentages reported by the Census are "not significantly higher in 1992 than 1991." Also, if the Census had not included social security and welfare payments, the poverty increase would have been larger.

Second, Primus claims the data are not so bad when compared with the sharper increases in poverty during the 1980–82 recession. Observe the shift in comparisons. Instead of the *New York Times'* comparison of Canada, Primus selects the previous American recession. Yet, take another look at the *Times'* informative chart. Two earlier recessions (1960–61 and 1970) showed smaller increases in poverty than in 1990–91. Again, the carefully chosen comparison determines the desired conclusion.

The political right has its own spin. In *The San Jose Mercury News* article, Robert Rector of the Heritage Foundation dismisses the Census report altogether. He sees it as a political effort "to exaggerate the amount of poverty" to promote more spending for the poor. He regards the Census definition as too generous, because it includes only cash income. It also should include, he argues, such assets as home ownership and non-cash benefits. Left unsaid is that home ownership among the poor is not extensive, and his own Foundation opposes most non-cash benefit programs.

Observe that none of the commentators question the accuracy of the report's data. The two accounts mention that a huge survey of 60,000 households provided the data, though they give no response rate. This one point of general agreement is testimony to the high esteem in which they hold the Census. Studiously non-partisan and employing the most advanced techniques in social research, the U.S. Census richly deserves such respect. Its definition of poverty, however, receives criticism from all sides.

Pity the Census officials! They *must* assign operational terms to measure policy-related concepts. *Any* definition of poverty will in part be arbitrary, and no definition will satisfy everyone. The spin-doctors have a point in their critiques. As a careful consumer of social data, you need the healthy skepticism advocated in this volume to reach your own conclusions apart from conflicting commentators.

8.3.2 Comments on Story 2: Drug Emergencies Rise

The principal contention of this *New York Times* story is straightforward. Based on U.S. Government data, reported hospital visits for drug-related emergencies increased in 1992 in comparison with 1991. The data strongly support this disturbing conclusion. Sharp increases occurred in eight of nine major American cities for all three classes of drugs—marijuana and hashish, heroin and morphine, and cocaine. Moreover, longitudinal data back to 1978 show this increase is part of a long-term national trend. Indeed, the trend has been so rapid since 1985 that both cohort replacement and conversion processes probably underlie it.

Another strength of this article is the care with which it specifies its effects. Only the Harvard University drug expert claims these data show a rise in drug addiction. The *New York Times* reporter correctly limits his assertions to the precise indicator used—drug-related emergency visits. The importance of this specification becomes apparent when we consider why this increase in emergencies may not represent an increase in addiction. Newer, more powerful versions of the drugs, such as "crack" cocaine, could easily have created more emergencies from the same number of addicts.

Yet the article leaves out details that are essential for a full evaluation. Of course, such details make for dull reading for many newspaper readers. Nevertheless, their absence allows for plausible rival explanations for the results. Were the data collected from *all* hospital emergency services in the U.S., or was it a sample? If a sample, how was it drawn and what was the non-response rate for services that did not report their results? Did all the reporting services use the same criteria (operational definition) over the years for what constituted "drug-related emergencies?"

These questions are not hair-splitting concerns. Without knowing the answers, additional explanations for the results suggest themselves. Perhaps, an ever-increasing number of emergency services reported their data each year. This alone could account for the rise in drug cases since the mid-1980s. Remote as this may seem, some past governmental reporting suffered from precisely this obvious artifact. Some years ago, annual crime reports of the Federal Bureau of Investigation showed a steady rise in most types of crime in part because the Bureau was including ever-increasing numbers of reporting police departments. In the present case, the large increases from 1991 to 1992 make this rival explanation unlikely. Yet, without details of the study, we cannot rule it out with certainty.

Another rival explanation involves changing diagnoses. As drug addiction burst into crisis proportions by the 1980s, medical personnel became increasingly aware of drug emergencies. They may well have begun to diagnose cases as drug related more often and keep better data on them. The steady rise in drug-related emergencies could reflect in part, then, greater attention to drug effects by medical personnel. Again, the size of the 1991 to 1992 increases limits this possibility. Nonetheless, our healthy skepticism needs reassurance on this point.

In reviewing these data, you may have noted several intriguing points that receive no attention in the *New York Times* story. For instance, the data provided do not control for population size. When we apply a crude control for population, striking differences emerge among the cities. Note that Los Angeles reports less than half the cocaine-related emergency visits in 1992 than much smaller Philadelphia. Why? Asking such questions about data irregularities can lead to insights about the phenomenon under study, often suggesting causal factors for future testing.

A search for error cases in these data raises additional questions. Why did heroin and cocaine-related emergency visits *decline* in Washington, D.C. during 1992 when they were rising elsewhere? Similarly, why the drop in cocaine-related visits among 12- to 17-year-olds when it was rising for other age groups? Why the sharp decline in cocaine-related emergencies in 1990—the only annual decline in the data? While such questions go beyond what we can expect newspapers to provide, they represent the probing curiosity that thinking like a social scientist requires.

Thus, the newspaper article omits a description of methods, controls for population growth, and a discussion of error cases. What it does dwell on are the policy implications of the results. Such implications are of particular interest to readers, of course. Yet, too-quick acceptance of the findings, without the application of a healthy skepticism, make such policy implications premature.

8.3.3. Comments on Story 3: More Fear Being Murdered

This article presents a typical newspaper account of survey results. The text cites only a few selected data from the survey. The sensationalized headline is supported largely by dramatic quotations from crime victims—all selected to fit the story's theme. The lead paragraph adds to the headline by claiming "[N]early twice as many Americans worry about being murdered now than in 1981 . . . ." Two pages later, *U.S.A. Today* provides the data. The lead refers to 11% of respondents holding such fears in a 1981 survey and 19% in a 1993 survey (actually a 73% gain).

Chapter 5 prepared you for analyzing this story. There are two major problems of insufficient evidence—one involves sampling and non-response and the other question wording. The margin of error listed here (3%) refers only to sampling error. Recall that such a figure is highly misleading in that it assumes an unattainable response rate of 100%. The article gives no response rates for either the 1981 or 1993 surveys. Nor do we know if the 1,244 adults listed was the original sample drawn, or the final sample size after the non-respondents dropped out. If it were the latter, we need to know the size of the original sample.

The survey was a national telephone study conducted over a six-day period. The Gallup Poll is a highly-respected organization; but even its telephone surveys often suffer large non-response rates. This strong possibility means that the total error (including both sampling and non-response error) could be far larger than the 8% difference in those fearing murder between the two surveys. Without more information, the wary consumer should not accept the sensationalized conclusion.

We also need to know the actual questions asked. Were the order and wording of questions the same in the two surveys? If not, we know that even slight changes in question order and wording can create more than the 8% difference on which the headline rests (Schuman & Presser, 1981).

The careful consumer must see the actual question for another reason. If the question is "loaded"—that is, begs the answers, it may exaggerate the fear of murder. Suppose the question asked: "Many Americans worry about being murdered these days. How about you? Have you *ever* worried about being killed?" Such a brow-beating query is clearly inadequate, for it will yield an excessive percentage of respondents in agreement. Unscientific surveys conducted by political sponsors often use such loaded questions to shape the answers they seek.

The experienced Gallup Organization knows better than to ask such a loaded question. Yet it is difficult to ask about fears of murder so as not to lead respondents into over-reporting fear. A healthy skepticism demands seeing the actual questions asked before accepting the cited percentages.

8.3.4. Comments on Story 4: Family Life in Decline

Again, note the deceptive headline. The survey results do not and cannot show that family life has declined. They show only that many respondents *think* that it has declined. Nor can survey data provide "proof that problems with the family are driven by factors other then economics"—as claimed by the study's sponsor. Nor can they prove "Dan Quayle was right" about children doing best in two-parent families. Surveys reveal what respondents *think* about social conditions. We should never confuse such data with the conditions themselves. To do so is to commit the compositional fallacy.

The story's description of the survey's characteristics are sketchy. It does provide the wording for one of the key questions. We are also told that it is a telephone survey of "1,100 Americans." The story cites the standard and erroneous "margin of error" of 3%. It does not mention non-response.

This survey report illustrates the political misuse of surveys. A political center shapes the questions, selects the results it likes, and interprets these results to fit its political stance. In addition, the center conducts the survey itself and provides too few details of method to assess the study's quality. One should not confuse such "managed research" with social science. Newspaper editors might question whether such political surveys represent news worth printing or propaganda packaged to masquerade as social research.

8.3.5. Comments on Story 5: Guns and Homicides

This brief *New York Times* story appeared the same day the research article itself appeared in the *New England Journal of Medicine* (Kellerman *et al.*, 1993). The story adequately covers the basic method of the research. The study conducted detailed analyses, including interviews with those who knew the victims, of 420 urban homicides. This figure represents 94.6% of all homicides committed in or near the home in three urban counties studied over a 32-month period. The strength of the research lies in the care with which the study located the control group. The story accurately describes the many factors on which the controls matched the victim.

The criticism of the National Rifle Association spokesperson misses the target. The 99.8% figure cited for the harmless use of guns is suspect. Especially suspect is the absence of any details about how this convenient figure was attained. In any event, the point does not respond directly to the study's most publicized finding—the greater danger for those in homes with guns.

Still, there is a problem with this finding. Recall Chapter 5's discussion of selection bias. The *Times* account generalizes the basic conclusion to *all* American homes— "a handgun in a home almost triples the chances that someone will be killed there. . . ." Yet, the study did not sample homes in general. Rather, it focused on homes with a recorded homicide and controls from similar homes in only three urban counties.

The problem is that homes with homicide are not randomly located in American society. We must limit the conclusion: *homes with homicides in three major urban areas are far more likely to own a handgun than matched homes without homicide*. Though more modest, this conclusion is still important. It begs additional research with a national probability sample of American households.

Finally, the article mentions at its close a major finding of this research. Homes that experienced a homicide more often than control homes included an illicit-drug user, a person with prior arrests, or someone who had been hurt in a fight in the home. The researchers statistically controlled for these differences, and still found those homes with a gun had a 2.7 times greater risk of homicide than control homes.

8.3.6. Comments on Story 6: Working Moms' Sons

This article provides little information with which to judge the merits of the study. Apparently, a group of researchers conducted a secondary analysis of 1988 federal government data. Their re-analysis showed that single males, aged 15 to 19, with employed mothers *report* having had initial sexual intercourse earlier than other males. We are also told that those who had some sex education had on average initial intercourse at an older age. Most of the article assumes the headline's conclusion and discusses its policy implications. Yet, obviously, we should first be confident about the research finding before we concern ourselves with its implications.

This story offers an exercise in listing missing information. To start, the account gives virtually no information about the initial survey. From what study do the data come? What federal agency conducted it? We know the study interviewed 1,880 young, single males, but how were they sampled? What was the response rate? Would including married males have altered the findings? We cannot evaluate data from an unspecified survey.

The article provides two charts. Did you notice that these data are not directly relevant to the headlined conclusion? The charts show two national trends. (1) Between 1979 and 1988, the number of young American males who report having had sex slightly increased. (2) From 1983 to 1993, the number of mothers working full-time and part-time has steadily risen. (No control for population growth, however, is made in this chart.) Neither of these trends demonstrates the relationship cited in the headline. They speak only to increases over recent years in both factors, not to the association between them.

Story 6 also provides an instructive example of unstated assumptions. The data refer to the boys' *reports* of sexual activity. The article and the discussants all assume, without saying so, that these reports are accurate. Anyone who has ever endured the boasting of sexual exploits in a male locker room would surely question such an assumption! The critical issue is whether this reporting error relates in any way to the working patterns of mothers. It does not stretch the imagination to believe that it could. Suppose the sons of working mothers depend more on the acceptance and support of peer groups than other boys. This possibility could lead these boys to exaggerate their sexual experiences more than others.

Much of the policy discussion also assumes a *causal* relationship between the two variables. Chapter 4 warns us to be skeptical about such casual assumptions about cause. The study as described does not meet the minimum criteria for assuming cause. Some mothers could have begun working *after* their sons had their initial sexual contact. Moreover, a third variable, such as social class, could create the relationship between the two variables. In general, working-class youth have earlier sexual experience, and working-class mothers work more than other mothers. This is such an obvious possibility that the Urban Institute researchers undoubtedly controlled for it. Yet, the newspaper report does not reveal this important detail.

The article does mention one limitation of the analysis—namely, that the study did not investigate the fathers' employment status. Does this mean that the researchers did not control for this crucial variable? If so, this, too, would serve to undercut the story's too-facile assumption that mothers' employment *causes* the earlier sexual activity of their sons.

8.3.7. Comments on Story 7: Dour People Live Longer

The writer of this article, Daniel Goleman, is one of the most experienced reporters who pursues journalism's social science "beat." Unlike most American newspapers, the *New York Times* has long had skilled reporters who specialize in stories on social research. This has increased not only the quality but the frequency of such stories in the *Times*.

This story supplies important facts despite its brevity. The research by Howard Friedman and his associates (Friedman *et al.*, 1993) features a secondary analysis of a famous longitudinal study. This investigation reanalyzed data already collected in the Terman Life Cycle study conducted at Stanford University (Terman & Oden, 1947). This new analysis constructed new variables and multiple indicators of its major concepts. Begun in 1921, the Terman project followed 1,528 people through seven decades of their lives. Goleman describes the Terman project and prudently cites the central finding: "Cautious, dour people live longer."

This sentence describes the principal result and correctly avoids claiming a *causal* relationship. The research shows there are strong *relationships* between longevity and two personality traits measured in 1921 when the respondents were children—high conscientiousness and low cheerfulness.

As always, the causal implications of this finding are complex. The relationship could reflect no causal link at all. Thus, the link between conscientiousness and longevity may reflect only that both relate to a third variable— such as social class again. That higher social class may cause both conscientiousness and longevity is plausible. The economically comfortable may be more often socialized as children to be conscientious; they live longer on average because of better living conditions. In their technical paper, Friedman and his colleagues reject this possibility, because Terman's sample was predominantly middle class and remained so throughout their lives (Friedman *et al.*, 1993:178).

Goleman takes care to mention the chief limitation of the research. The study included only children with high scores on an I.Q. test, and most of them were middle-class white Californians. Even these participants were not a probability sample of highly-intelligent white children. Perhaps the study's intriguing findings hold only for more intelligent, middle-class whites. High I.Q. scores, race, and class, then, could act as moderators. If so, the personality association with long life would hold only for such people and not others. Moreover, this sample is all from the same cohort, having been born around 1910. Their results may not generalize to later cohorts who faced different conditions and life experiences. These possibilities beg for further research using probability samples of people of many measured intelligence levels and cohorts.

While the report stressed the two personality variables that predicted long life, it did not dwell on four other variables that failed as predictors. Often in science, what does not predict is as important to know as what does predict. The research also looked at sociability, physical energy and activity, self-esteem, and mood stability—all thought to relate to health. Yet, they did not predict longevity in these data.

The *Times* story omitted other important information. Women on average live longer than men, and this was true in this sample as well. However, the personality findings remained even after the analysis controlled for sex. That is, conscientiousness and low cheerfulness predicted longer lives for both women and men.

The technical paper also supplied comparative effect sizes for its principal results. The effects for conscientiousness and low cheerfulness as mortality risks are important. They roughly rank with such well-known risks as high systolic blood pressure and serum cholesterol. However, the danger of smoking one pack of cigarettes a day is considerably greater than these risks. Observe how such effect size comparisons provide understandable orders of magnitude that are useful for public policy.

Why should these two personality traits predict longer lives? Friedman and his colleagues offer several interesting speculations. Perhaps, people who are conscientious and those who are less cheerful and optimistic avoid risks and stressful situations. In addition, they also may develop better self-care and healthful behaviors and reject the "it cannot happen to me" defense.

8.4 A FINAL WORD

A final caveat is in order. Thinking like a social scientist is, of course, only one among many ways of thinking. The book makes no claim that it is the best or preferred way to think. There are many roads to truth; different modes of thought have different purposes. Social science thinking aims to gain an understanding of the complexities of the social world. It is a way of thinking we all encounter—especially as consumers. The author hopes this volume has helped you to gain an appreciation of the basic ideas that underlie *how to think like a social scientist.*

References

Abrahamsen, D. 1970. *Our Violent Society.* New York: Funk & Wagnalls.

Adorno, T. W., Frenkel-Brunswik, E., Levinson, D. J., Sanford, R. N. 1950. *The Authoritarian Personality.* New York: Harper & Row.

Allen, J. 1989. The 1990 Census: Counting everybody. *Focus, 17* (7), 5–6.

Allport, F. H. 1962. A structuronomic conception of behavior: Individual and collective. I. Structural theory and the master problem of social psychology. *Journal of Abnormal and Social Psychology, 64,* 3–30.

Allport, G. W. 1968. The historical background of social psychology. In G. Lindzey & E. Aronson (Eds.), *The Handbook of Social Psychology.* 2d ed. Vol. I. Reading, MA: Addison-Wesley.

Allport, G. W., Pettigrew, T. F. 1957. Cultural influence on the perception of movement: The trapezoidal illusion among Zulus. *Journal of Abnormal and Social Psychology, 55,* 104–113.

Almond, G. A., Verba, S. 1965. *The Civic Culture.* Boston: Little, Brown.

Alwin, D. F., Cohen, R. L., Newcomb, T. M. 1991. *Political Attitudes Over the Life Span: The Bennington Women After Fifty Years.* Madison, WI: University of Wisconsin Press.

Archer, D., Gartner, R. 1984. *Violence and Crime in Cross-National Perspective.* New Haven, CT: Yale University Press.

Aronson, E. 1988. *The Social Animal.* 5th Ed. New York: Freeman.

Aronson, E., Blaney, N., Stephan, C., Sikes, J., Snapp, M. 1978. *The Jigsaw Classroom.* Beverly Hills, CA: Sage.

Aronson, E., Brewer, M., Carlsmith, J. M. 1985. Experimentation in social psychology. In G. Lindzey & E. Aronson (Eds.), *Handbook of Social Psychology.* 3d ed. Vol. I. New York: Random House.

Associated Press. 1994. Holocaust poll "was flawed." *San Jose Mercury News,* May 19, 1994, 27A.

Atkinson, J. W., Hoselitz, B. F. 1958. Entrepreneurship and personality. *Explorations in Entrepreneurial History, 10,* 107–112.

Bales, R. F. 1970. *Personality and Interpersonal Behavior.* New York: Holt, Rinehart & Winston.

Bateson, G., Jackson, D. D., Haley, J., Weakland, J. 1956. Toward a theory of schizophrenia. *Behavioral Science, 1,* 251–264.

Berlinski, D. 1976. *On Systems Analysis.* Cambridge, MA: M.I.T. Press.

Blalock, H. M., Jr. 1969. *Theory Construction: From Verbal to Mathematical Formulations.* Englewood Cliffs, NJ: Prentice-Hall.

Blalock, H. M., Jr. 1984. *Basic Dilemmas in the Social Sciences.* Beverly Hills, CA: Sage.

Blau, P. 1955. *The Dynamics of Bureaucracy.* Chicago: University of Chicago Press.

Braddock, J. H., II. 1989. Social psychological processes that perpetuate racial segregation: The relationship between school and employment desegregation, *Journal of Black Studies, 19,* 267–289.

Braddock, J. H., II, Crain, R. L., McPartland, J. M. 1984. A long-term view of racial desegregation: Some recent studies of graduates as adults. *Phi Delta Kappan, 66,* 259–264.

Braddock, J. H., II, McPartland, J. M. 1987. How minorities continue to be excluded from equal employment opportunities: Research on labor market and institutional barriers. *Journal of Social Issues, 43,* 5–39.

Campbell, D. T. 1974. Evolutionary epistemology. In P. A. Schilpp (Ed.), *The Philosophy of Karl Popper* (Vol. 14, 1 & 2), *The Library of Living Philosophers* (Vol. 14, 1). La Salle, IL: Open Court Publishing.

Campbell, D. T., Stanley, J. C. 1966. *Experimental and Quasi-Experimental Designs for Research.* Chicago: Rand McNally.

Chafetz, J. S., Ebaugh, H. R. F. 1983. Growing conservatism in the United States? An examination of trends in political opinion between 1972 and 1980. *Sociological Perspectives, 26,* 275–298.

Chaudhuri, A., Stenger, H. 1992. *Survey Sampling: Theory and Methods.* New York: Dekker.

Cohen, B. P. 1992. Paradigms and models. In E. F. Borgatta & M. L. Borgatta (Eds.), *Encyclopedia of Sociology.* Vol. 3. New York: Macmillan.

Cook, T. D., Campbell, D. T. 1979. *Quasi-Experimentation: Design and Analysis Issues for Field Settings.* Chicago: Rand McNally.

Cotton, P. 1990. Examples abound of gaps in medical knowledge because of groups excluded from scientific study. *Journal of the American Medical Association, 263* (8), 1051–1052.

Davis, J. A. 1975. Communism, conformity, cohorts and categories: American tolerance in 1954 and 1972–73. *American Journal of Sociology, 81,* 491–513.

Davis, J. A. 1980. Conservative weather in a liberalizing climate: Change in selected NORC General Social Survey items, 1972–1978. *Social Forces, 58,* 1129–1156.

Davis, J. A. 1985. *The Logic of Causal Order.* Beverly Hills, CA: Sage.

Davis, J. A. 1992. Changeable weather in a cooling climate atop the liberal plateau: Conversion and replacement in 42 General Social Survey items, 1972–1989. *Public Opinion Quarterly, 56,* 261–306.

Davis, J. A., & Smith, T. W. (1991). *General Social Surveys, 1972–1991: Cumulative Codebook.* Chicago, IL: National Opinion Research Center.

Dawes, R. M. 1980. Social dilemmas. *Annual Review of Psychology, 31,* 169–193.

Dawson, V. L., Zeitz, C. M., Wright, J. C. 1989. Expert-novice differences in person perception: Evidence of experts' sensitivity to the organization of behavior. *Social Cognition, 7,* 1–30.

Durkheim, E. 1951 [1893]. *Suicide.* Glencoe, IL: Free Press.

Dwyer, J. H. 1983. *Statistical Models for the Social and Behavioral Sciences.* New York: Oxford University Press.

Eagly, A. H. 1978. Sex differences in influenceability. *Psychological Bulletin, 85,* 86–116.

Eagly, A. H., Carli, L. L. 1981. Sex of researchers and sex-typed communications as determinants of sex differences in influenceability: A meta-analysis of social influence studies. *Psychological Bulletin, 90,* 1–20.

Elder, G. 1974. *Children of the Great Depression.* Chicago: University of Chicago Press.

Emery, F. E. (Ed.) 1976. *Systems Thinking.* Baltimore, MD: Penguin Books.

Erikson, E. H. 1958. *Young Man Luther.* New York: Norton.

Erikson, E. H. 1963. *Childhood and Society.* New York: Norton.

Erikson, E. H. 1968. Life cycle. In D. L. Sills (Ed.), *International Encyclopedia of the Social Sciences.* Vol. 9. New York: Macmillan.

Erikson, E. H. 1969. *Gandhi's Truth.* New York: Norton.

Farley, R. 1984. *Blacks and Whites: Narrowing the Gap?* Cambridge, MA: Harvard University Press.

Festinger, L., Carlsmith, J. 1959. Cognitive consequences of forced compliance. *Journal of Abnormal and Social Psychology, 58,* 203–210.

Field, M. 1983. Bradley's narrow loss attributable to success of Republicans in getting party members to vote absentee, presence of Proposition 15 on ballot, low turnout of minority groups, as well as white racism. *The California Poll,* Release no. 1201.

Flacks, R. E. 1967. The liberated generation: An exploration of the roots of student protest. *Journal of Social Issues, 23,* 52–75.

Franklin, J. H. 1956. *The Militant South: 1800–1861.* Cambridge, MA: Harvard University Press.

Franz, C. E., McClelland, D. C. 1994. Lives of women and men active in the social protests of the 1960s: A longitudinal study. *Journal of Personality and Social Psychology, 66,* 196–205.

Friedman, H. S., Tucker, J. S., Tomlinson-Keasey, C., Schwartz, J. E., Wingard, D. L., Criqui, M. H. 1993. Does childhood personality predict longevity? *Journal of Personality and Social Psychology, 65,* 176–185.

Giles, M. W., Buckner, M. A. 1993. David Duke and black threat: An old hypothesis revisited. *Journal of Politics, 55,* 702–713.

Gleick, J. 1987. *Chaos: Making a New Science.* New York: Viking.

Gluckstern, N. B., Packard, R. W. 1977. The internal-external change agent team: Bringing change to a "closed institution." *Journal of Applied Behavioral Science, 13,* 41–52.

Gnagey, W. J. 1960. Effects on classmates of a deviant student's power and response to a teacher-exerted control technique. *Journal of Educational Psychology, 51,* 1–8.

Gorer, G. 1943. Themes in Japanese culture. *New York Academy of Science, 5,* 106–124.

Granovetter, M. S. 1973. The strength of weak ties. *American Journal of Sociology, 78,* 1360–1380.

Granovetter, M. S. 1982. Alienation reconsidered: The strength of weak ties. *Connections, 5* (2), 4–16.

Granovetter, M. S. 1983. The strength of weak ties: A network theory revisited. *Sociological Theory, 1,* 201–33.

Greeley, A. M., Rossi, P. H. 1966. *The Education of Catholic Americans.* Chicago: Aldine.

Gurwitz, J. H., Col, N. F., Avorn, J. 1992. The exclusion of the elderly and women from clinical trials in acute myocardial infarction. *Journal of the American Medical Association, 268* (11), 1417–1422.

Hardin, G. 1968. The tragedy of the commons. *Science, 162,* 1243–1248.

Harding, P., Jenkins, R. 1989. *The Myth of the Hidden Economy.* Philadelphia: Open University Press.

Hirschman, A. O. 1981. *Essays in Trespassing: Economics to Politics and Beyond.* New York: Cambridge University Press.

Huck, S. W., Sandler, H. M. 1979. *Rival Hypotheses: Alternative Interpretations of Data Based Conclusions.* New York: Harper & Row.

Huff, D. 1982. *How to Lie With Statistics.* New York: Norton.

Hutton, W. 1986. *The Revolution That Never Was: An Assessment of Keynesian Economics.* New York: Longman.

Inkeles, A. 1969. Making men modern: On the causes and consequences of individual change in six developing countries. *American Journal of Sociology, 75,* 208–225.

Inkeles, A. 1978. National differences in individual modernity. *Comparative Studies in Sociology, 1,* 47–72.

Inkeles, A., Smith, D. 1974. *Becoming Modern: Individual Change in Six Developing Countries.* Cambridge, MA: Harvard University Press.

Institute for Social Research. 1991–92. The Bennington study. *I.S.R. Newsletter, 17,* 4–6.

Jackson, J. K. 1956. The adjustment of the family to alcoholism. *Marriage and Family Living, 18,* 361–369.

Jaynes, G. D., Williams, R. M., Jr. (Eds.). 1989. *A Common Destiny: Blacks and American Society.* Washington, DC: National Academy Press.

Jennings, M., Niemi, R. 1975. Continuity and change in political orientations: A longitudinal study of two generations. *American Political Science Review, 60,* 1316–1335.

Johnson, S. 1994. Court ruling on census count could help cities. *San Jose Mercury News,* August 11, 1994, 1B–2B.

Judd, C. M., Smith, E. R., Kidder, L. H. 1991. *Research Methods in Social Relations.* New York: Holt, Rinehart & Winston.

Katz, D., Kahn, R. L. 1966. *The Social Psychology of Organizations.* New York: Wiley

Kellerman, A. L., Rivara, F. P., Rushforth, N. B. Banton, J. G., Reay, D. T., Francisco, J. T., Locci, A. B., Prodzinski, B. A., Hackman, B. B., Somes, G. 1993. Gun ownership as a risk factor for homicide in the home. *The New England Journal of Medicine, 329* (No. 15), 1084–1091.

Kelley, H. H. 1983. The situational origins of human tendencies: A further reason for the formal analysis of structures. *Personality and Social Psychology Bulletin, 9,* 8–30.

Kercher, K. 1992. Quasi-experimental research designs. In E. F. Borgatta & M. L. Borgatta (Eds.), *Encyclopedia of Sociology.* Vol. 3. New York: Macmillan.

Keynes, J. M. 1920. *The Economic Consequences of the Peace.* New York: Harcourt, Brace & Howe.

Keynes, J. M. 1930. *A Treatise on Money.* London: Macmillan.

Keynes, J. M. 1936. *The General Theory of Employment, Interest and Money.* New York: Harcourt, Brace.

Kiecolt, K. J. 1988. Recent developments in attitudes and social structure. *Annual Review of Sociology, 14,* 381–403.

Kiesler, C. A., Lowman, R. P. 1980. Hutchinson versus Proxmire. *American Psychologist, 35,* 689–690.

Kohn, M. L. 1969. *Class and Conformity: A Study in Values.* Homewood, IL: Dorsey.

Kohn, M. L. 1977. Reassessment, 1977. In *Class and Conformity.* 2d ed. Chicago: University of Chicago Press.

Kohn, M. L., Schooler, C. 1969. Class, occupation and orientation. *American Sociological Review, 34,* 659–678.

Kohn, M. L., Schooler, C. 1973. Occupational experience and psychological functioning: An assessment of reciprocal effects. *American Sociological Review, 38,* 97–118.

Kovel, J. 1970. *White Racism: A Psychohistory.* New York: Pantheon.

Kroeber, A. L. 1948. *Anthropology.* New York: Harcourt, Brace & World.

Kuhn, T. S. 1970. *The Structure of Scientific Revolutions.* 2d ed. Chicago: University of Chicago Press.

Lantermann, E. D. 1993. Value systems and integration success of resettlers. Unpublished paper presented at University of Muenster Summer School Conference, Reisensberg, Germany on July 22, 1993.

Lieberman, S. 1950. The effects of changes in roles on the attitudes of role occupants. *Human Relations, 9,* 385–403.

Lerner, M. J. 1980. *The Belief in a Just World.* New York: Plenum.

Mann, L., Janis, I. L. 1968. A follow-up study on the long-term effects of emotional role-playing. *Journal of Personality and Social Psychology, 8,* 339–342.

Mannheim, K. 1952. The problem of generations. In K. Mannheim (Ed.), *Essays in the Sociology of Knowledge.* London: Routledge and Kegan Paul.

McClelland, D. C. 1961. *The Achieving Society.* Princeton, NJ: Van Nostrand.

Michotte, A. 1963. *The Perception of Causality.* New York: Basic Books.

Middleton, R. 1976. Regional differences in prejudice. *American Sociological Review, 41,* 94–117.

Midway Data Associates. 1991. *The General Social Survey for the PC.* Chicago: Midway Data Associates.

Milgram, S. 1974. *Obedience to Authority.* New York: Harper & Row.

Miller, D. (Ed.) 1985. *Popper Selections.* Princeton, NJ: Princeton University Press.

Myers, D. G. 1993. *Social Psychology.* 4th Ed. New York: McGraw-Hill.

Myrdal, G. 1944. *An American Dilemma.* New York: Harper & Row.

Newcomb, T. M. 1943. *Personality and Social Change.* New York: Dryden Press.

Newcomb, T. M., Koenig, K. E., Flacks, R., Warwick, D. P. 1967. *Persistence and Change: Bennington College and Its Students After 25 Years.* New York: Wiley.

New York Times. 1993. Poverty and callousness in America. *The New York Times,* October 7, 1993, A–18.

Parsons, T. 1937. *The Structure of Social Action.* New York: McGraw-Hill.

Parsons, T. 1951. *The Social System.* New York: Free Press.

Parsons, T. 1970. Some problems of general theory. In J. C. McKinney & E. A. Tiryakian (Eds.), *Theoretical Sociology.* New York: Appelton-Century.

Parsons, T., Bales, R. F., Shils, E. 1953. *Working Papers in the Theory of Action.* New York: Free Press.

Parsons, T., Shils, E. (Eds.) 1951. *Toward a General Theory of Action.* Cambridge, MA: Harvard University Press.

Pearlin, L. I., Kohn, M. L. 1966. Social class, occupation and parental values. *American Sociological Review, 31,* 466–479.

Pettigrew, T. F. 1958. Personality and socio-cultural factors in intergroup attitudes: A cross-national comparison. *Journal of Conflict Resolution, 2,* 29–42.

Pettigrew, T. F. 1959. Regional differences in anti-Negro prejudice. *Journal of Abnormal and Social Psychology, 59,* 28–36.

Pettigrew, T. F. 1961. Social psychology and desegregation research. *American Psychologist, 16,* 105–112.

Pettigrew, T. F. 1964. What "white backlash"? *Nieman Reports, 18* (4), 7–9.

Pettigrew, T. F. 1979. The ultimate attribution error: Extending Allport's cognitive analysis of prejudice. *Personality and Social Psychology Bulletin, 5,* 461–476.

Pettigrew, T. F. (Ed.) 1980. *The Sociology of Race Relations: Reflection and Reform.* New York: Free Press.

Pettigrew, T. F. 1985. Can social scientists be effective actors in the policy arena? In R. L. Shotland & M. M. Marks (Eds.), *Social Science and Social Policy.* Beverly Hills, CA: Sage.

Pettigrew, T. F. 1988. Influencing policy with social psychology. *Journal of Social Issues, 44* (2), 205–219.

Pettigrew, T. F. 1991a. Advancing racial justice: Past lessons for future use. In H. J. Knopke, R. J. Norrell & R. W. Rogers (Eds.), *Opening Doors: Perspectives on Race Relations in Contemporary America.* Tuscaloosa, AL: University of Alabama Press.

Pettigrew, T. F. 1991b. Normative theory in intergroup relations: Explaining both harmony and conflict. *Psychology and Developing Societies, 3,* 3–16.

Pettigrew, T. F. 1991c. The importance of cumulative effects: A neglected emphasis of Sherif's work. In D. Granberg & G. Sarup (Eds.), *Judgment and Intergroup Relations: Essays in Honor of Muzafer Sherif.* New York: Springer-Verlag.

Pettigrew, T. F. 1991d. Toward unity and bold theory: Popperian suggestions for two persistent problems of social psychology. In C. W. Stephan, W. G. Stephan & T. F. Pettigrew (Eds.), *The Future of Social Psychology.* New York: Springer-Verlag.

Pettigrew, T. F. 1993. How events shape theoretical frames: A personal statement. In J. H. Stanfield II (Ed.), *A History of Race Relations Research: First-Generation Recollections.* Newbury Park, CA: Sage.

Pettigrew, T. F., Coltrane, S., Archer, D. 1995. Selective non-response in California energy surveys. Manuscript under review.

Pettigrew, T. F., Meertens, R. W. 1995. Subtle and blatant prejudice in western Europe. *European Journal of Social Psychology, 25,* 57–75.

Pettigrew, T. F., Spier, R. B. 1962. The ecological structure of Negro homicide. *American Journal of Sociology, 67,* 621–629.

Platt, J. 1973. Social traps. *American Psychologist, 28,* 641–651.

Pool, I. de S., Abelson, R. P., Popkin, S. L. 1964. *Candidates, Issues and Strategies: A Computer Simulation of the 1960 Presidential Election.* Cambridge, MA: The M.I.T. Press.

Popper, K. R. 1959. *The Logic of Scientific Discovery.* New York: Basic Books.

Ragosa, D. 1985. Analysis of reciprocal effects. In T. Husen & N. Postlethwaite (Eds.), *International Encyclopedia of Education.* London: Pergamon.

Reno, R. 1993. More poor: Wretched figures amid a "recovery." *San Jose Mercury News,* October 7, 1993, 7B.

Reynolds, P. D. 1971. *A Primer in Theory Construction.* Indianapolis, IN: Bobb-Merrill.

Riley, R. T., Pettigrew, T. F. 1976. Dramatic events and attitude change. *Journal of Personality and Social Psychology, 34,* 1004–1015.

Robey, B., Rutstein, S. O., Morris, L. 1993. The fertility decline in developing countries. *Scientific American, 269* (6), 60–68.

Robinson, W. S. 1950. Ecological correlations and the behavior of individuals. *American Sociological Review, 15,* 351–357.

Rosenberg, M., Pearlin, L. I. 1978. Social class and self-esteem among children and adults. *American Journal of Sociology, 84,* 53–77.

Rosenthal, R. 1991. *Meta-Analytic Procedures for Social Research*. Rev. Ed. Newbury Park, CA: Sage.

Rosenthal, R., Jacobson, L. 1968. *Pygmalian in the Classroom*. New York: Holt, Rinehart & Winston.

Rosenthal, R., Rosnow, R. L. 1975. *The Volunteer Subject*. New York: Wiley.

Ross, L. D. 1977. The intuitive psychologist and his shortcomings: Distortions in the attribution process. In L. Berkowitz (Ed.), *Advances in Experimental Social Psychology*. Vol. 10. New York: Academic Press.

Rotter, J. 1966. Generalized expectancies for internal vs. external control of reinforcement. *Psychological Monographs, 80* (1). Whole no. 609.

Ryder, N. B. 1968. Cohort analysis. In D. L. Sills (Ed.), *International Encyclopedia of the Social Sciences*. Vol. 2. New York: Macmillan.

Scheaffer, R. L., Mendenhall, W., Ott, L. 1986. *Elementary Survey Sampling*. 4th ed. Boston: PWS–Kent.

Schelling, T. 1971. The ecology of micromotives. *Public Interest, No. 25*, 61–98.

Schelling, T. 1978. *Micromotives and Macrobehavior*. New York: Norton.

Schuman, H., Kalton, G. 1985. Survey methods. In G. Lindzey & E. Aronson (Eds.), *Handbook of Social Psychology*. 3d ed. Vol. I. New York: Random House.

Schuman, H., Presser, S. 1981. *Questions and Answers in Attitude Surveys: Experiments on Question Form, Wording, and Context*. New York: Academic Press.

Schuman, H., Steeh, C., Bobo, L. 1985. *Racial Attitudes in America: Trends and Interpretations*. Cambridge, MA: Harvard University Press.

Scripps-Howard News Service. 1993. More single women are saying "I don't." *San Jose Mercury News*, July 29, 1993, A17.

Sears, D. O. 1986. College sophomores in the laboratory: Influences of a narrow data base on social psychology's view of human nature. *Journal of Personality and Social Psychology, 51,* 515–530.

Sewell, W. H., Hauser, R. M. 1975. *Education, Occupation, and Earnings: Achievement in the Early Career*. New York: Academic Press.

Sherif, M. 1966. *In Common Predicament*. Boston: Houghton Mifflin.

Smelser, N. J., Smelser, W. T. 1981. Group movements, sociocultural change, and personality. In M. Rosenberg & R. Turner (Eds.), *Social Psychology: Sociological Perspectives*. New York: Basic Books.

Smith, A. 1952 [1776]. *An Inquiry into the Nature and Causes of the Wealth of Nations*. Chicago, IL: Encyclopedia Britannica [No. 39 of the *Great Books of the Western World*].

Smith, T. W. 1982. General liberalism and social change in post-World War II America: A summary of trends. *Social Indicators Research, 10,* 1–28.

Smith, T. W. 1990. Liberal and conservative trends in the United States since World War II. *Public Opinion Quarterly, 54,* 479–507.

Snyder, M., Swann, W. B. 1978. Behavioral confirmation in social interaction: From social perception to social reality. *Journal of Experimental Social Psychology, 14,* 148–162.

Spitz, R. T., MacKinnon, J. R. 1993. Predicting success in volunteer community service. *Psychological Reports, 73,* 815–818.

Stevens, S. S. 1968. Measurement, statistics, and the schemapiric view. *Science, 161,* 849–856.

Stouffer, S. A., Suchman, E. A., DeVinney, L. C., Star, S. A., Williams, R. M., Jr. 1949. *The American Soldier: Adjustment during Army Life*. Vol. I. Princeton, NJ: Princeton University Press.

Sykes, G. 1958. *The Society of Captives*. Princeton, NJ: Princeton University Press.

Taylor, S. E., Koivumaki, J. H. 1976. The perception of self and others: Acquaintanceship, affect, and actor-observer differences. *Journal of Personality and Social Psychology, 33*, 403–408.

Terman, L. M., Oden, M. H. 1947. *Genetic Studies of Genius: IV. The Gifted Child Grows Up: Twenty-Five Year Follow-Up of a Superior Group*. Stanford, CA: Stanford University Press.

Turner, J. H. 1990. *The Structure of Sociological Theory*. 5th Ed. Belmont, CA: Wadsworth.

U.S. Bureau of Labor Statistics. 1992. *B.L.S. Handbook of Methods*. Bulletin 2414. Washington, DC: U.S. Government Printing Office.

U.S. Bureau of the Census. 1975. *Historical Statistics of the United States, Colonial Times to 1970*. Part 1. Washington, DC: U.S. Government Printing Office.

U.S. Bureau of the Census. 1979. *The Social and Economic Status of the Black Population in the United States: An Historical View, 1790–1978*. Washington, DC: U.S. Government Printing Office.

U.S. Bureau of the Census. 1991. *The Black Population in the United States: March 1990 and 1989*. Washington, DC: U.S. Government Printing Office.

U.S. Bureau of the Census. 1992a. *Statistical Abstract of the United States*. 112th Edition. Washington, DC: U.S. Government Printing Office.

U.S. Bureau of the Census. 1992b. *The Black Population in the United States: March 1991*. Washington, DC: U.S. Government Printing Office.

von Bertalanffy, L. 1975. *Perspectives on General System Theory Scientific-Philosophical Studies*. New York: Braziller.

Waddington, C. H. 1977. *Tools for Thinking*. London: Jonathan Cape.

Walker, I., Pettigrew, T. F. 1984. Relative deprivation theory: An overview and conceptual critique. *British Journal of Social Psychology, 23*, 301–310.

Webb, E. J., Campbell, D. T., Schwartz, R. D., Sechrest, L., Grove, J. B. 1981. *Nonreactive Measures in the Social Sciences*. 2d ed. Boston: Houghton Mifflin.

Weber, M. 1930 [1904–05]. *The Protestant Ethic and the Spirit of Capitalism*. Translated by T. Parsons. New York: Scribner.

Weinberg, G. M. 1975. *An Introduction to General Systems Thinking*. New York: Wiley.

Williams, E. N. 1980. Census Bureau must adjust minority count. *Focus, 8*, (10–11), 5–6.

Williams, L. F. 1989. What the Census means in money and power. *Focus, 17* (7), 7–8.

Williams, R. M., Jr. 1976. A neglected form of symbolic interactionism in sociological work: Book talks back to author. *American Sociologist, 11*, 93–101.

Wilson, C. G., Golub, S. 1993. Sexual abuse prevention programs for preschool children: What do parents prefer? *Psychological Reports, 73*, 812–814.

Yarrow, M. R., Clausen, J. A., Robbins, P. R. 1955. The social meaning of mental illness. *Journal of Social Issues, 11* (4), 33–48.

Glossary

ACHIEVED STATUS is the ranked position and roles in society that people attain by their own efforts. See **ascribed status.**

ADDITIVE EFFECTS occur when the effects of the independent variables simply add up to explain the total effect on the dependent variable. See **interaction effects.**

ALLOCATION processes determine how a society's resources are divided and granted to its members. These structural processes are the means by which societies select who gets what.

ARCHIVAL DATA are data gathered earlier for another purpose, such as census data, legal records, and voting results. See **secondary analysis.**

ARTIFACT is a problem in a study's method or statistical analysis that leads to an erroneous result. See **threats to validity.**

ASCRIBED STATUS is the ranked position and roles in society that people are born with, such as race and sex. See **achieved status.**

BETWEEN SUBJECTS COMPARISONS are made between experimental and control groups when subjects serve in either group, but not both. See **within subjects comparisons.**

BIAS refers to any influence that distorts the accuracy of research results or human perception. See **constant error** (under **error**), **fundamental attribution bias, non-response bias, threats to validity,** and **ultimate attribution bias.**

BOTTOM-UP CAUSAL PATHS are theoretical explanations that extend from the micro- and meso-levels up to the macro-level of analysis. These paths imply that changes at the individual and situational levels lead to changes at the societal level. See **top-down causal paths.**

CATHARSIS is a term from Freudian theory that refers to individuals reducing their aggressive energy through the expression of aggressive behavior.

CAUSAL ATTRIBUTION involves the processes by which people use information to determine the causes of events. See **dispositional causal attribution, fundamental attribution bias, situational causal attribution,** and **ultimate attribution bias.**

CLOSED SYSTEMS. See **systems.**

COHORT is an age cluster of people who experience a significant event about the same time in their lives. See **cohort replacement, echo effect, conversion, generation,** and **life-cycle.**

COHORT REPLACEMENT represents a shift in attitudes and cultural norms caused by younger cohorts reaching maturity and replacing older cohorts that are dying. Unlike the conversion process, replacement changes are slow and gradual. See **cohort** and **conversion.**

COMPOSITIONAL FALLACY occurs when an analyst considers only data on individuals, but draws conclusions about the entire society. This procedure is a fallacy, because the micro-level units are inadequate and too small to represent phenomena and processes at the societal level. See **ecological fallacy.**

CONCEPTS are abstract terms that social scientists use in their theories to refer to such general ideas as ascribed status, markets, and roles. They are also called constructs. Primitive concepts are the most basic terms, but the hardest to define precisely. Shared agreement about primitive concepts is vital, because other concepts cannot describe them. Derived (or nominal) concepts are derived from primitive concepts. See **operational definitions** and **variables.**

CONSTANT ERROR. See **error.**

CONSTRUCTS. See **concepts.**

CONTROL GROUP consists of those subjects in an experiment who undergo exactly what a comparable experimental group experiences, except for the independent variable(s) under test. The basic idea of controls is to exclude plausible alternative explanations for the results. See **experimental group** and **plausible rival hypotheses.**

CONVERGENT VALIDITY. See **validity.**

CONVERSION represents a shift in attitudes and cultural norms across all cohorts. Unlike replacement, conversion changes are sensitive to immediate events and can be rapid and volatile. See **cohort** and **cohort replacement.**

CORRELATION COEFFICIENT is a measure of association between two variables. It ranges from 0 (no relationship) to +1.0 (perfect positive relationship) or −1.00 (perfect negative relationship). See **multiple regression analysis.**

CRITERION VALIDITY. See **validity.**

CROSS-SECTIONAL RESEARCH collects data on the dependent variable at only one point in time. See **dependent variable** and **longitudinal research.**

DECOMPOSITIONAL FALLACY is another name for the ecological fallacy. See **ecological fallacy.**

DEPENDENT VARIABLE is the factor predicted to change as a result of changes in the independent variables. In cross-sectional research, it is measured only once. In longitudinal research, it is measured two or more times. See **cross-sectional research, independent variables,** and **longitudinal research.**

DERIVED CONCEPTS. See **concepts.**

DISPOSITIONAL CAUSAL ATTRIBUTION involves our perceiving people's actions as caused by their internal dispositions, such as traits, attitudes, or abilities. See **causal attribution, fundamental attribution bias, situational causal attribution,** and **ultimate attribution bias.**

DIVERGENT VALIDITY. See **validity**.

DOUBLE BLIND STUDY involves an experiment in which neither the subject nor the experimenter knows whether the subject is participating in the control or experimental group. See **single blind study**.

DYNAMIC means continuous motion and change—a property of all social systems. See **dynamic equilibrium**.

DYNAMIC EQUILIBRIUM refers to a social system's state when its various components and processes reach a delicate, if ever changing, balance. With this dynamic balance, the basic character of the system remains about the same. See **dynamic** and **systems**.

ECHO EFFECT refers to a large cohort providing a new large cohort at child-bearing age. See **cohort**.

ECOLOGICAL FALLACY occurs in social analysis when only data from large macro-units are available, yet the analyst draws conclusions about individuals. This procedure is a fallacy in that the macro-units are too large to represent individual differences within the unit. See **compositional fallacy**.

EFFECT SIZES gauge the practical importance of the effects of the independent variables on the dependent variable. They assess differences largely independent of the size of the sample studied. Only sample size distinguishes between effect sizes and significance tests: significance test = effect size + sample size. Studies with large sample sizes aimed at applications find effect sizes to be useful. See **meta-analysis** and **statistical significance**.

ENTROPY is the universal process in which all forms of organization move toward destruction. People die, organizations dissolve, and nations perish. Negative entropy is the resistance to this natural tendency to run down and expire.

ERROR refers to any deviation in data from the "true" result—as in measurement error and sampling error. In its statistical sense, it does *not* mean "mistake." There are two general types of statistical error. Variable error is random error. Research can reduce it by having larger numbers of observations. Constant error is non-random error that deviates in one direction from the "true" data. Simply increasing the number of observations or subjects only magnifies constant errors. See **measurement error, reliability,** and **validity**.

ERROR CASES are instances where the theory's predictions are clearly incorrect. Such cases inform us about the weakness of the theory under test. Many error cases of a particular type suggest improvements for the theory.

EXIT POLLS question only known voters by sampling people as they leave the voting place on election day.

EXPERIMENTAL GROUP consists of those subjects in an experiment who undergo exactly what a comparable control group experiences as well as the independent variable(s) under test. See **control group**.

EXPERIMENTAL REALISM involves an interesting experimental situation that thoroughly involves the subjects. See **mundane realism**.

EXTERNALITIES are the social benefits or costs of an economic activity that occur without the explicit agreement of those affected. Adam Smith's markets, guided as if by an *invisible hand,* have *positive* externalities. Social dilemmas, such as overgrazing of the commons, have *negative* externalities. See **markets** and **social dilemmas**.

EXTERNAL VALIDITY. See **threats to validity**.

FACE VALIDITY. See validity.

FEEDBACK. See negative feedback.

FUNDAMENTAL ATTRIBUTION BIAS is the human tendency to exaggerate the importance of dispositional causes and disregard situational causes. People are salient. They are in the foreground of our visual field; thus, they impress us as causal agents. By contrast, situational factors are usually in the background and out of view. See bias, causal attribution, dispositional causal attribution, situational causal attribution, and ultimate attribution bias.

GENERALIZATION is the expanded application of research results or theory to other types of people, situations, or cultures.

GENERATION refers to the structural and cultural aspects of family lineage and parent-child relationships. See cohort and life-cycle.

HISTORY. See threats to validity.

INDEPENDENT VARIABLES are the factors under study as the predicted causes of changes in the dependent variable. In experiments and quasi-experiments, the researcher controls the timing and form of the independent variable. In passive research designs, the researcher has no control of the independent variables. See dependent variable, passive research designs, predictor variable, and quasi-experiments.

INSTRUMENTATION. See threats to validity.

INTERACTION EFFECTS occur when the effect on a dependent variable of one independent variable is not the same at every level of another independent variable. So, the joint effects of the independent variables are not additive. See additive effects.

INTERNAL CONSISTENCY RELIABILITY. See reliability.

INTERNAL VALIDITY. See threats to validity.

LIFE-CYCLE involves the course of human life moving through a sequence of developmental stages from birth to death. See cohort and generation.

LONGITUDINAL RESEARCH collects data on the dependent variable at more than one point in time. See cross-sectional research, dependent variable, and panel studies.

MACRO-LEVEL OF ANALYSIS involves the study of societal-level entities—organizations and institutions, *not* individuals or situations. These entities are more than mere collections of people, for their structures and functions are different in kind from entities at other levels. See meso-level of analysis and micro-level of analysis.

MARGINAL UTILITY. See utility.

MARKETS, in their pure state, involve buyers and sellers who determine prices through uncontrolled individual exchanges. These exchanges stabilize prices to their "true" value through supply and demand processes. Producers of goods supply their products in response to the demand for them. Sellers compete with each other to attract buyers; buyers seek the lowest prices. The desirable result is stable, reasonable prices with products in supply as wanted by consumers. See externalities and social dilemmas.

MATURATION. See threats to validity.

MEASUREMENT refers to the assignment of numbers to objects or events so that we can study them systematically. Such number assignment must be done according to established rules if it is to make sense. See measurement error.

MEASUREMENT ERROR refers to any distortion in a measure in how it reflects the concept it is supposed to be representing. See concepts, error, measurement, reliability, and validity.

MEDIATOR VARIABLES mediate *between* the independent and dependent variables and help to explain *how* and *why* they relate to each other. See dependent variable, independent variables, and moderator variables.

MESO-LEVEL OF ANALYSIS involves the study of face-to-face situations. See macro-level of analysis and micro-level of analysis.

META-ANALYSIS provides a statistical analysis of the results of many independent studies of a single phenomenon. It estimates the effect size of a phenomenon across many studies and conditions. It is most effective when it reviews research that uses diverse types of subjects, measures, and methods. Meta-analysis summarizes all the known research on a given topic with greater precision and objectivity than subjective reviews of the same studies. See effect sizes.

MICRO-LEVEL OF ANALYSIS involves the study of individuals considered one at a time. See macro-level of analysis and meso-level of analysis.

MODERATOR VARIABLES moderate *when* and under what conditions the independent and dependent variables relate to each other. They help to predict *when* and *where* the relationship will hold. See dependent variable, independent variables, and mediator variables.

MORTALITY. See threats to validity.

MULTIPLE REGRESSION ANALYSIS is an extension of correlational analysis to more than one independent variable. It is a major means of controlling for related variables in non-experimental research. It is also important in assessing statistical significance in both experimental and non-experimental research. See correlation coefficient.

MUNDANE REALISM refers to the degree to which an experimental setting approximates a real-life setting in the subjects' lives. See experimental realism.

NEGATIVE ENTROPY. See entropy.

NEGATIVE FEEDBACK is information *fed back* to a central mechanism that reports disturbances and deviations in a system. Then, the central mechanism triggers corrective adjustments in the system's processes. The room thermostat that controls temperature typifies a regulatory mechanism that uses negative feedback. See systems.

NOMINAL CONCEPTS. See concepts.

NON-RESPONSE BIAS involves two conditions. (1) Selective non-response occurs; that is, particular types of people selected for the sample do not respond to a survey. (2) These non-responding types relate systematically to the variables under test. There are two chief types of selective non-response. *Not-at-home sample members* are often busy, younger people. *Refusals* are usually older and simply refuse to participate. See bias and constant error (under error).

NORMS are widely-shared expectations regarding how people should think and act in particular situations. *Formal* norms are the shared expectations of what *ought* to occur. *Informal* norms are the shared expectations of how people *actually* behave.

OPEN SYSTEMS. See systems.

OPERATIONAL DEFINITIONS are the procedures for measuring variables. Thus, they uniquely specify the meaning of a concept (or construct). For example, an IQ test provides an operational definition of intelligence. See **concepts** and **variables**.

PANEL STUDIES are longitudinal studies that use the same subjects throughout the study. See **longitudinal research**.

PARADIGMS are broad scientific perspectives. They suggest new theories and types of research and pose new problems while solving old ones.

PASSIVE RESEARCH DESIGNS involve research where the independent variable is out of the researcher's control and subjects cannot be assigned randomly to condition. Social research in such restricted settings require as many control comparisons as are possible. See **independent variables** and **quasi-experiments**.

PLACEBO is a pill or other substance that causes no physiological effects when ingested by subjects. Experimenters often use a placebo for control groups in experiments to test for expectancy effects. See **control group**.

PLAUSIBLE RIVAL HYPOTHESES are alternative explanations for a phenomenon to that provided by the researcher. Control comparisons are necessary to exclude such rival hypotheses. See **control group** and **threats to validity**.

PREDICTOR VARIABLE is another name for independent variable. Non-experimental research, such as surveys, uses the term. See **independent variables**.

PRESOCIALIZATION refers to the process by which we prepare ourselves in advance for a new role before we occupy it. See **roles**.

PRIMITIVE CONCEPTS. See **concepts**.

PROBABILITY SAMPLES provide each person in the population of interest (such as voting age citizens) with an equal (or known) chance of being selected.

QUASI-EXPERIMENTS are research studies that cannot assign subjects randomly to condition (the key element of true experiments). However, they allow multiple comparisons and control over the independent variables. See **independent variables** and **passive research designs**.

REACTIVITY refers to human beings constantly reacting to their environment. In reacting, they affect what caused them to act in the first place. Hence, the subject matter of social science is in perpetual flux. See **self-fulfilling prophecy**.

RECIPROCAL CAUSATION happens when two or more variables mutually influence each other. It is best studied with longitudinal designs. See **longitudinal research**.

REFERENCE GROUP is a group that you use to compare yourself and your group. See **relative deprivation**.

RELATIVE DEPRIVATION refers to the tendency to compare your lot in life with others rather than judging it in absolute terms. *Individual* relative deprivation involves feeling dissatisfied when comparing what you have with similar other individuals within your group. *Group* relative deprivation involves feeling dissatisfied when comparing what your group has with other reference groups. See **reference group**.

RELIABILITY refers to the problem of variable (random) error. There are two types. Test-retest reliability involves the stability of measures recorded at different times. Internal consistency reliability gauges the cohesion of a measure recorded at one point in time. See **error, measurement error,** and **validity**.

REPLACEMENT. See **cohort replacement**.

REPLICATION occurs when a researcher repeats a study with a fresh sample of subjects. It increases the power of statistical methods and more firmly establishes research findings.

ROLES are positions that people occupy in the social world—such as student or store clerk. Roles involve duties as well as privileges, and they specify how to behave in a specific context. Thus, roles specify who does what, when, and where.

SECONDARY ANALYSIS involves the reanalysis with new hypotheses of old data gathered for another purpose. See archival data.

SELECTION BIAS. See bias and threats to validity.

SELECTIVE NON-RESPONSE. See non-response bias.

SELF-FULFILLING PROPHECY occurs when expectations about future events lead people to act in a way that verifies the expectations. See reactivity.

SIMULATION involves operating a model that attempts to replicate an actual social process. Usually such models test how a system's variables respond to change in other variables of the system. See system.

SINGLE BLIND STUDY involves an experiment in which the subjects do not know whether they are participating in the control or experimental group, but the experimenter does know. See double blind study.

SITUATIONAL CAUSAL ATTRIBUTION involves our seeing people's actions as caused by the situation, such as pressures to conform or economic incentives. See causal attribution, dispositional causal attribution, fundamental attribution bias, and ultimate attribution bias.

SOCIAL DILEMMAS occur when individual and societal interests conflict—as in resource depletion and pollution. They share two features. First, each individual benefits more from making the selfish choice than for the socially cooperative choice. Second, everyone is better off if all cooperate than if all defect. See externalities and markets.

SOCIAL LOCATION refers to where we are located within society. Such characteristics as sex, race, occupation, and social class determine our social locations.

SOCIAL STRUCTURE involves relatively persistent social patterns. These patterns are interrelated events that complete a system's cycle of activities. See macro-level of analysis and systems.

STATISTICAL SIGNIFICANCE determines whether the effects of the independent variables on the dependent variable are so large that the possibility of their happening by chance is minimal. Only the sample size distinguishes between significance tests and effect sizes: significance test = effect size + sample size. Studies with small sample sizes find statistical significance to be especially useful. See effect sizes, multiple regression analysis, type I errors, and type II errors.

STRUCTURAL DIFFERENTIATION refers to how expanding open systems develop further components with increasingly specialized functions—not unlike cell division in biology. This differentiation process also leads to a hierarchical (up-down) arrangement of the components within systems. See systems.

SURPLUS MEANING refers to the extra meanings and ideas conveyed by concepts and theories that go beyond their formal definitions and statements.

SYSTEMS are sets of components and the relations between them. The essential points are the cohesion of a system's components, their interaction, and their interrelationships. Closed systems are self-contained and do not interact with the environment. Open systems are in constant communication with the environment. Both living and social systems are open systems. See **dynamic equilibrium, macro-level of analysis, negative feedback, simulation, social structure,** and **structural differentiation.**

TESTING. See **threats to validity.**

TEST-RETEST RELIABILITY. See **reliability.**

THREATS TO VALIDITY include all the biases and artifacts that distort social research and thus provide plausible rival hypotheses. There are two types of validity. External validity entails the generalization of a study's results to other situations. Internal validity concerns the accuracy of a study's results and conclusions. Chapter 3 details six types of threats to internal validity. The first is history: a specific event influences the dependent variable at the same time as the independent variable. Maturation refers to changes in the subjects from the passage of time. Testing effects occur when we measure the dependent variable twice, and the first test influences the second. Instrumentation problems arise from any change in the measures used to gauge the dependent variable. Selection and mortality refer to different types of people being assigned to (selection) or dropping out of (mortality) the experimental and control groups. See **artifact, bias, plausible rival hypotheses,** and **validity.**

TOP-DOWN CAUSAL PATHS are theoretical explanations that extend from the broadest macro-level of analysis down to the narrower meso- and micro-levels. These paths imply that changes at the societal level lead to changes at the situational and individual levels. See **bottom-up causal paths.**

TURNOUT refers to the percentage of Americans who are registered that come out to vote in an election.

TYPE I ERRORS occur when researchers *incorrectly* accept their hy-

potheses as supported. See **statistical significance** and **type II errors.**

TYPE II ERRORS occur when researchers *incorrectly* reject their hypotheses as falsified. See **statistical significance** and **type I errors.**

ULTIMATE ATTRIBUTION BIAS is the tendency to think the worst about the causes of behavior by members of disliked outgroups. Following a negative act by an outgroup member, we attribute it dispositionally—"that's the way those people are." If the outgroup member acts positively, we maintain our prejudice by either denying it or explaining it away situationally—"what else could they do in that situation?" See **bias, causal attribution, dispositional causal attribution, fundamental attribution bias,** and **situational causal attribution.**

UNDERGROUND ECONOMY refers to informal economic activity that takes place in every society, but that goes unrecorded in official data. See **non-response bias.**

UTILITY, from value theory in economics, refers broadly to the satisfaction that a person gets from a particular good or service. Marginal utility refers to the additional satisfaction that a person gets from consuming one more unit of that good or service. The principle of diminishing marginal utility holds that the value of anything eventually declines as you have more of it.

VALIDITY refers to constant error. It focuses on how well a measure captures the essence of the abstract construct. Face validity is just a matter of judgment: Does the measure look (on the *face* of it) as if it measures the construct? Convergent validity asks if the measure relates positively with other measures of the same construct. Divergent

VALIDITY *continued*

validity is exactly the opposite. It checks to see if the measure *fails* to relate with measures of *other* constructs. Finally, criterion validity asks: Does the measure relate with other variables as theory holds the construct should? See **concepts, error, measurement error, reliability,** and **threats to validity.**

VARIABLE ERROR. See **error.**

VARIABLES are the concrete representations of concepts. They have two or more categories that *vary* over time and samples, as opposed to constants whose values remain fixed. Age and years of education are examples of variables. See **concepts** and **operational definitions.**

WITHIN SUBJECTS COMPARISONS are made between experimental and control conditions when the same subjects serve in both groups. See **between subjects comparisons.**

ZEITGEIST is a German word that means *the spirit of the times,* the typical outlook of a particular period in history.

ZERO-SUM refers to situations where there is a finite (limited) resource. So, when we divide this fixed resource, the more one side receives, the less the competitor gets.

Name Index

Page numbers in italics indicate charts or illustrations.

Subject Index

Page numbers in italics indicate charts and illustrations.